EMPOWERING OLDER PEOPLE

EMPOWERING OLDER PEOPLE

An International Approach

Edited by
Daniel Thursz, Charlotte Nusberg, and Johnnie Prather

Published in cooperation with
the International Federation on Ageing

AUBURN HOUSE
Westport, Connecticut • London

Library of Congress Cataloging-in-Publication Data

Empowering older people : an international approach / edited by Daniel
    Thursz, Charlotte Nusberg, and Johnnie Prather.
            p. cm.
        "Published in cooperation with the International Federation on
    Ageing."
        Includes bibliographical references and index.
        ISBN 0–86569–238–6 (alk. paper).—ISBN 0–86569–258–0 (pbk.)
        1. Aged—Cross-cultural studies.   2. Power (Social sciences)—
    Cross-cultural studies.   3. Autonomy (Psychology)—Cross-cultural
    studies.   I. Thursz, Daniel.   II. Nusberg, Charlotte.
    III. Prather, Johnnie.   IV. International Federation on Ageing.
    HQ1061.E46   1995
    305.26—dc20   94–29714

British Library Cataloguing in Publication Data is available.

Library of Congress Catalog Card Number: 94–29714
ISBN: 0–86569–238–6
      0–86569–258–0 (pbk.)

First published in 1995

Auburn House, 88 Post Road West, Westport, CT 06881
An imprint of Greenwood Publishing Group, Inc.

Printed in the United States of America

The paper used in this book complies with the
Permanent Paper Standard issued by the National
Information Standards Organization (Z39.48–1984).

10 9 8 7 6 5 4 3 2 1

Copyright Acknowledgments

The authors and publisher wish to thank the following for use of material from:
Tarek Shuman, ed., *Population Aging: International Perspectives: Proceedings and Recommendations of the International Conference on Population Aging*, copyright 1993 by the University Center on Aging, San Diego State University, San Diego, California.
"Empowerment: An Aging Perspective" by Ken Tout, pp. 221–274, reprinted with permission.
"Empowerment—Families—Older Persons" by Brigid Donelan, pp. 275–292, reprinted with permission.
"Empowerment and Participation in Development" by Mukunda Rao, pp. 293–320, reprinted with permission.
"Senior Organizations and Seniors' Empowerment: An International Perspective" by Henry J. Pratt, pp. 321–360, reprinted with permission.
Takako Sodei, "Tradition Impedes Empowerment in Japan," *Ageing International*, Volume XX, No. 1, March 1993, reprinted with permission.

Contents

Preface

Charlotte Nusberg

Older people are one of the last groups with which the notion of empowerment has become associated. Yet the privileges it represents—the ability to make informed choices, exercise influence, continue to make contributions in a variety of settings, and take advantage of services—are critically important to the well-being of the elders. These are choices often taken for granted by working-age adults, but they have eluded older persons for a variety of reasons, including poverty, poor health, low educational levels, lack of transportation and access to services, negative stereotypes about aging, and overt and subtle age discrimination. As the world's population lives longer and more independent lives, it is clear that having choices and maintaining control over personal decisions has taken on new meaning and importance for older persons everywhere.

Empowering Older People: An International Perspective represents the first examination of the possibilities and limitations of empowerment as it applies to older people around the world. What does empowerment mean in a developed country? In a developing country? How does it play out across cultures, political boundaries, and widely disparate economic scenarios? How is it arrived at by older individuals and by the organizations that represent them?

The contributions in this volume do not offer definitive answers to these questions. They can and do, however, present the complexities of the debate and demonstrate the importance of empowerment to the lives of older people. Part I examines the concept of empowerment and its applicability to older persons. Part II demonstrates the experience of organizations representing elders in becoming empowered. Part III looks at various paths to personal empowerment on the part of older individuals. Part IV explores the relationship of empowerment to social and economic development, and Part V explores the use of research as a tool of empowerment. Perspectives are presented from Canada, Chile, Denmark, the

Dominican Republic, Mexico, Pakistan, South Africa, Sri Lanka, Thailand, the United Kingdom, and the United States.

This volume is an outgrowth of a workshop organized by the International Federation on Ageing, the U.S. National Council on Aging, Inc., and the UN Centre for Social Development and Humanitarian Affairs, during the 1992 UN Conference on Population Aging held in San Diego, California. Not only did we want to give a public airing to the issue of empowerment and aging, but it was our hope that the discussions and recommendations emanating from the workshop would impact upcoming UN world conferences on population, social welfare, and women. The UN's *International Plan of Action on Aging* and the *UN Principles for Older Persons* already espouse the rights of older persons to some extent, but their influence needs to be extended to the mainstream of policy and program planning.

A special thanks should be extended to the contributors to this volume, many of whom came from the far-flung corners of the world to share their findings and thinking with us in San Diego, and to the Center on Aging at San Diego State University, which organized the 1992 UN Conference on Population Aging and provided the opportunity to hold a meeting on this subject. Thanks also to the Research Division of the American Association of Retired Persons (AARP) for making staff time available to complete this volume. Particular thanks go to Teresa Abrams and Michael Berens, of the Research Division of AARP, for their help with the editing of this book, and Lillian Wilson, who prepared the camera-ready copy with skill and patience.

Introduction

Daniel Thursz

Despite a great deal of progress in the efforts to end the myths surrounding the aging process, there are still some powerful images that govern both policies and programs dealing with older people. None is more manifest than the view that older people are increasingly dependent, need protection from their environment, and eventually from themselves. It is this notion that creates enormous barriers to the development of policies based on the strengths of the individual and his or her right to self-determination.

Clearly, there are older persons who are frail, some of whom cannot make decisions for themselves. There are older persons who need protection from exploitation by forces in society, sometimes from relatives, and even from themselves. However, this is not the case with the overwhelming majority of older persons who are not only capable of self-determination but insist on maintaining their independence and dignity, even in the face of physical difficulties. The fact is that most older persons are like everybody else. They seek autonomy and participation in decision making. They do not perceive themselves as clients or patients. They are not willing to abandon their judgment for the judgment of others and want to maintain control of their own destiny.

In order to live out their lives as they wish, they have to struggle against both popular and professional biases. Often, these barriers to self-determination are created by well-meaning individuals, be they children, relatives, or social workers. "At your age, you should not attempt this . . ." is probably the most repeated admonition heard by older persons.

The concept of empowerment is based on the conviction that there must be an alternative force against the popular myths of dependence of older persons. It is not based on the assumption that power can be granted to older persons by the provider of service or the family. On the contrary, it is self-empowerment that is sought.

Nevertheless, the provider of service, as well as the policy maker, must develop a sensitivity to this need. Opportunities must be created for self-determination of individuals as well as collective action by groups of older persons.

We recognize that in many parts of the world these are not common concerns. Where elementary needs—such as money, food, and health services—require Herculean efforts on behalf of older persons, it is understandable that self-determination and community participation may be perceived as luxuries. In other parts of the world, the very term "power" will conjure up a political force that will bring about suspicion and even countermeasures.

Even in the United States, the term "empowerment" has been seen with suspicion.

Writing in 1920, John Daniels attempted to define the Americanization of immigrants. Foremost among the tasks required by their new host country was participation in community: "Participation in American life, therefore, involves loyalty to America, devotion to this American idea of democracy, and a responsible share in the activity through which this ideal is measurably realized in practice and present fact. Such participation is the very essence of Americanism," he wrote.

Fifty years later, despite the strong democratic foundation of the United States, the "War on Poverty" and the 1964 Economic Opportunity Act raised apprehension regarding "maximum feasible participation of the poor." At that time, this writer attempted to calm such fears about the concept of "power" in a government publication:

> Somehow, the word power has become suspect and has acquired a sinister overtone . . . An accurate use of the terms "black power" or "poor power" ought not to bring on undue fears and reactions. If black people band together to affect their conditions, they are acting in the best traditions of a democratic system. Most issues in a democracy are not resolved through an intellectual process—not through a mystical approach. They are resolved by the actions and reactions of power systems—that occasionally coalesce, struggle with each other, or compromise . . . Consumer groups have as their primary purpose the development of power—acquired through larger membership and through their use of various methodologies that renders them more effective (powerful).

It should be obvious that even where there are strong democratic traditions, there are many forces that stand in the way of self-empowerment.

Providers of service to older persons can easily fall prey to a desire to control, out of the most altruistic motives. The problem is generic to the helping professions and affects persons of all ages. Dr. Charles D. Cowger, Associate Professor at the School of Social Work at the University of Illinois-Urbana, in a recent article (1994, 263), argues against the focus in social case work on treatment, dysfunction and therapy metaphors. He writes, "Clinical practice that considers social and economic justice suggests a type of practice that explicitly deals with power and power relationships. This perspective understands client empowerment as central to clinical practice and client strengths as providing the fuel and energy for that empowerment. Client empowerment is characterized by two interdependent and interactive dynamics: personal empowerment and social empowerment." Cowger defines personal empowerment as similar to the traditional clinical notion of self-determination whereby clients give direction to the helping process, take charge and control of their personal lives, get their "heads straight," learn new ways to think about their situations, and adopt new behaviors that give them more satisfying and rewarding outcomes (1994). In a very valuable contribution to the discussion of empowerment, Cowger defines the social empowerment dynamic as related to societal resources and opportunity. He concludes, "Clinical practice based on empowerment assumes that client power is achieved when clients make choices that give them more control over their presenting problem situations and, in turn, their own lives."

Concern for both older persons' control over their own lives and social justice, and marshaling resources and opportunity for that vulnerable population should be the hallmark of professional practice with older persons. This approach is not limited to social workers but should guide the work of senior center directors, hospital administrators, physicians, and nurses.

In recent years, a new occupational group has been created to work with older persons. Known as "case" or "care" managers, these individuals can work with a wide range of clients. Ideally, they can operate with the same concern for self-determination that social case workers demonstrated in earlier times. Yet they can also be vested with power and decision making by the bureaucracies that employ them—making decisions for people rather than responding to the wishes of their clients. The dilemma is real and can be modified by clear appeal procedures, empowerment education for clients, and ombudsmen with sufficient leverage to challenge case managers. Older persons do not want to be "cases" and don't want to be managed. If "empowerment" can lead to some semantic distortions, the term "case manager" conjures up a totally opposite image.

While much of the discussion of empowerment has focused on individuals and their right to self-determination, there is another aspect of the subject that can be classified as "collective empowerment." It is part of the democratic ethos that groups with similar interests or goals can organize for common action. In the United States, such groups as the American Association of Retired Persons, the Older Women's League, the Gray Panthers, the National Council of Senior Citizens, and many other groups participate in the political process arguing for certain legislation, protesting what they perceive as injustices, and arguing for improved resources and opportunities for their members. There are counterpart groups in many other countries. A critical issue is the danger that when funding comes from government, such groups lose autonomy and may be controlled by the very forces that they wish to challenge.

Autonomy is indeed a difficult element to maintain in the lives of individuals or organizations. Older people need to find, among providers of service and public policy leaders, allies who will be willing to open channels for self-empowerment. These allies will have to be equally adept at containment—and resist the temptation to give too much advice or to suggest, by verbal and nonverbal means, that their counsel is crucial to the decision making by older persons. The greatest role that can be played by providers is to help educate older persons to continue to make critical decisions independently of them, and to organize with persons in similar circumstances to affect the milieu in which they live.

REFERENCES

Cowger, Charles D. 1994. "Assessing Client Strengths: Clinical Assessment or Client Empowerment." *Social Work*, May 1994.

Daniels, John. 1920. *America Via the Neighborhood*. New York and London: Harper & Brothers.

Thursz, Daniel. 1969. *Consumer Involvement in Rehabilitation*. Washington, DC: U.S. Department of Health, Education, and Welfare.

Part 1

THE CONCEPT

Chapter 1

The Aging Perspective on Empowerment

Ken Tout

Liberty! Equality! Fraternity! Emancipation! Enlightenment! Empowerment!

We live in a world where emotive words are used to stimulate us to great deeds and urgent action. However, often the essential meanings of watchwords and slogans are little more clear than the symbolic significance of the colors in some national flags. In beginning our examination of the word "empowerment," we should consider the two groups of words already quoted.

Liberty, equality, and fraternity are, according to their purest meanings, primitive substantive factors that have their own sufficient existence and do not depend on some previous negative or pernicious experience. Liberty, equality, and fraternity could have existed in an original Garden of Eden situation where all in the garden was lovely and no taint of human sin had introduced baser factors.

This concept throws up into clear relief the inherent significance of the other group of words. Emancipation might be termed derivative and dependent in that it presupposes a prior state of slavery from which emancipation must be achieved. Enlightenment could not possess its meaning unless there existed a prior state of intellectual darkness that needed the light of reason on it. So empowerment necessarily implies a previous negative state that can be described as lack of power.

Empowerment must therefore be considered not only as to whither it leads, but also as to whence it comes. What is the primitive state or negative circumstance that makes empowerment necessary?

In exploring the essence of the word and, as it were, extracting the flesh of its meaning, it is tempting to use the skeleton of its bare letters as a structure, an acrostic by which to detail the need for empowerment, the nature of the power, and the negotiation of a continuing status.

THE NEED FOR EMPOWERMENT

Taking the first two letters of the word skeleton empowerment, the *e* and *m* will highlight a study of the essence of, and the motivation for, empowerment.

The essence of empowerment lies in the questions: whence it comes? Whither it leads? It might appear that a study of primitive, or let us say preindustrial attitudes to aging, is not relevant to current issues of a graying population in the United States or Western Europe. But if aging is studied as an international reality, it is seen that most all countries are sailing to a wind of change that blows, with gale force in some quarters and a light breeze in others. The Ships of State must note this factor, with its presage of possible storms to follow. In gerontology, an awareness of origins is as important as a concept of destinations in setting sail appropriate to the present wind in navigation.

There is some debate as to whether elders were ever the revered and powerful leaders of primitive society they were often supposed to be. In the 1940s, Leo Simmons, an early investigator in the field, found that in 56 out of 71 preindustrial tribes old people were serving as chiefs (Simmons, 1945). At the same time, he identified 50 percent of tribes where what might be described as cruelty to older people existed. In some cases this consisted of logical measures to accelerate death of a member for whom the society could prescribe no chronic care.

In more recent times, Glascock and Feinman (1981) found 26 instances of old people being summarily killed in 42 developing communities. Maxwell and Silverman (1981) and others found similar instances. Foner (1985), summing up such research, gave the opinion that "as long as children and other kin in non-industrial societies must shoulder the caretaking burden, so long will relationships with the incapacitated elderly remain as they are: a complex and tangled web of attachments, reciprocities, tensions, and antagonisms." This present paper will not pretend, therefore, that every preindustrial society was a Garden of Eden experience for incapacitated elderly.

However, much evidence does emerge that in some primitive societies the elder had a very special role and a traditional level of prestige. Gerontologists in today's transitional societies ascribe much of the elderly person's current woes to the transitional state from a more respectful society to a more competitive system. In these last years an enduring primitive society, the Bambara of West Africa, has been intensively researched by Rosenmayr (1990), the former an Austrian and the latter a national of Mali. They stated that "the often repeated assumption that old people in tribal society are respected because they are wise is misleading. It is not old age as such that is respected but the seniority principle in tribal society which merits respect as the central model for survival and 'filtered change.'"

Alberta Ollennu of Ghana makes an interesting observation along the same lines: "When picking a Chief, it is the Queen Mother of the clan who indicates the right procedure for king making. When any traditional matter arises the Queen Mother is brought in. Normally her word is law" (Payne, 1991).

Developing country gerontologists are explicit in their reaction to the trends away from traditional structures, insofar as those trends affect the elderly in an adverse manner. Nana Araba Apt, president of the African Society of Gerontology, has said (1985), "Modernization with increased physical and social mobility is shifting people from the traditional patterns of family and clan settings," and "certain trends in present day economic and social policies are leading to a deterioration [in the family] and not an improvement in that well-being" (1991).

An Asian perspective agrees that "the position of the elderly has been undermined by such factors as changing values, growing individualism, smaller numbers of children, the migration of the young to cities in search of employment, housing shortages in urban areas, the increasing participation of women in the labor market, and the devaluation of the knowledge and experience of the elderly" (United Nations, 1986, para. 33).

These regional judgments on current transitional trends enable a wider world comment, owing much to James Schulz (United Nations, 1991).

> Shifts from nuclear families may imply the loss of older persons' roles as heads of families and a loss of decision-making functions and financial responsibilities. In rural areas, new patterns of land ownership and mechanization of agriculture reduce the opportunities for older farmers to adjust their work-load and carry out smaller tasks as their strength diminishes. In urban settings, the substitution of wage labor for independent work makes it difficult to adapt working conditions to the needs of aging. Access of the young to modern education can impair intergenerational ties undermining the status of older people by making their experience and attachment to tradition appear outmoded and irrelevant to technical progress.

If gerontologists in developing countries are pointing to this "depowerment" or "dispowerment" as a major, if not the major, crisis factor for the increasing numbers of elderly people, gerontologists from industrialized societies may well reflect on the extent to which such a dispowerment factor affects older people, including the native-born who still live by norms and expectations of two or three generations back, and aging persons of more recent waves of migration from developing countries into the heartlands of industrialization.

It is tempting at this point to cite two of my own research findings, which are quoted extensively in a 1989 publication, and refer to the impact of transition on two sites that appear fairly adjacent on a normal map of the South American continent.

Vilcabamba, the famous "Valley of the Aged," is located in an area of southern Ecuador where environment and culture are propitious for human survival: clean air, pure water, a pleasant climate, mainly vegetable diet, lack of modern time and task pressures, absence of industrialization, good intergenerational relationships, and so on. Potosi, in the highlands of Bolivia, is not a nice place to live. As long ago as 1550 a Dominican priest described it as "the Mouth of Hell." Extreme altitude, the need to import lower-land workers who do not easily acclimatize, exacting weather conditions, brutish labor requirements of mining work at an altitude of about 15,000 feet, alienation of workers from their own cultures and extended families, and so on, make it the antithesis of Vilcabamba in that its activities relate to commercial convenience rather than human welfare.

The striking finding of my research (K. Tout, 1989a), since justified by the experience of welfare programs put in place, relates to both longevity and aging. People live a long time in Vilcabamba. There is debate around exaggerated early longevity myths. But it is common in that valley to find people of 90 and 100 years of age actively pursuing their daily labor and displaying an alertness of mind, an articulate participation in general debate, and even a pronounced sense of fun, which maintains the highest regard in which the elders are held by younger generations. In Potosi it is not uncommon to discover male miners who, at 35 or 40 years of age, are burn-out cases, unable to sustain their daily tasks due to accidents, respiratory diseases, malnutrition, or simply the effects of living where they do.

This comparison does not necessarily prove anything, but it does highlight two factors. One is the impact of industrialization on a primitive society (Potosi) compared to a control site virtually unaffected by modernization (Vilcabamba) of very similar cultures. The other, an important factor but not necessarily central to this present review, reflects on the need for practitioners, as distinct from demographers, to judge who is aged by other than artificial age barriers such as 60 plus, or even an old-old definition. Funders of programs in Vilcabamba and Potosi recognize this latter factor and rely on, for their identification of aged, empirical judgments.

Modern thinking often relates dispowerment and the need for empowerment with the circumstances of population minorities. It might therefore be instructive to consider the elderly in minority situations caused by the trends already referred to. The following is a list for further thinking about groups of elderly who may have been disenfranchised, or who are poorly represented in current dispensations.

It would be an error to consider the elderly (as a group of, say, people over 60 years of age) to be a minority. A minority in respect of what majority? A majority of people under 60? That would be an unfair and indiscriminate comparison. Some demographic statistics clearly show that there is no homogeneous under-60 group. In some industrialized cities and resorts, an over-60 population accounting for 30 percent of the total population is by no means likely to be a minority when compared to those under school age or of school age. When such percentages of over-60s are taken into account, we must not only consider the areas of the industrialized world that have been unkindly designated "Costa Geriatric," but also emergent "gray" cities such as Buenos Aires, Shanghai, or Singapore.

The "old-old" or "fourth age" appear to qualify as a minority in terms of their increased demand per capita for health and social services, and also their relatively few numbers. However, this designation needs to be treated with reservation as the immediate reaction of demographers is to try to label old-old as over 75 or 80, when old-old in Potosi and similar societies may mean 40-plus.

Although conceding the need for demographers and program planners to consider the minority requirements of the old-old, it is pertinent to refer to casual disablement, in the sense of groups of long-term disabled, elderly persons within elderly cohorts enjoying generally much better fitness. The stereotyping of need groups results in such anomalies as the home-help service for a disabled adult in an English county being exchanged for another system, style, and cost of home help for the same person with the label of an "elderly person" (disabled or not) on passing the magical 60th birthday.

Other minority groups within the general orbit of aging, and who can profit from more general minority campaigning, include rural elderly, such as those farmers disadvantaged as described earlier, and ethnic elderly.

Some minority groups do not spring so readily to mind. In some developing countries with scarce service resources, a group needing support and empowerment will be the grandparents, mainly grandmothers, surviving the scourge of hetero-sexually transmitted AIDS. Where the parent generation has been annihilated the grandmother is increasingly being perceived as the potential savior of family, and even of the local community, although she is not politically empowered or educationally prepared for the consequences of an AIDS pandemic.

A further minority group relates to massive refugee movements, of which a number have been seen in recent years. Leaving aside consideration of the immediate specific needs of the elderly refugee on arrival at the reception camp, an area where HelpAge International is effectively operating when permitted or enabled, there are two other minority situations of great concern. A minority of elderly persons may remain behind in the depopulated disaster zone, either because they choose to or because they cannot travel. A further minority of elderly has, very tragically, been produced by the selective measures applied by host third countries—the countries of final resettlement—when offering permanent refuge only to skilled, working-age persons with their nuclear families. In such circumstances older people can be left in a permanent limbo for the remainder of this life at least.

Further minority classification might be given to two groups, and there will be others who are, amid their peers, actual majorities. One of these groups is widows, especially in societies where old age welfare may depend partially on late re-marriage, which may be accessible to the male of the species but not to the female. The widows are a considerable majority over the widowers, but, in such societies, they suffer from radical dispowerment.

A majority of elderly in some societies consists of nonpensionable peasants. Where new farming techniques result in the inability of the peasant to continue to make profits, or even leads to landlessness, and where access to goods in the changing society more and more requires cash, the majority peasant may find life increasingly intolerable.

This may have appeared to be a prolonged, and sometimes remotely related, manner of distilling the essence of the word empowerment as related to elder interests. However, its legitimacy rests on the fact that, at least in a considerable number of societies and cultures, there has been a history of, and an impact from, dispowerment of older people to some extent, within living memory. For the older generations this constitutes a rationale for seeking empowerment.

Continuing with the skeleton acrostic of the word empowerment, the letter *m* denotes the motivation that spurs on every great and urgent cause.

The motivation for seeking the empowerment of the elderly lies in two main considerations. The first is the continuing increase in the gross numbers of elderly people and their increasing percentage proportion of the total population. The second and more emotive reason will emerge from individual case studies of the actual plight of persons trapped in the converging forces of modernization of societies.

The facts about the graying of populations are now so well known that at this point the only additional observation will be to underline the often ignored fact that the graying will, over the next two decades, be more rapid in developing countries than in the already gray nations. Countries in North America and Western Europe will continue to age at a locally significant rate. One useful, although inevitably oversimplified, statistic issued by the United Nations has the over-80 population of developed countries increasing by 108 percent. The corresponding figure projected for developing countries is 377 percent. Within the developing countries category there is the further disparity of an increase in tropical South America at 405 percent and Southeastern Asia at 409 percent compared to North America at 60 percent.

If the budgets of the mighty economies of North America and Europe (cited as 90 percent increase in the above data) envisage complex problems of pension, Social Security, health, and personal social services provisions over the period, what will be the financial burden on less developed economies, where the forces of modernization drive inexorably toward cash economy and technical processes that undermine traditional cultures, and also require instant provision of nontraditional structures?

Also, whereas the strong, sometimes imperial and/or capitalist economies of the North were able to introduce aging programs over a protracted period of time, the factors detailed are impacting gravely on weaker economies at an accelerated rate and over a greatly reduced period in comparison. Some measure of this disparity can be gathered from two statistics. Out of 27 Caribbean countries, 20 have less than a quarter of a million inhabitants while only one, Cuba, has a population as large as New York or London. Each of those countries has to maintain a full national infrastructure on a budget not greater than that of a local community in the North.

In Bangladesh, which is not normally designated as a very rapidly developing economy, landlessness among the peasants, mentioned above as nonpensionable, has increased from 20 to 50 percent in the course of only three decades. Also, "the old feudal lords were replaced by a new class of exploitative surplus farmers combining the roles of farmer-cum-trader-cum-money-lender" (Ibrahim, 1985).

This development was seen as partially the result of international modernization trends, and partially a result of poorly planned use of additional official aid funding. And the Bangladesh scene was further darkened by the regularity of natural disaster, which is a another factor that tends to afflict developing countries more than the industrialized societies of the North.

In listing the individual plights of elderly persons, one must be extremely selective and inevitably represent the extremes of community disregard and individual incompetence. Having said that, the agency from whose files the following four cases are presented has similar records, or has access to networks, for many tens of thousands of such examples.

Case 1. From a Caribbean culture comes the instance of a woman approaching her 80th birthday, and being responsible for nine small children. Their dwelling is the smallest of shanties, composed of wreckage from other abandoned shanties. Their total stable resource is the woman's Social Security payment. Their plight is related to the migration to the United States of the two parent couples to whom the children belong. The two couples had traveled to the United States to pursue the mirage of easy wealth as often perceived in less favored countries. It had seemed a sensible strategy to leave the children at home in the care of the grandmother, whose lot would soon be relieved by an influx of American dollars.

Unfortunately, the two couples concerned had none of the basic education, technical skills, or adaptability required for success in the new society. They discovered that merely maintaining life in the more expensive milieu left them with no spare cash to remit home. To all intents and purposes they disappeared into the whirlpool of unqualified immigrants swimming desperately to keep their own heads above water.

At home the family continued to exist on the maximum Social Security payment available from the scarce resources of government funds, about $1.60 per week. So the old woman who, according to established myth, should have been cared for safely within the bosom of the extended family, had to continue as breadwinner, housekeeper, home mother, and security guard for small children growing up in a poor and perilous neighborhood.

Case 2. Among the 10 percent of older people in their South American country fortunate enough to qualify for a retirement pension, were the General, on a substantial income, and his servant the Corporal, with income enough for a few luxuries. Neither of their pensions was index-linked. The national economy passed through some years of enormous strain with inflation climbing at times to 2,000 percent per annum. The value of the pensions decreased, and neither of the ex-military men had any particular skill that might have generated income in their new sphere of life.

They moved into more meager quarters and then into a single, dilapidated room. The pension was not now sufficient to purchase a reasonable diet. The Corporal fell seriously ill, so the General, unskilled in domestic chores, became the servant and nurse. Their plight was exacerbated by the comparison with days of relative wealth, and by comparison also with the standard of life of those of similar professional skills still actively employed.

Case 3. An African widow has a single son of her old age. Her husband had taken advantage of his traditional option of deserting her and seeking a younger, more able wife or maybe more than one such wife. The son was left with the widow, as he was mentally unstable and not able to work at consecutive tasks. The boy was prone to fits, which caused him to throw himself to the ground and act irrationally. The villagers diagnosed his condition as devil-possessed.

The widow and son were driven from the village, where they were among the poorest, and had to confine themselves to wandering in the forest. Their normal sustenance consisted of roots, berries, or, in time of less plenty, leaves and twigs from the trees.

Case 4. A great-grandmother is living in a large Indian city. The granddaughter had three children. She worked in the local market but her income was insufficient, so the children and their great-grandmother spent their time sitting on the edge of the pavement begging. Then the granddaughter died and her husband, who had appeared from time to time, was no longer to be found.

The great-grandmother was quite old, so the eldest of the children virtually became the supporter of the family by leading the begging as they sat in the street. Concerned local people contacted social workers who arranged for the children to be boarded in a home. Nuns tried to minister to the old woman. But she was so inured to living as a vagrant in the open air that she would not tolerate life in a regulated institution, and so absconded back to a cardboard shelter in her old haunts.

In a world ostensibly concerned about human rights, it should be argued that such end-of-the-line cases should no longer be permitted to suffer unaided, in whatever country their destiny may have placed them. It is perhaps a criticism, particularly of the British media, that great emphasis and priority is put on such issues as saving particular species of wild animals or a variety of tree, yet these instances of human elder suffering do not merit a mention. In some way, it seems, the media share the shame of the sufferer and cannot find a means of expressing it.

Yet, surely here is emotive stuff enough for a noble campaign. But if the cases cited appear to criticize the lack of services in certain developing countries (which happen to have been mentioned only as examples and not as particular transgressors), let me add a more recent case from my own experience. My wife was alerted, a few weeks back, to the case of an elderly woman reposing at 2 A.M. in a police cell, where she had been taken for shelter, warmth, and a temporary bed. Well-dressed but possessing no evidence of identity, and unknown to local social services, she had been found wandering at that hour of the morning with only a Christian name to quote, and no idea of where she was or whither she came. Exhaustive inquiries failed to produce any fond relatives, concerned neighbors, or searching social services departments who had noted her absence. This occurred in sophisticated, modernized Britain.

THE NATURE OF POWER

Having considered factors that might suggest a need for empowerment of older people, it will also be instructive to dwell for a while on the nature of the power that is to be achieved. Our word "skeleton of empowerment," moving beyond the essence and the motivation factors, can provide an outline of factors such as political aspects, opportunities for elders, welfare of the less able, education in aging, and relationships.

Political Aspects

The world is aware of the power of movements like the "Gray Panthers." Older people, it appears, can be empowered in the political world of today. However, this is not to support the facile assumption that if 20 percent of the population is over 60 years of age they may, in a certain situation, band together to cast 20 percent of the nation's votes in an election for the same cause, thus bringing down governments or causing palpitations in the breasts of complacent politicians.

Political power has a much wider range than the act of voting. Binstock and others (1981) have pointed out that

> images of the aging as a powerful voting bloc are inaccurate . . . populations of older persons are politically, socially and economically heterogeneous. . . . Analyses of age as a variable in political attitudes and voting patterns have consistently shown that the differences within age groups are greater than the differences between age groups . . . [but] most discussions of the political activities of aging-based membership organizations similarly depict them as relatively powerful forces and likely to become still more powerful.

In modern society, as Thursz (1969) points out, the direct intervention in elections for political appointments is only one of many options open to pressure groups.

> Power is increased or reduced according to a whole range of factors. Unlike the ballot box, which grants to each citizen an equal share of power, government—and, indeed, service systems—react differentially to various individuals and groups. The Governor of the State of New York has considerably more influence than an aged widow in Jackson Heights. Service systems react to requests on the basis of an instantaneous diagnosis of the power of the individual or group.

Clearly, there are levels of empowerment of the elderly, as well as of provision for the elderly, which are only within the capability of governments or supra-governmental organizations, and ways must be found to convince those organizations of the importance of this. One important area of such levels of response is indicated in a Pan American Health Organization (1989) report on "The Challenge of Ageing in Latin America." This states that

> our response to the challenge of aging population therefore requires not simply an expansion of professional services but the adoption and implementation of the principles of primary health care advocated by the World Health Organization—namely the development of services to focus on the whole population, appropriate use of resources and technology, the involvement of all sectors and agencies in the development of services, and, most important of all, the participation of elderly people themselves.

Nana Apt (1991), in Ghana, identifies another great sector of influence that, if related to low-key relationships, still requires a considerable national intervention to realize.

> Two factors, namely large numerical increases of older persons and their tendency to live in rural areas, have policy implications for African governments' long term plans for the provision of health, housing, social welfare and social security. . . . There is obviously a need to recognize the potential force of an integrated family structure and an urgency to institute concrete measures to strengthen the economic capacity of families to continue to care for their elderly members.

The extent of the problem of reinforcing traditional structures was discussed in a conference primarily concerned with women's issues.

> The issue of caring for the elderly at home stimulated reactions from many in the audience. Several Africans, as well as Indian, Pakistani and Indonesian participants acknowledge the dichotomy between social expectations and reality on this question. . . . while the traditional standard of family care was not denied, many participants from developing nations questioned whether it could be sustained. . . . thus far, nongovernmental sources are unable to fill the gap. . . . in many countries there are no government-enforced standards for such home care. (American Association for International Aging, 1986)

If the general world need for government action is acknowledged, the methodology of persuasion of political authorities is still to be refined. One observer (Schumacher, 1974) speaks of the complaints of the underprivileged being conveyed "in the language of terrorism, genocide, breakdown, pollution, exhaustion." We live, it seems, in a unique period of convergence. It should, no doubt, be asked whether elders would ever combine to speak in such language, or even have recourse to the desperate methods of British suffragettes, by committing suicide under the hooves of the king's horse at the racecourse. Some observers (Choucri, 1974) have suggested that older persons are less prone to violent methods than younger groups. "Positive aspects of aging which might be universalized in an older population include emotional stability, serenity, objectivity, loyalty, discipline, honour and patience" as opposed to youthful traits like "indocility, rivalry, lack of awareness of dangers personal and communal, and so on" (Flores Colombino, 1982).

It might be supposed therefore that older action groups could be looking to such weapons as community skills accumulated through a lifetime, sagacity, patience, and understanding in negotiations, as well as such elements of prestige and respect as still adhere to the modernized concept of aging. Such respect would be engendered by the records of older people as musicians, writers, and artists; as continuing able business people; and as successful politicians, even though some actions of certain so-called gerontocracies have appeared to demonstrate a proclivity toward abuse, either physical or moral.

However, in negotiating towards empowerment, the older generations are generally seen as being in a situation of weakness. They tend to lack the resource of armed force, massed disciplined trade unions, or the implied threat of mobile terrorism. Additionally, the sector of elderly who enjoy massive wealth tends to be alienated from the vast majority who subsist either at the normally meager retirement pension level or sometimes without established income.

In this kind of political give-and-take, the argument of mutual interests tends to be somewhat weak. The Brandt Report (1980) pointed out that "the 'haves' are rarely willing to relinquish their control and their resources and share them with the 'have-nots.' . . . Further . . . even where both sides stand to gain, either may feel unwilling to give in, because they are not gaining enough, or because the other gains too much. This is especially true in negotiations between unequals, where, if inequity is to be redressed the gains cannot be equal."

The older generations might, therefore, be expected to approach the question of political empowerment with some sense of hopelessness as commencing from a point of political "have-nots." New strategies for influencing the powers that be need to be worked out. Among these, two might be briefly referred to here. Politicians and government planners will not be influenced unless the quality of information provided is at least equal to that offered by other pressure groups. Research in aging, in both its demographic and sociological aspects, is still far from impressive, particularly in the developing world. Much of the lacuna of information is related to dearth of funding. The Catch-22 situation exists whereby funding agencies in the North will not approve and disburse funding without the type of submitted information which can only be provided through adequate funding— which means vastly more funding than at present. It is understandable that non-government organizations, in particular, tend to respond to the call to rush into urgent welfare situations with what is often termed "fire brigade" action, when perhaps a painstaking squad of detectives would be more appropriate as a first approach.

The second thought on new strategies relates to the recruitment of highly profiled personalities of younger age groups to reinforce the appeal of the older luminaries, who bring respect and attention to the aging cause. Pop stars have contributed greatly to general emergency fund-raising for causes such as famine relief in Africa in recent years. It should not be beyond the ability of leaders of older age groups to recruit such stars to what is, to a great extent, an inter-generational concern. The willingness of the much admired Princess Diana to act as patron to HelpAge in Britain has not only enhanced the image of that voluntary agency but also drawn much additional media and public attention to the question of aging in a modern society.

The incorporation of younger groups into elder concerns has a two-way effect. It not only uses the influence and charisma of the younger performers and notables, but also causes them to become more knowledgeable about the fundamentals of the cause that they are espousing.

Opportunities for Elders

If we accept that much of what is regarded as aging is little more than a convenient demographic classification, and that a majority of persons in the respective age bands maintain a reasonable ability to enjoy life, then the opportunities which elders will desire will cover most aspects of normal life. Persons of what is normally considered extreme age have been involved in parachute jumping, mountain climbing, marathon running, and other exhausting physical pursuits, just as other elders have achieved great feats of artistic achievement or academic distinction. A complete list of opportunities that some elder or other might at some time require would be an inventory of almost every human activity and ambition.

For the present survey, the opportunities referred to will cover three important fields of interest but in no way preclude any other items. The three fields of interest are work and income, social outlets for those with restrictive circumstances, and freedom of choice within more institutionalized regimes. Immediately, one is aware of many other opportunities that lay urgent claim to consideration, such as the opportunity for a widow to find and marry a suitable male partner in societies that currently deny or impede this right.

The question of discrimination against elderly workers, and the lack of alternative income possibilities in many societies, probably shares with the problem of social isolation and loneliness the stigma of being the major mass problem facing elderly people on a world scale at this time. The question of freedom of choice within institutions concerns only a tiny minority numerically, but it is the cause of some of the most acute personal and group problems that can be placed under the description of institutionalization.

Power—personal, group, and community—lies in the ability of older people to continue to provide for themselves both economically and in terms of mental stimulus. This latter aspect is aptly described by the Indian philosopher Kumarappa (1958), "If the nature of work is properly appreciated and applied, it will stand in the same relation to the higher faculties as food is to the physical body. It nourishes and enlivens the higher man and disciplines the animal in him into progressive channels. It furnishes an excellent background for man to display his scale of values and develop his personality." But if it is almost impossible to raise funds for starving elderly refugees, it is likely to be even more difficult to arouse enthusiasm for soul starvation of elders, however deleterious this may be.

A more pragmatic and technological stance is displayed in an Israeli report (Eisenbach and Sabatello, 1991). "The aging of the population, increased life expectancy of the elderly at age 65, and claims that successive cohorts of elderly are healthier, better educated, and less disabled, all question the wisdom of compelling the elderly to retire from principal places of employment at a fixed age or of encouraging such retirement with economic incentives." On the other hand, the report continues, "Technological progress: While some changes greatly reduce the amount of physical effort required, thus making work easier for older workers, productivity changes reduce the overall need for workers, and technological changes can cause skill obsolescence, particularly among older workers."

That mainly urban portent could be balanced by a brief repetition of an earlier quote. "In rural areas, new patterns of land ownership and mechanization of agriculture reduce the opportunities for older farmers to adjust their work-load and carry out smaller tasks as their strength diminishes" (United Nations, 1991).

The problem of age discrimination is not confined to the workplaces of the older industrialized countries. Characterized by a Pre-World Assembly on Aging technical meeting (Mahar, 1979) as "the increasing informational and social obsolescence" of the older person in the modern work function, this same tendency is revealed in two studies from Brazil. One of these, from Sao Paulo, showed that the only group in which unemployment was increasing rapidly was that of older workers, as employers generally preferred the greater physical potential of the younger worker. Workers over 40 years of age could expect to be discriminated against because of their "aging," but surprisingly, this discrimination effect was found mainly among qualified and semiqualified older workers, and not to the same extent with unqualified laborers.

In Rio Grande do Norte, an agricultural worker captured the agony of discrimination in his testimony (CERIS, 1981). "When you leave off producing you lie around like an outcast till you die. . . . The old man after a certain age no longer finds work; nobody wants to give him any work."

Some of the response to this problem will need to come from the ultimate strength and sanction of government legislation, some from informed discussion with trade unions and employers' confederations, and some from mass exposure of the problem. Clearly, an individual worker in present-day Britain will benefit from high pressure support and considerable legislative reference in cases of sex discrimination, race discrimination, and disablement discrimination, but almost no sympathy—much less support—in cases of age discrimination. Until comparatively recent, times the much-vaunted welfare state even reduced the pension of a retired person who dared venture out to work beyond a certain minimal remuneration, even though there was no moral or legal justification for reducing a contributory pension.

Again the problem of social isolation, and its possible remedies, is so vast as to defy brief analysis. There are psychosocial factors related to stress-impelled events or situations, and other psychosocial factors in connection with lack of social support. In the first instance, this could be bereavement of the spouse, a late-life divorce, or compulsory retirement, especially at an early age. In the second instance, this could be physical isolation, lack of community integration, and absence of intimate relationships (Kees and Knipschseer, 1988).

Attempts to respond to such isolation often take the form of casual and irregular or ill-planned voluntary involvement with the isolated person. Psychologists warn of the danger of disappointment of expectations aroused by such interventions. Where, as in the case of elders with no family, "expectations for social support will be quite high, to meet the expectations . . . will be much more difficult. As long as somebody's standard of social support expectations is not met, there is an incongruity between the support given and that expected; this incongruity will prohibit the buffering effect of the social support given the message" (Kees and Knipscheer, 1988). The message is for caution in other than well-planned, continuous, and sensitive interventions in cases of perceived loneliness.

There are wide variations possible in providing opportunities in elder groups. The tendency of some day centers to hope that provision of a pack of cards will provide for all pensioners' interests is very far from reality. A specialist report reminds that

> the older the age group being considered the greater the diversity within it. For example, the range of physical and psychological abilities of a group of 60-year-old people is greater than that found in a group of 20-year-old people. Similarly the range of physical and psychological abilities in a group of 80-year-old people is greater than that found in a group of 60-year-old people. (Pan American Health Organization, 1989)

Moving from a rather generalistic view of a major problem to a concern of a minority (possibly 4 percent of older people in some countries), there is the matter of freedom of choice for the less able elderly who are confined to an institution and prone to the symptoms of that premature rigor mortis known as institutionalization.

Muriel Skeet (1989) encompasses the subject nicely by saying, "Where patients live in any type of building that is larger in scale than ordinary domestic accommodation, opportunities for them to determine their own lifestyles and to make choices about their daily lives are limited. Residential care emphasizes the disabilities and dependency of patients and reduces opportunities for choice, whereas, if there is adequate professional and practical support, care at home develops patients' abilities and independence: it leaves patients and their families in control." It might be added that, outside the institution, the elder is a person rather than a patient or client.

Let's consider the key worker system in an elderly persons' home. A consultant (Bond, 1992) found, "Time is crucial in creating a therapeutic relationship. Professional careers in group settings are unlikely to have enough time to do the things they would like with residents at their own pace and at the moment when intervention is most needed." But when she arrived at a home to advise on introducing the key worker idea, "staff were suspicious of proposed changes. Care staff were sometimes run off their feet just trying to get everyone up, dressed, fed and into bed at night" merely to conform to an arbitrary system based on custom and practice. And to whose advantage?

Consulting with my wife on the routine in a particular home, I discovered that such pressures could be relieved by the simple method of allowing residents to choose their own individual timetables. Once staff had been convinced that this would not lead to some form of genocide for which they would be held responsible, it was found that irregular gettings-up, dressings, bathings, and feedings spread the load of work much more amenably for staff and made life more pleasant for residents.

So, in such a home, "nobody has a right to intrude into any of the [individual bed-] rooms without due permission from the residents who get up when they feel like it and have a wide choice of menu. If they prefer to dine out there is a restaurant" in the center section of the complex (J.R. Tout, 1991). Surprisingly, such freedom of choice is still the exception rather than the rule in many instances in many lands.

The elimination of choice and opportunity can even be carried to the extent observed in a home in Peru (and not confined to that country by any means). There, when married couples are admitted, they are split up. The man is sent to the male section, and the woman goes to the female area. Their only meeting is a sighting across the aisle of the chapel at daily worship. Although the building is magnificent, the levels of medical care superb, and the food nutritious, the feelings of the suddenly and forcibly divorced married couples can be imagined. The reason given by the matron of the home for this particular aberration of institutionalization was simply, "Well, you know what old men get up to."

To strike a most serious note, an Asian study contains a warning.

> In the future the prolongation of life through sophisticated medical technology is likely to generate debate on the financial burden of maintaining life at the margin. The cost of sustaining a sick elderly person through his or her remaining years in pain and misery would probably be evaluated, at both societal and individual levels, against the benefits of the person remaining alive. . . . the central issue of medical care for the elderly in the future is not about the advancement in medical technology but rather on the financial costs of such care, and the values and philosophies associated with the preservation of life into extreme old age. (Cheung, 1989)

The Asian warning may appear a little exaggerated until we remember that even the British National Health Service found itself in the quandary, some years ago, of committing some discreet form of "geronticide," by restricting kidney dialysis to patients below a certain age. Not so long ago a Nazi government considered the decent elimination of those incapable of full mental participation in life to be an all too logical solution.

Perhaps it is necessary, having in mind also the covert methods of geronticide by starvation or other neglect to which numbers of elderly are condemned, to postulate another opportunity to which the elderly should be empowered: simply the opportunity to live out their individual natural span of life.

Welfare of the Less Able

It is necessary to differentiate between the provision of sufficient opportunities for those many older people who are able to enjoy them, and the provision of welfare care for the minority of older persons who cannot fend or care for themselves. The failure to fend represents an economic inability (plus normally a mental inability to cope), and requires some economic support. The failure to care will be normally due to psychological or physiological problems or a combination of these.

The interface between the opportunities and welfare considerations becomes particularly evident in attempts to mobilize elderly people to individual or group action. Sometimes this appears to be wasted effort. "It is in the very nature of aging to retard the activity of [some] individuals and to dull their perceptions, which means that to involve [such] elderly people directly in planning new initiatives requires much time and patience, when the needs of the program proscribe such considerations. . . . The very urgency of need makes it seem more feasible to relegate the majority of elderly to the role of passive recipients, but this in turn militates against the most sacred objectives of the program: the independence and usefulness of the elderly person" (K. Tout, 1988).

A conclusion drawn from research in the United States was that

the consensus to be drawn from different streams of research is that while most people in the U.S. have the basic ingredients for social support, sizable subgroups exist for whom lack of imbeddedness in social networks, or disruptions in traditional sources of social support, may have deleterious physical, mental and emotional health consequences. The "oldest old" (persons 85 and above); recently bereaved widows; individuals suffering from chronic brain disorders; low income, inner city residents; and the rural elderly have been found to be among such groups. (Minkler, 1987)

There is a certain commonality of experience among such deprived and disadvantaged groups of elderly. I had to brief a retired Peace Corps volunteer on work with dependent elderly people in a remote region of Belize. After a year of working in the region, the Peace Corps volunteer informed me that she found conditions of the elderly in remotest Belize hardly dissimilar from conditions with which she had worked for years in remote areas of Washington State in the United States.

It might be assumed that services in North America and Europe would be available to meet the basic needs of those who require welfare support (in the forms of income support, health care, and social intercourse) due to their dependency. There would no doubt be debate as to the *adequacy* of existing services. In many developing countries there is no question but that even basic services of some types do not yet exist, and that in some places there is no immediate prospect of their coming into being.

"In developing countries the ability to organize community response often varies inversely to the traditional strengths of the community, which lie in family and clan ties which are organic and innate, and do not require the systematic planning and implementation of infrastructures requisite to formal social services" (AGECO Reports, 1989/1990). Hence those countries do not possess cadres of planners and organizers to meet the increasing requirements for care programs.

On a national scale the provision of sufficient services, to empower those elderly toward maximum life enjoyment who cannot ensure this for themselves, is surely a sine qua non of so-called civilization in countries with adequate economies. However, in many developing regions the emerging problem can only be met by international commitment of funds and constancy resources. Given the current wide discussion of the world village concept, this respect and service, for those whom modernization has most impoverished, should be high on the agenda of empowerment measures to be considered by world citizens.

EDUCATION IN AGING

This title has two meanings: general education for people who are at an age where they become aware of their so-called aging state (although technically aging may be said to commence at birth), and education about the realities of aging for those who have never prepared themselves for later life as prescribed by their society.

For many retired people—as for many in developing societies who have no constant source of support—the acquisition of further education can mean more than a useful leisure pastime. It may enable a significant buttering of the daily bread. That being so, it is still helpful to consider the empowerment or enrichment of lifestyle which education for its own sake can bring to later years.

A recent review, owing much to G. H. Mead, sums up this experience.

> The aging process will be experienced as positive or negative (life-enhancing or life-restricting) according to two basic factors. First the richness and complexity of self, which is a significant interpersonal resource, will depend on the ability of the individual to imaginatively and flexibly take on the roles of others. Secondly . . . the greater the complexity,

flexibility and sophistication of a society the greater the potential of the individual to develop a complex and richly layered self. (Hepworth, 1991)

If this argument is accepted, it continues, "The processes of self-development in and through later life are not the sole responsibility of the older members of the population but a two-way transaction involving the active and imaginative participation of those networks of interacting individuals of all ages that we call 'society.' "

Another aspect of later life education is the extent to which it can combat elitism. There is perhaps no wider variation in human living than the disparity between the poorest old and the most affluent old. The figure of the tycoon, liberated from the day-to-day shackles of his business diary, but still able to enjoy his vast range of expensive, deluxe leisure options, contrasts vividly with the picture of the aged beggar woman, sitting on a dirty pavement, sleeping under a cardboard shelter, and unable even to enjoy the dubious delights of a basic institution because of her life-long induction into beggary. At no other stage of life (except maybe at the burial, which is only life's reflection) can the contrast be so stark, or unrelieved by hope of restitution or rehabilitation.

Education per se cannot prohibit the tycoon from using his private jet or luxury yacht, nor can it hand a bowl of rice to the aged beggar. But education is often the first ingredient which moves the wealthy to consider more seriously the lot of others, and which can help all but the most derelict a step forward from the cardboard shelter on the dirty pavement.

A welfare program that I was monitoring failed to understand why a Belizean woman, receiving a regular sum of $20 a month from a son in the United States, was still living in relative poverty and discomfort. She received the 20-dollar check regularly; a kind neighbor went to the bank to change the check for her, since she had never entered a bank in her life; the neighbor handed her the Belize dollars honestly; and she spent them all each week as her son insisted.

It was only after much closer scrutiny that the truth emerged. At that time a U.S. dollar was worth two Belize dollars. But the kind neighbor had seen a means of profit and was bringing home to the old woman just 20 Belize dollars for 20 U.S. dollars, thus depriving her of 50 percent of her income. Lack of education resulted in the woman being still unable to understand why eventually she was receiving 40 dollars from a more reliable visitor when she only received a 20-dollar check. She did not refuse the additional cash, of course. This may seem a very minor incident, but it begs the question, "Would lack of education mean my income being cut by half?"

A recent study in Guatemala (Arias de Blois, 1991) throws up several interesting sidelights on education levels of older people. The literacy rate for males over 60 years of age was 43.1 percent and for females, 30.5 percent. But when those figures took account of rural residence and indigenous ethnicity, the literacy rates decreased in males from 43.1 percent to 16.8 percent, and for females from 30.5 percent to only 2.8 percent. Perhaps of equal interest is a discovery about the worth of education about education, that is to say, making people aware of the value of education. Over a period of only eight years, when elderly people were asked to declare their reason for nonemployment (in a society where continued income is a requisite for most persons), the number who blamed lack of education had risen nearly 700 percent.

In less modernized societies illiteracy is not to be equated with ignorance. In the more academically oriented societies of the North, an illiterate person will often feel under the constraint of giving an explanation, such as parental disregard for education, lack of finance, migration, poor mental health, or whatever. In many preindustrial societies, the system of reading and writing was either of no importance at all or was restricted to specifics such as religious observances.

An illiterate person from a peasant society may well be highly skilled in the agricultural processes, the indicators of weather, the science of construction, and many other useful matters. The illiterate female may have a considerable store of knowledge about health, medicines, female life systems, clan procedures, catering, and horticulture. So a literacy class in a rural area of a developing country does not have to assume that its elderly pupils are ignorant; they may be highly informed members of their own society. Literacy classes, sometimes seen by educators as the lowest form of educational life, should in those situations be seen as "continuing education," perhaps of a postgraduate value to the pupils. I insist on this point, having had need to remonstrate more than once with well-intentioned, youthful teachers of third world literacy classes for elders, where the teacher displayed a rather supercilious attitude to what were assumed to be ignorant, unintelligent peasants.

The movement toward greater educational opportunities for older people is to be welcomed. This is a phenomenon not merely of the North, but also in a number of developing countries. For instance, Pro Vida, the Colombian age care agency, has negotiated with Colombian universities access for older people to some one hundred normal academic courses in subjects ranging from ecobiology to philosophy, and from food engineering to business administration. The same agency has also organized literacy classes for 2,000 elderly people at a time.

A warning note is sounded by one writer (van der Veen, 1990, 101) who feels that, if segregation of older students leads to courses of lesser academic standards, then "third age universities run the risk of becoming inferior universities and this is straightforward ageism . . ." but, on the other hand, a normal university "can be indeed called elitist when it is not sufficiently active in demolishing the barriers that prevent older students from participating in higher education." Yet again, "a system for education for older adults can be elitist, particularly when it does not organize a balanced offering of educational opportunities at all levels, and instead concentrates on forms of higher education."

If, in the North, preretirement courses are considered essential to buffer the shock of compulsory separation of the worker from the workplace and work routine, how much more so in the South? In many developing countries there are areas where the concept of retirement is still unknown, or, as in the case of those intrepid centenarian workers in Vilcabamba, is thought to be relevant at maybe 150 years of age (quoted to author in Vilcabamba).

The Costa Rican voluntary organization for age care, AGECO, has been approached by local business concerns with a unique problem. Having no armed forces and no defense budget, Costa Rica has wisely developed one of the best national social welfare systems in the developing world. More than 80 percent of its people already enjoy retirement benefits. But, say the business representatives, "We are telling our workers, many of whom are rural people migrated into the city, that they must now retire, and they do not know what retirement means." So AGECO has been contracted to organize substantial preretirement classes, at the expense of business firms, so that workers can approach this unfamiliar experience with a confidence that expresses itself in the continuing quality of their work in the last days before retirement (AGECO).

Relationships

So much is said in defense of the family as a first resource and last resort for elderly people that it might seem strange to speak of empowerment of the older person within the more intimate relationships of everyday life. The fact is that, in all the underresearched segments of gerontology, possibly no segment is less adequately investigated than the true quality of family care, especially in less developed societies. Some personal experience suggests that the quality of care is sometimes very inadequate. This can sometimes relate to the attitude or condition of the elderly persons themselves.

The problem of quality of family care may have been the basis for a recommendation from an international forum in Kiev.

> Although the family has primary responsibility for the care of its elderly members, it is recommended that local authorities should enhance the care of the elderly by enforcing the general observance of by-laws regulating the minimum quality of housing, the maintenance of public services, and sanitation; such observance could be assured through care-givers without adversely affecting the circumstances of the elderly themselves. (United Nations, 1986)

The interface between family relationships and official intervention is often a sector of human enterprise fraught with negative potential, to the extent of nullifying the best empowerment intentions. It has been said that "the family, for its part, is the antithesis of bureaucracy. . . . family members, unlike the staff of a bureaucracy, are not inter-changeable. The loss of a family member is felt immediately by all other members. . . . In all developed countries, however, functions which may once have been the unique province of the family are now becoming shared functions of the family and bureaucracy" (Shanas, 1981).

A Beijing conference pointed out that a

> factor taxing the resources of families as care providers, is the increase in numbers of the *extreme* aged, who may require intensive nursing and other support. While family members may wish to continue care for very elderly relatives, they will, in most cases, lack the skill and physical capacity to provide continuous nursing supervision. Linked to the growing prevalence of the extreme aged is the increasing probability of families encompassing four or five generations. (United Nations, 1989)

The same conference details a fair summary of major factors on which continued extended family care will depend: "cultural or legal prescriptions and the level of adherence to those prescriptions; the demographic availability of family members; the geographic availability of family members; the economic capacity of families to provide support; the willingness of family members to provide support."

A fascinating, if somewhat sad, illustration of aspects of family care quality and elder capability comes from Guatemala. The Comité Nacional Pro Ciegos y Sordomudos de Guatemala (Committee for Blind and Deaf) discovered numbers of blind elderly people abandoned as beggars on the streets. A separate unit was established adjacent to the ophthalmic hospital. Although rescue was too late to cure most of the blind beggars, a twofold training system was introduced so the beggars enjoyed residence under a decent roof. The mode of daily living for the blind was taught, but, in addition, there was useful training in such aspects as housekeeping, child care, cooking, and an income-generating handicraft.

As the news spread about this initiative, suddenly the families, who had ejected the elders from their homes, began to appear at the door of the unit, saying, in effect, "Please may we have our Granny back. We do love her and want her at home." In its wisdom, the Committee responded that families who had ejected the elder could only receive him or her back again if they themselves as a family attended a specially conceived course in intergenerational relationships. The placement would then be closely monitored.

This example reflects the dire straits of poverty that, in most cases, was discovered to be the major cause for ejection of the extra mouth needing to be fed. It also gives evidence of the extent to which relationships in such circumstances become tolerable when the rejected elder is transformed into a clean, capable, productive member of the household.

Where permanent breakdown in families has occurred as, for instance, by death of all younger family members, or distant migration, "a number of intergenerational pilot projects have pointed the way towards wider strategies for either reinforcing the existing family system while there is still time or identifying *surrogate* family structure based on the commitment of individuals or communities."

For instance, teaching about aging in schools can "lead on to action programs, part of which consists in the child being introduced to an old person or persons who have no relative. These sensitive relationships depend on the most simple but essential elements such as the child reading the daily newspaper to the illiterate 'grandparent.' . . . In return the 'grandparent' shares with the child a rich store of cultural traditions, memories, songs, dances, games, for which there may be no written tradition" (K. Tout, 1989b).

Such programs have developed more permanent relationships with firm, mutually satisfying links extending through the pupil to the pupil's own family, who eventually "adopt" the older person. The countries cited as having programs of this type were India, Sri Lanka, Kenya, and Colombia, but the application is worldwide.

Reference has already been made to the increased probability of four and five generational families. The Bonn study (Lehr) produced two particularly significant factors. One was that out of 411 families, 402 enjoyed the continuing presence of great-great-grandmothers (average age 90.5), but only 15 had great-great-grand-fathers still living. Only 4 percent of the great-great-grandparents lived in areas where *no other* member of the five generations was settled. Added to this factor, or rather subtracted from that, was that 4 percent was the number of great-great-grandparents for whom modern methods of communication render mere distance an insignificant consideration. Thus, we perceive a factor that may, at some time and in some cases, obviate or reduce the need for empowerment action from external sources. The same factor is seen in reverse in Paillat's observation (1981) that in France in the eighteenth century one became an orphan of both father and mother at an average 29.5 years of age, while today the equivalent age is more than 55. There will also be more cases where a fourth or even fifth generation, fit and able elder may exercise care for a younger grandparent within the family hierarchy, thus giving Paillat's orphan statistic some substance.

The Beijing conference, while itself exploring the value of family support, also adds a rider to the effect that "an over-emphasis on family support as a solution to the problems of an aging society detracts from the need for inputs from other areas such as from aged persons themselves, from the numbers of economically active persons who do not have surviving parents, from employers and from the State. The State must increasingly adopt a more interventionist, coordinating role" (United Nations, 1989).

Such interventions must take the form of relationships, in other words, two-way responses involving the elderly themselves to the extent possible, and not regimes imposed by financial budget-setters or sociological trendsetters.

Nana Apt (1991) again says, "Many people in Ghana" [as elsewhere] "continue to extol the virtues and strengths of the extended family system in its provisions for the welfare of elderly people. Whether the traditional extended family will be able to meet the needs of its older members is a question that has yet to be answered."

We have sought to explore the nature of the power that is sought through the themes of politics, opportunities, welfare, education, and relationships. The empowerment word "skeleton" now leaves us to look at the negotiation of a worthy and permanent status through:

- mobilization of the constituency;
- enlightenment of the general public;
- national infrastructure and support; and
- transition strategies.

NEGOTIATION OF A CONTINUING STATUS

The word "negotiation" is used here advisedly, as there will be very rare opportunities for elderly people to impose solutions outside their own constituency. Older heads of state like Ballaguer or Paz Estenssoro may give personal support to the movement for empowerment of the elderly, but routes of detailed negotiation will continue to be through politicians and civil servants who may not look kindly on attempted demonstrations of gray power. Funding will have to be sought through intricate and prolonged processes, and the opinion and support of the general public will have to be wooed. In many of these confrontations the mere principle of seniority may count for little.

There will have to be sensitive exchanges with representatives of other causes so that specialization does not lead to conflict. Above all, there will be a need to respond to many variations of opinion, objectives, and actual requirements of the elderlies' own constituency, including the question of many of appropriate age who may not wish to acknowledge the various categorizations of aging. The first imperative may therefore be mobilization of the constituency.

Mobilization of the Constituency

It is important to regard this constituency as composed not of "aged" but of the "aging." In this way the entire human population will be included, and the grand design will be seen to incorporate such other aspects as preretirement concerns, problems of youth needing intergenerational relationships, and basic, biological research into the mystery of life itself.

This approach also provides a philosophical exit from the high-conflict dilemmas of individuals versus masses, small groups versus large movements, one good cause versus another, and so on. But these potential flash points must be addressed in detail as well.

It has been said that "nobody really likes (the) large-scale organization yet, it seems, (the) large-scale organization is here to stay . . . the fundamental task is to achieve smallness *within* (the) large organization any organization has to strive continuously for the orderliness of *order* and the disorderliness of creative *freedom*" (Schumacher, 1974). In this respect it is useful to consider a militant pressure group in terms of military units: platoons, companies, battalions, and divisions, of variable size but each dependent on the others for greatest efficiency of operation.

There also has to be the variation of interdependent units, such as infantry, cavalry, artillery, and logistics, each proud of its own identity but recognizing the indispensable value of the others. The United States has its own blueprint for a mighty army of retired persons in the American Association of Retired Persons (AARP) who, in their individual aims, lifestyles, allegiances, and rates of aging must represent myriad variations. Some instances of mobilization at a lower numerical level and in less developed infrastructure may also be pertinent.

A pleasant instance of elder empowerment comes from the port area of Lima in Peru. Some years ago a group of nursing mothers gathered together to hold discussion sessions and generally enjoy each others' fellowship. In due course the mothers became grandmothers. At that point they decided to transform their society into a Grandmothers Club. Instead of being concerned with prenatal and postnatal subjects, they would give attention to the circumstances of older women in their area. The major problem was quickly diagnosed as lack of enough food to eat on the part of many older people. So the social club for nursing mothers grew into a meals service for the very old and frail, and thence into a mouthpiece for the needs of elderly people in their locality (Malley, 1990).

A Mexican program drew its inspiration from the Council of Elders formed by seven Nahuatlacas tribes during a migration that began in the year 1160. At the magical age of 52 the person was considered to have become an Elder, due to honor and privileges. Some 800 years later, social workers drew on the ancient idea to form groups of interested people who would be trained in special workshops so that they would develop fairly consistent models of councils.

One of the aims of these councils is, as the name implies, to discuss affairs relating to aging. A further aim is to inform the authorities and the general public of the outcome of such debates. But, because of the urgency of need in rapidly urbanizing areas, as well as rapidly depopulated rural areas, the councils became action centers where primary health and other services could be made immediately available to other people.

In view of previous references to the valley of the aged in Vilcabamba, Ecuador, it should be noted that when the Committee for the Defense of the Elderly of Vilcabamba was constituted, half of the committee were themselves elderly people, in Vilcabamba terms, over 80 years of age. This is in direct contrast to a meeting that I attended in London some years ago, composed of nearly 30 civil servants, academics, social workers, geriatricians, and voluntary agency leaders. After some long discussion of the national destinies of the aged, I was constrained to remark that there was not one person present who could be considered, demographically, an elderly person. Were they being condemned in absence?

There must be the overall concept of humanity as an entity, right as a primal force, welfare as an indivisible benefit available to all underprivileged groups of all chronological ages, in every country of the world. While maintaining individual identity, a movement of the elderly toward empowerment can claim common cause with other groups, and may even draw surprising support from unsuspected quarters, such as children's organizations with intergenerational interests.

A prophetic thought on mobilization of the constituency is heard from an Asian source.

In the future the bulk of the elderly will have received more education and will be more participative in social, economic and political activities. As they become aware of their rights, the demand for a reallocation of resources in their favor may become a rallying point, mobilizing them into a political force. However, the full manifestation of their political power may be constrained by the nature of political regimes in the region. The response of governments to these issues will be critical to overall societal stability and progress. (Cheung, 1989)

Having mobilized the constituency, the next objective will be to enlighten the public.

ENLIGHTENMENT OF THE PUBLIC

There appears to be some agreement that, as a prior requisite of public education on the matter of world aging, more research and more adequately presented information are needed. A United Nations survey (1991) admits,

There are huge gaps in our knowledge. Despite the fact that gerontological research has increased dramatically over the past three decades, we still do not know some of the most basic facts about the lives of the elderly in most countries, especially the developing countries. This means that the discussion that follows is more impressionistic than scientific in nature.

As implied earlier, we have not yet come near to a satisfactory definition of words like aged or elderly or very old. Concepts differ widely. "The concept of a physiological index of age is appealing," writes one commentator (Tobin, 1981), "since we have often said that someone 'looks younger than his age' or 'performs better than people his age.' Inherent in these statements is the implicit notion that we know how someone of a given age should look or perform, that we know what is normative or standard. Within the discipline of human physiology, this determination is frequently difficult.

To proceed, having at least a minimum resource of information available,

one way of changing society's negative attitudes to aging and the aged is to motivate the latter to participate in more activities at all levels and in all areas of society . . . more use could be made of television to promote such initiatives as well as to give information on preventing diseases and disabilities. . . . In relation to the mass media . . . its representatives should be consulted and brought into discussions of needed publicity at an early stage of planning. (Skeet, 1989)

If it is important for the elderly themselves to portray a more attractive image of "elderliness," then it is almost as important to produce charismatic and articulate spokespersons from among the constituency itself. "For too long the disabled and disadvantaged had to depend on well-meaning affluent or non-disabled spokesmen to argue their case. Despite the sincerity of such individuals and organizational spokesmen, most had little real contact with the people for whom they were speaking and none was, in any meaningful way, responsible or accountable to them" (Thursz, 1969).

In publicizing matters that are essentially mainly individual, family, or local, the grand campaign of great impact has to be national and even international. There are now bodies of debate and sources of funding which are multinational or international, and many of those agencies will respond most readily to other groupings at a similar level. As one who has worked with governmental co-funding at the national and international level, I am always impressed by the fact that the best project is often the smallest one that provokes least attention at high level, unless the approach is suitably reinforced; whereas, on occasions, other projects of more dubious worth may be processed rapidly, simply because of the sheer size or hierarchical standing of the proposers.

An international debate on this subject saw that

> the interplay of economic and political relations in today's world gives rise to a much more complex interdependence, involving the growing impact of domestic policies on other nations and of international developments on domestic policies. . . . international institutions need to communicate to an audience wider than the community of persons which participates in their discussions and negotiations. . . . resolutions and declarations will only be effective if they influence the public at large. (Brandt, 1980)

In this latter respect the world of active gerontology should, in car-racing parlance, start in pole position. It is a constituency whose nature means that most human beings will enlist in it, excepting only accidental or epidemic mortality, for most other human mortality tends to be preceded by a period of what might be termed accelerated aging, however brief and at whatever age of adulthood. Large numbers deny that allegiance, because of the traditional stigma attaching to current concepts.

To put it another way, the expectation for the average person of "contracting" aging is far higher than that of contracting AIDS, blindness, venereal disease, or even cancer or heart disease. If we say that people are repelled from the aging cause because of stigma or fear, why is its lobby less persuasive than those for AIDS or cancer?

If this section of the survey appears to be unduly pessimistic, it might be timely to end the section on enlightenment of the public with a reminder from a professional body about the wonders of changes of attitude and allegiance that can be wrought with such speed and efficiency in the tightly networked world of today. Communications networking will be even more frighteningly efficient and instant in the tomorrow of our own aging.

It will not be a great surprise to know that research tends to confirm that media coverage can change the public's thoughts and behavior in as little as two weeks or in as much as six months. In our recent experience, a very dramatic example of the sheer power of the press has become evident. One of the most effective press campaigns of all time changed the normal peace-loving, humane and tolerant nations into warring societies in less than six months. The run up to the Gulf War . . . one of the most interesting aspects of the whole period was the shift in perception from war as being fundamentally anti-peace to war as the only means of bringing peace. (Phillips, 1992)

Those comments may be thought appalling if the instrument of public opinion-forming is used for ill, but enthralling if used for good, as, for instance, to bring about public enlightenment on the positive aspects of aging and to recruit and mobilize action on the negative aspects.

Supposing the elderly constituency to have been mobilized, and a campaign of public enlightenment to have been successfully carried through, any resultant public assertion of the empowerment of older people and any voluntary initiatives aiming at supplying evident requirements will need a governmentally established or authorized infrastructure to survive. Such government support could be in terms of legislation, funding, and service delivery programs in particular.

National Infrastructure and Support

"The well being of elderly people in a rapidly changing society will gradually but steadily become a crucial problem which deserves urgent government attention now," says Nana Apt (1991). But Paul Cheung (1989), responding from an Asian viewpoint, finds that

this is essentially a planner's problem, as the majority of the population, including the policy-makers and politicians, find little meaning in worrying about a scenario that is not going to occur in the near future. Political initiative and support for old age programs are generally lagging across the region. . . . The growth of the elderly population as a public concern is far from prominent among the developing countries in the region, and this accounts for the pervasive lack of infrastructural support for the elderly.

It should be noted that Cheung gives Hong Kong, Japan, and Singapore plus marks for action on aging.

A study of legislative strategies by a legal expert indicates two major principles of government legislation. The first is as a statement of enacted principles.

A fundamental basis for strengthening protection of the health of the elderly is sound legislation. Official policies are generally expressed in laws. When a government adopts an official policy through enactment of legislation, implementation can begin energetically. Even if personnel, facilities and financing for services are limited, steps can be taken to organize and utilize direction provided by legislation can provide a strong springboard for their [health workers'] efforts. (Roemer, 1982)

The other function of legislation is to set in motion services and provisions nationally, either as a direct government service or in a way that carries national authority for other action.

The purposes of legislation are to establish an official policy of government on a particular problem, to develop resources to carry out the policy adopted, to establish programs of service, to provide for financing and to set forth means of managing and regulating the services provided ... while the progression of the aging process affects different individuals at different rates and in different ways, ultimately all aged persons need the umbrella of protective services." (Roemer, 1982)

Another Beijing conference (United Nations, 1990) considered the problems of disablement but also had recommendations relevant to other groups such as the aged, some of whom may also have an interest in disabled welfare.

Governments should play a leading role in increasing resources, enacting and improving disability legislation, facilitating access to knowledge, information, and upgrading of skills, in order to develop talents and potential ... training of expertise, methods for policy development, and ways to strengthen [voluntary] organizations. ... These elements should be incorporated into national development planning and programming.

The World Assembly on Aging of the United Nations was held in Vienna in 1982. From it emerged the Vienna International Plan of Action on Aging. This constitutes an adequate basic blueprint for any government which sincerely desires and plans to enlarge its base of support for the elderly. The outcome of periodic review and appraisal programs, which require governments to report on the international plan, reveal some progress in some countries. In other places, little progress is reported, and the international plan still poses many principles, strategies and objectives that need to be achieved.

The actual delivery of services need not be undertaken by the government, itself, but can be the role of an agent organization, duly appointed, authorized, and supported by the national government. In its report to the United Nations on its focal point for aging matters, Belize, like some other nations, indicated that an agent organization, a voluntary age care movement, was the responsible and empowered body in that country. The voluntary agency, HelpAge Belize, was set up in line with a government-sponsored survey and strategy plan authored by the author of the present paper and his wife. An extract from the original plan will illustrate this empowered agency method.

> A major factor in the planning of services in a country of the size and development of Belize is the relationship between official and voluntary services . . . in major social welfare countries the problem is fragmentized or localized to an extent by the various horizontal and vertical boundaries between authorities and specialized organizations. In unserviced countries the preponderance of voluntary enterprise is such that there is little clash of responsibilities in the actual delivery of service between official and voluntary bodies. Any clash tends to be rather in the political, legal, financial or bureaucratic fields. . . . On the government/professional side there could be a justifiable reluctance to utilize voluntary endeavor in a programmed manner if the voluntary sector is disorganized, contentious or under-trained. Given the need eventually to expand and improve services to cope with an increased age population there should be no fear on the part of professional post incumbents that the use of voluntary manpower might threaten jobs. . . . The first requisite for a truly national strategy on aging is therefore a forum where official and voluntary services can come together for discussion without prejudice. (Tout and Tout, 1985)

Some of the principles enunciated above could have much wider application, even where long-established, centrally planned, and delivered services are seen to be failing to take the strain which current and future demographic changes will impose. There are systems, of course, where nongovernmental services are more properly divided into voluntary agencies on the one hand and private or commercial sectors on the other. In all cases, the weal of the persons within the population being served should be the overriding consideration, rather than political convenience, agency promotion, or private profit.

Now, if we have successfully mobilized our constituency, enlightened public opinion, and evolved adequate national infrastructures and support services, what more do we need? One of the limits of too rigorous and static an empowerment is that virtually overnight its provisions would begin to lose their impact and relevance. Already 2,500 years ago, the Greek philosopher Heraclitus was declaring that all is born of strife, and all is in constant flux. The brilliant discoveries and inventions of these last decades have accelerated that state of societal flux. Successful empowerment of today would need further *repowerment* tomorrow.

TRANSITION STRATEGIES

In spite of the odds that appear to be stacked against the empowerment of elderly people, there are hopeful signs. "Existing projects have provisionally proven that the oldest people in developing countries will respond to planned activities in which they can enjoy a meaningful participation. . . . However, much research is still needed to ensure an accurate assessment of local situations, as well as more evaluative work on existing projects" (PAHO, 1989). The hopeful signs always point forward through more transitional stages toward varying goals.

A Latin American report underlines the inevitability of transition.

> The social characteristics of old people will change. Many of the professionals currently reading this document. . . . will themselves retire during the next 20 years and they will obviously have different views of the needs of older people than those who are older today. . . . [they] will have higher standards and expectations will be better educated and more accustomed to working in groups as members of planning teams. (PAHO, 1989)

China sees an urgent need to monitor the transition of the family into new forms. "We should keep abreast of the trend of the changes in family structure and advocate the establishment of network families *according to circumstances.* Confronted with objective reality we should neither rigidly adhere to the traditional family pattern of the past, nor should we let things slide" (United Nations, 1989).

A recent British commentator (Blaikie, 1992) notices rapid changes in elder behavior that are likely to continue. "The 'chronological bonds' which once bound people to age-appropriate behaviors are being loosened . . . so grandmothers begin to dress like their daughters and grandfathers jog with their sons . . . older people are encouraged not just to dress young, but to exercise, have sex and socialize in ways often indistinguishable from their children's generation."

Technologically, the oldest generations are in a transitional state that can only continue.

> The present generation of older persons has been witness to, and participants in the greatest marvels of human ingenuity . . . to characterize them as "technophobic" is not logical. . . . the *coming* generations of older people will be the most technically sophisticated generations in all of recorded history. As thoughtful humans, we must be prepared to answer these challenges creatively and humanely . . . a fertile area for research as technological progress continues to provide new options. The concept of coping must give way, in a new decade and a new century, to an expanded understanding of rehabilitation. (Engelhardt, 1989)

Unfortunately, the opportunities for fuller living which new research and technologies will offer may be offset by new problems, some of them as unanticipated as the AIDS problem was so few years ago. For example, there is an indication that the rate of elder suicide may rise substantially.

> The elderly have higher suicide rates than any other age group. . . . Younger people today [commit] suicide more frequently than did our

elders in their youth. As the elderly are the fastest growing segment of the population, we can expect that both the rate and the absolute number of late life suicides will increase through the early part of the next century. The limited available data suggest that the profile of suicide changes with increased age, including an ever greater male to female ratio; an increasing lethality of suicide attempts, with more use of violent means; and a greater association with physical illness and affective psycho pathology. (Conwell et al., 1991)

The study here quoted identifies the over-75 group as having a higher suicide rate than the 65–69 group.

Improved methods of diagnosis may reveal more conditions requiring expensive services and tend to bias available resources toward demands at present unperceived. An instance is in borderline personality disorder where "our existing diagnostic yardsticks suffer from a lack of fit. . . . If there are individuals with borderline personality disorder in old age, as clinicians know there are, then we need to adapt our yardsticks to be able to identify them." And, the writer goes on, "Given the chronicity of some degree of personality disorder throughout life, and the increase in prevalence of specific stresses in age, as well as the remarkable shift in demographics to the older end of the life course, there is real concern about the ratio of service demands to service supplies and the efficacy of interventions and treatment" (Rosowsky and Gurian, 1991).

In conclusion, aging may be "one of the potential crisis subjects of the future" (K. Tout, 1993), unless the elders themselves are fully involved in their own destiny. However, there already exist many worthy models for action in which official departments can collaborate with community groups, voluntary agencies, and elders themselves, to offset the threat of catastrophe before it fully develops.

REFERENCES

AGECO Reports. 1989/1990. AGECO, Apartado 5956-1000, San Jose, Costa Rica.

American Association for International Aging. 1986. *Conversations in Nairobi*. Washington, DC: AAIA.

Apt, N. A. 1985. *Aging in Ghana*. Legon: University of Ghana.

————. 1991. "The Myth of the Extended Family." *ageACTION* 4.

Arias de Blois, J. 1991. *Aging in Guatemala (A Demographic Analysis)*. Paris: CICRED, and Valletta: INIA.

Binstock, R. H. 1981. "The Aging as a Political Force: Images and Resources," A.J.J Gilmore (ed.), *Aging: a Challenge to Science and Society*, vol. 2. Oxford: L'Institut de la Vie and WH0.

Blaikie, A. 1992. "Whither the Third Age?" *Generations Review* 2(1), 3.

Bond, M. 1992. "Time Is on Our Side." *Social Work Today*. February 27, 24.

Brandt, W. (Chairman) 1980. *North-South: A Programme for Survival*. London: Pan.

CERIS. 1981. *Report on Old People's Homes in Brazil*. Rio de Janeiro: CERIS.

Cheung, P. P. L. 1989. *Planning for the Elderly in Development*. United Nations, ESCAP.

Choucri, N. 1974. *Population Dynamics and International Violence.* Lexington, MA: Lexington Books

Conwell, Y., K. Olsen, E. D. Caine, and C. Flannery. 1991. "Suicide in Later Life: Psychological Autopsy Findings." *International Psychogeriatrics* 3, 59.

Eisenbach, Z, and E. F. Sabatello. 1991. *Demographic and Socio-Economic Aspects of Population Aging in Israel.* Paris: CICRED, and Valletta: INIA.

Engelhardt, K. G. 1989. "Computers, Artificial Intelligence, Robotics, and Aging Humans." *International Journal of Technology and Aging* 2(1), 3.

Flores Colombino, A. 1982. "Psychology of the Third Age," in A. C. Morelliet al. (eds.), *Bio-psycho-social Third Age.* Montevideo: Libreria Medica Editorial.

Foner, N. 1985. Old and Frail and Everywhere Unequal. Care for the Aged in Nonindustrial Cultures. New York: Hasting Center Report, April.

Glascock, A., and S. Feinman. 1981. "Social Asset or Social Burden: An Analysis of the Treatment of the Aged in Non-Industrial Societies." C. L. Fry. (ed.), *Dimensions: Aging, Culture and Health.* New York: Praeger.

Hepworth, M. 1991. "Positive Ageing and the Mask of Age." Journal of Educational Gerontology 6(2), 100.

Ibrahim, M. 1985. Tradition and Modern Development in Bangladesh Society. Dhaka: Bangladesh Association for the Aged.

Kees, C. P. M., and P. Knipscheer. 1988. "Social Support and Isolation as Health Related Variables," in *Danish Medical Bulletin.* Special Supplement Series no. 6, 24.

Kumarappa, J. C. 1958. *Economy of Permanence.* Rajghat, Kashi: Sarva-Seva Sangh Publications.

Lehr. Ursula. 1989. Personal Communication.

Mahar, D. J. 1979. *Frontier Development Policy in Brazil: A Study of Amazonia.* New York: Praeger.

Malley, J. 1990. "The Grandmothers to the Aid of Grandmothers." *ageACTION* 2, 2.

Maxwell, R. J., and P. Silverman. 1981. "Geronticide." Paper prepared for American Anthropological Association, Los Angeles.

Minkler, M. 1987. *Community Based Initiatives to Reduce Isolation and Enhance Empowerment of the Elderly.* Berkeley: University of California.

Paillat, P. 1981. *"Influence de l'évolution demographique sur la constitution de la famille et sur la place des personnes âgées."* in A. J. J. Gilmore, et al. (eds.), *Aging: A Challenge to Science and Society.* Vol. 2. Oxford University Press: L'Institut de la Vie and World Health Organization.

Pan American Health Organization. 1989. *The Challenge of Ageing in Latin America.* Washington, DC: PAHO.

Payne, K. 1991. "Meet Mrs. Alberta Ollenu." ageACTION. London: HelpAge International 3, 7.

Phillips, D. 1992. "Recession Enhances the Value of Measurement." *The Institute of Public Relations Handbook.* London: Kogan Page.

Roemer, R. 1982. *Basic Principles and Legislative Strategies to Promote the Health of the Elderly.* Copenhagen: WHO (Europe).

Rosenmayr, L. 1990. "The Position of the Old in Tribal Society," in M. Bergener, et al (eds.), *Challenges in Aging.* London: Academic Press.

Rosowsky, E., and B. Gurian. 1991. "Borderline Personality Disorder in Late Life." *International Psychogeriatrics* 3(1), 39.

Schumacher, E. F. 1974. *Small Is Beautiful. London: Abacus.*

Shanas, E. 1981. "The Elderly: Family, Bureaucracy, and Family Help Pattern," in A. J. J.

Gilmore et al. (eds.), *Aging: A Challenge to Science and Society.* Vol. 2. Oxford: L'Institut de la Vie and World Health Organization.

Simmons, L. 1945. *The Role of the Aged in Primitive Societies.* New Haven, CT: Yale University Press.

Skeet, M. 1989. *Small Area Planning for the Elderly.* Copenhagen: WHO (Europe).

Thursz, D. 1969. *Consumer Involvement in Rehabilitation.* Washington, DC: U.S. Department of Health, Education and Welfare.

Tobin, J. D. 1981. "Physiological Indices of Aging" in A. J. J. Gilmore et al. (eds.), *Aging: a Challenge to Science and Society.* Vol. 1. Oxford: L'Institut de la Vie and World Health Organization.

Tout, J. R. 1991. "An Integrated Service." *ageACTION* 5, 5.

Tout, K. 1988. "Aging: Social Supports and Community Interventions in Developing Countries." *Danish Medical Bulletin.* Special Supplement Series, No. 6, 69.

Tout, K. 1989a. *Ageing in Developing Countries.* Oxford: Oxford University Press.

Tout, K. 1989b. "Intergenerational Exchange in Developing Countries," in S. Newman and S. W. Brummel (eds.), *Intergenerational Programs: Imperatives, Stratagies, Impacts, Trends.* New York: Haworth, 74.

Tout, K. (ed.). 1993. *Elderly Care: A World Perspective.* London: Chapman and Hall.

Tout, K., and J. R. Tout. 1985. *Perspectives on Ageing in Belize.* OPEC/HelpAge International.

United Nations. 1986. *Report of the Interregional Seminar to Promote the Implementation of the International Plan of Action on Aging-Kiev.* New York: United Nations.

United Nations, 1989. *International Symposium on Aging: Policy Issues and Future Challenges-Beijing.* New York: UNFPA:CPR/85/P54.

United Nations. 1990. *International Meeting on the Roles and Functions of National Co-ordinating Committees in Disability in Developing Countries.* Beijing, November 1990. New York: CSDHA/DDP/NDC/4.

United Nations. 1991. *The World Aging Situation.* United Nations Office at Vienna.

van der Veen, R. 1990. "Third Age or Inter-Age Universities?" *Journal of Educational Gerontology.* (2), 101.

Chapter 2

Empowerment: As Illustrated by a Bear, Napoleon, and Others

Brigid Donelan

A BEAR STORY

A bear is given to a city, caged. The citizens build a park for it, which takes a year. When the park is ready, the cage is removed. Surrounded by the wide spaces of the park, the bear continues to walk the now imaginary confines of the cage. The cage's boundaries are etched on its mind, restricting its movements.

The bear story illustrates two sides of empowerment: it resides within, in the psyche, and it lies without, in the environment.

Governments and development agencies generally try to create the environmental conditions for empowerment. Educators and psychologists try to release the inner drive. Ultimately, it is only the self who empowers. Napoleon provides an infamous example of self-empowerment: when about to be crowned head of the Holy Roman Empire, he took the crown from the Pope's hands and crowned himself.

The *Oxford Dictionary* expresses another dichotomy in addition to this inner/outer one. It says that empowerment means both "to give power to" and "to make able." To give power to has a clear political connotation; to make able a more practical one. The political empowerment of many new nations in the past 50 years, regardless of their size or wealth, establishes the climate for guaranteeing the same rights to individuals: individual sovereignty regardless of power or wealth. Individual sovereignty or autonomy suggests a right to participate in shaping the social and political environment—which is different from that of having to adjust to a prevailing order established by others.

The practical or "making able" aspect of empowerment was stressed over the past 20 years in development programs promoting popular participation. Popular participation sought to make able mostly through small-scale, self-help activities.

In the present paper, the term empowerment encompasses its practical, political, environmental, and psychological (including emotional and interpersonal) dimensions. Growing awareness and practice of these facets of empowerment is effecting a deep change, if not a paradigm shift, in the exercise of power—principally from power as an exclusive good held by the few toward power as a common good shared by the many.

Power sharing lies at the heart of many current development efforts and is the basis of such slogans as: from top-down to bottom-up, from hierarchy to participation, from formal to informal organization, from conferred to elected authority, and from ascribed to earned status.

The concept of empowerment will be understood and practiced in as many ways as there are countries or groups. It may go wrong. It may be used as a mobilizing slogan, while subtly coopting support for centralized decisions. It may be promoted courageously and altruistically, only to empower actors who subsequently disenfranchise others. It may give rise to institutional structures that empower one group to empower others—such as social services—which too often inadvertently create or perpetuate dependency.

Empowerment may be a topic of heated debate in some places and taboo in others. It may be taboo for several reasons, including a custom of social deference, alternative means of influencing decision making, reluctance to assume additional responsibility, or a lack of consultative skills.

Just as the increase in newly independent countries gave rise to a need for new mechanisms of consultation and cooperation between them, expanding the role of the United Nations, so is it with individuals. As the numbers of active decision makers increase, mechanisms are needed to replace domination that formerly gave order and direction to affairs. One important mechanism is the frank exchange of views in a "free market of ideas."

So it has been in the context of the International Year of the Family (IYF), 1994. IYF gave rise to debates, often heated debates, on what is the family. However, family forms are too varied and fluid to submit to a neat order or one definition. A slogan used in promoting IYF suggests that democracy is an important common denominator for families throughout the world. In a widely used poster for IYF, a caption reads, "Building the smallest democracy at the heart of society."

Democratization, participation, interdependence and other words in the lexicon of "empowerment" are found in recent reports and recommendations on social and economic development. Some complain that the many conferences and debates on development end just there: with words. However, there is a necessity of such "talking shops" at which a consensus on common global values is emerging.

All talk of an eventual peaceful and orderly world is but pious cant or sentimental fantasy unless there are, in fact, some simple but powerful beliefs to which all men hold, some codes or canons that have or can obtain universal acceptance (Kluckhohn, 1962).

FAMILIES: FIRST RESOURCE AND LAST RESORT

Definitions

Family forms are varied and complex across the world, and change over time. No one definition of family prevails, and no final explanation of the marital relationship has been made. In the view of one author, a family is "a unit composed not only of children, but of men, women, an occasional animal, and the common cold" (Ogden Nash as quoted by Metcalf, 1986). Another author simply says that "the reason husbands and wives do not understand each other is because they belong to different sexes" (Dorothy Dix as quoted by Metcalf, 1986). Communications in the family can resemble global events: "We do not squabble, fight or have rows. We collect grudges. We're in an arms race, storing up warheads for the domestic Armageddon" (Hugh Leonard as quoted by Metcalf, 1986).

Perhaps men and women speak different languages. "Male-female conversation is cross-cultural communication. . . . From the time they're born, they're treated differently, talked to differently, and talk differently as a result. . . . These cultural differences include different expectations about the role of talk in relationships" (Tannen, 1986).

It has been said that democracy is government by discussion, which is only effective if people stop talking. Listening is a good part of democratic communication. The balance between listening and talking can be achieved by an attitude of "self-otherness" that is neither selfish nor selfless, but something in between (Cannon, 1992).

Demographic Change Brings Democratic Change

Demographic change in the family is improving democratic practices. As the horizontally extended family of three well-populated generations gives way to a vertically extended family of four, five, and even six smaller generations (the "beanpole" family), the traditional hierarchy of parent-child and husband-wife relationships is changing.

The authority and decisiveness that parents need to exercise in socializing their young children must give way to a more equal, or mature, relationship with adult offspring, a relationship that can now last twice the number of years devoted to child rearing. Mature children may find it difficult to maintain a close relationship with parents if the latter continue to treat them as immature.

Similarly, a married couple may find it difficult to sustain a close relationship with each other in the 20 or 30 years after child rearing if they fail to establish mutual understanding beyond the needs of parenting. As well, a mutually supportive and enabling relationship is important to establish in the middle years, when it may not be so essential, in anticipation of older years when it may be crucial.

Older Women's Challenge

In preindustrial societies, age usually empowers women in the family and the community. Older women in these societies need not conform to the same rules of modesty as younger women and may engage in a wider variety of activities. They have, for example, "more possibility to challenge men in the councils, engage in commerce and trade beyond the boundaries of their villages, and collaborate in organizational activities" (Chaney, 1990).

Roles that empower older women in preindustrial societies include: midwife and healer; administrator of household resources, lands, and other property; trader and businesswoman; and master of traditional skills. While older women in these societies are themselves quite liberated, they often help perpetuate the submissiveness of younger women.

Industrialization limits older women's power in the family and community. Agribusiness makes small holdings unprofitable. Manufactured goods replace handicrafts. Medical services replace traditional midwifery and curing arts. Innovations make wise council seem dull. Radio and cinema tell stories with striking visual and sound effects. New technologies, then, gradually erode the role, income security, and status of older persons. Additionally, when at all portrayed in film, the old are usually shown in negative stereotype, especially older women. Older women of industrial and postindustrial societies may well wish for the pastoral past, or feel compelled to work toward a better future.

Some older women, working toward a better future, have been changing the global agenda. The 33-million-strong American Association of Retired Persons (AARP) was started by one such woman, the "Gray Panthers" by another. Many more young women entering public life will make a correspondingly greater impact on public policy as they age.

Older Men, in the Family and Out

Empowerment with regard to older men in traditional societies would imply a need for them to empower others, that is, to share power with others, including in the family. In industrial and postindustrial societies, after the rigors of 25 years in a mine or boardroom, many older men are happy to "cross over," becoming more gentle, relaxed, sensitive and emotional—while their erstwhile, housebound wives start a business, return to school, or run for mayor. Both sexes begin to take care of "unfinished business" by developing capabilities they often had to neglect in the child-rearing years.

Where divorce is widespread, as in industrial and postindustrial societies, older men are more likely than older women to lose touch with their children and other family members. Several research findings point to a relatively high rate of suicide among single older men (Fattah and Sacco, 1989). This most final of acts, often triggered by a combined sense of uselessness, hopelessness, and helplessness, may have its origins in unrealistic early conditioning for manhood that exaggerates power and neglects emotion. It may be a manifestation of an imbalance where a man is empowered politically and economically but feels powerless before his own emotions and in his interpersonal relationships. Conversely, women could be—by nature or nurture—more empowered psychologically and interpersonally than men, while having less legitimated power over their economic and political destiny.

Powerlessness in any area "sets in motion a series of self-reinforcing defeats that have been described in the literature as learned helplessness, loss of self-esteem and feelings of hopelessness" (Evans, 1992). Felt powerlessness may persist long after opportunities for power are available, as in the case of the bear with which this paper began.

Occasionally, and usually in jest, someone asks why the United Nations has no program for men, since it has programs for women, youth, disabled persons, aging, and the family. As global development moves up a ladder of basic needs, from physiological and security needs to love and self-esteem, there may come a time to establish a program for men.

Picasso's Paradox

Empowerment occurs throughout the life course as a result of acquiring knowledge, experience, and confidence. Rejuvenation can result from this, as noted by Pablo Picasso, who once remarked that it takes a long time to grow young. Picasso was creative into his 90s. Invention and creativity are generally equated with youthfulness; responsibility and understanding are equated with old age. From such a perspective, there are many who are old in youth, others who are young in old age, and some who are both simultaneously.

The eight stages of the life cycle (Erikson, 1985) provide a useful working concept of individual development. In each stage—infancy, early childhood, play age, school age, adolescence, early adulthood, adulthood, and old age—we have something to learn: trust, autonomy, initiative, industry, identity, intimacy, generativity and, in old age, ego integrity. Each earlier learning experience can mature into a different facet of wisdom in old age. For example, if trust is learned in infancy, it matures into appreciation of interdependence and relatedness in old age. Initiative, if learned in the play age, leads to humor, empathy, and resilience in old age, and so on.

Several cultures have tried to mark off the life course in stages. The Comanches (Native Americans) had five life stages; the Kikuyu of Kenya, six for males and eight for females; the Andaman Islanders, 23 for men; and the Incas had ten (Falk and Tonashevich, as quoted by Chaney, 1990).

We have much to gain from seeing the life cycle as continuous empowerment: a gradual denouement of innate capabilities and an expanding responsiveness to opportunities in the environment. For those who reach very old age, the process may seem paradoxical in that it can require accepting decline in intellectual, physical, or social powers on the one hand, while possibly gaining in humility, patience, and humor on the other. Although old age may compel us to accept decline and possibly dependency, it does not require anyone to accept abuse or negative stereotyping.

Ultimate Powerlessness

The ultimate powerlessness in the family occurs with abuse: physical, psychological, or financial abuse. It is exacerbated when there is no recourse. In recent years, much abuse of older persons in the family or domestic setting has come to light.

Causes of elder abuse are complex, arising from any one of the following: the abuser's personality, the older person's behavior, family dynamics, or environmental pressures. One distraught abuser asked:

What do you do when you find the Nana you have known and loved for 33 years is somebody you don't like. When you find that this cherished person is lazy, dirty and completely uncaring for anybody else. . . . You are weary of coping with endless demands, endless complaints and endless feigned illnesses not to mention endless emotional blackmail . . .? (Eastman, 1984, 36).

Under the burden of care, the caregiver lashes out. In other cases, the caregiver may be settling old scores, after the "fall of the tyrant," taking revenge on a once-powerful parent for real or imagined slights and hurts sustained in childhood.

Traits found in abusers of the elderly include: low self-esteem, poor coping mechanisms and communication skills, drug or alcohol abuse, and mental illness. The abuser may feel trapped and resent loss of career, friends, and leisure time; disappointment at inadequate recognition or rewards for caregiving; and outrage at the injustice of an unshared caregiving burden within the family.

The traits found irritating and provocative in the dependent older person have been identified as selfishness, self-pity, masochism, sadism, complaining, feigned illnesses, indulging in amateur dramatics, begging for overdoses, or to be smothered or killed.

Family dynamics contributing to abuse include poor family integration, cycles of violence inherited by each generation, sibling feuds, and social isolation removing the family from the controlling factor of neighborhood disapproval.

Environmental factors contributing to elder abuse may include unemployment, inadequate housing, migration, and man-made and natural disasters.

Gathering information on domestic elder abuse is usually difficult. Anxiety or withdrawal symptoms can easily be misinterpreted as age-related feebleness. Family loyalty and dependency keep older persons from reporting abuse. In some cases, reporting abuse could further strain family relationships and result in institutionalization of the older person (a course of action to be avoided except when necessary for medical care). Neighbors, neighborhood groups, and service professionals, particularly primary health care staff and general medical practitioners, are probably best placed to observe and report the incidence of abuse.

A multidisciplinary team approach is often recommended for assessment and treatment of domestic elder abuse, with well-identified tasks for all team members and a designated key worker to keep in regular contact with the client. Prevention of abuse is an important focus for public policy requiring an empowering environment from birth to enable individuals to achieve their full potential and support for the family to remain or become a democratic institution where problems are discussed and the burden of care is shared.

FAMILY CARE

Who Cares?

Who will provide care for the rising proportion of the very old? How will it be provided?

As long as older people can function independently in daily life, family care is not an issue. It becomes one as frailty or dementia sets in and is critical if public supports are weak or missing. Frailty and dementia increase with age, affecting mainly the oldest old, those 80-and-above. The oldest old comprise the fastest growing population group in the world, jumping from 13 million in 1950 to over 50 million today and a projected 137 million in the year 2025. In that period, the total population will have increased three times, the 60-and-above six times and the 80-and-above ten times. Unlike caring for children, caring for feeble elderly involves increasing dependency and degeneration. It can stretch over a 24-hour day for 365 days a year, for years on end. It can deprive the primary caregiver of career, friends, leisure, freedom, privacy, sleep, money, and, accumulatively, of basic human rights.

In so far as it has been assumed that the primary caregiving burden would fall on a female, usually the wife or a daughter, it could be argued that women were therefore born less equal than men, an equality promised in the International Bill of Human Rights. It proclaims, in Article 1, "All human beings are born free and equal in dignity and rights." While the primary family caregiver is still usually a wife or a daughter, sons and brothers often provide instrumental or secondary support. However, writers Philip Roth and Robert Anderson, who were their fathers' primary caregivers, may help to broaden the identity of caregivers through their works, "Patrimony," and "I Never Sang for My Father," respectively.

Most if not all governments prefer home care over institutional care for the feeble old, since it is usually more humane for the elderly and more economical for the government. Home or family care, often a euphemism for female care, may be inhumane in the extreme on the caregiver and it may bankrupt the family. As the numbers of the very old increase, and other demographic and social changes take place in the family and society, families must be empowered to care for their old. Community support, if not a fully fledged community response, is needed.

However, not every community response is equally commendable. In the fifth century A.D., the Massagetae folk group of the northern Caucasus had, in their own way, a community response. Torn between honoring their elders and being burdened by them, the Massagetae ceremonially killed and ate their elders—and it was held a misfortune not to have lived long enough to be sacrificed (Minois, 1989).

A simple but useful model of community care sharing has been described as a series of concentric circles surrounding an older person, with each circle "containing a different kind of support, ranging from informal at the center to formal at the periphery ..." (Cantor, 1989: 103). In the outermost circle lie political and policy-making entities that determine an elder's entitlements. A little closer are the governmental and voluntary service agencies. Still closer are the nonservice organizations or "mediating structures" that include religious, cultural, and neighborhood groups as well as individuals such as mail carriers, shopkeepers, and building superintendents. Finally, the innermost circle comprises the informal support system of neighbors, friends, and kin—with a major role usually played by one primary caregiver.

Trends suggest that as development proceeds, old age security shifts from family support to public support, or from personal transfers to public transfers, although there are signs of a reversal in recent years. As society becomes more aware of the importance of internal security, and as we attempt to establish collective security to minimize external threats, then governments can be expected to allocate more resources to the various community and family caregiving structures increasingly needed as societies age. Since caregiving has been a woman's burden, greater participation by women in government could be expected to produce a greater public response to this issue.

SUMMARY AND CONCLUSION

The aging of individuals and populations is one of the sweeping changes of our time, impacting on the values, norms, and organization of community life. It calls for important activities such as life-long individual development, intergenerational dialogue, collective family caregiving, community programs, and cooperation between the formal and informal sectors. It should lead us to become more wise, inclusive, and far-reaching in our endeavors, and to embrace sustainable development forms.

Values are in flux worldwide, but a consensus is slowly emerging at the global level on which ones can be held in common. An example is democracy in the family, as promoted by a slogan for the International Year of the Family, "Building the smallest democracy at the heart of society." The building of values is in process in varying ways in the many family forms throughout the world. Democracy implies empowerment.

Empowerment has many interpretations in concept and practice. It can mean "to make able" or "to give power to." It can be brought on by something in the environment or come from within the individual psyche. For all its complexity, empowerment is a simple cry for a more egalitarian, democratic, and humanitarian social order. It may go back to the beginning of time for "there is nothing new under the sun." We can hope that it lies ahead as a promise of the next millennium. In this pivotal decade between two millennia, the concept of universal empowerment is an important component of a paradigm shift from a world dominated by the few toward a world shared more or less equitably by all.

REFERENCES

Cannon, Nona H. 1992. "Self-Otherness: A Goal For The Family." Abstract of background paper delivered at the Seminar On Family Life Education For Peace. University for Peace, Costa Rica, January 12, 1992.

Cantor, Marjorie H. 1989. "Social Care: Family And Community Support Systems." *The Annals of the American Academy of Political and Social Science*, vol. 503, May 1989.

Chaney, Elsa M. 1990. *"Empowering Older Women: Cross-cultural Views."* American Association of Retired Persons and International Federation on Aging.

Eastman, Mervyn. 1984. *Old Age Abuse*. Mitcham, Surrey: Age Concern England.

Erikson, Erik H. 1985. *The Life Cycle Completed: A Review*. New York: W. W. Norton.

Evans, Estella Norwood. 1992. "Liberation Theology, Empowerment Theory And Social Work Practice With The Oppressed." *International Social Work*, vol. 35. London: SAGE.

Fattah, E. A. and V. F. Sacco. 1989. *Crime and Victimization of the Elderly*. New York: Springer-Verlag.

Kluckhohn, Clyde. 1962. *Culture and Behavior*. New York: The Free Press of Glencoe, a division of the Macmillan Company.

Metcalf, Fred (compiler). 1986. *The Penguin Dictionary of Modern Humorous Quotations*. London: Penguin Books.

Minois, Georges. 1989. *A History of Old Age: From Antiquity to the Renaissance* (translated by Sarah Hanbury Tenison). Oxford: Polity Press, in association with Basil Blackwell, Ltd.

Tannen, Deborah. 1986. *That's Not What I Meant: How Conversational Style Makes Or Breaks Relationships*. New York: Ballantine.

Chapter 3

A Second Opinion

James T. Sykes

The concept of empowerment, unfortunately, embodies elements of the patronizing that set elders aside as individuals to whom "we" give certain authority or standing. Thoughtful advocates have offered various definitions of the term empowerment, and provided compelling cases for empowering the elders of society to feel capable of directing their own lives, and to use their individual and cohort "power" effectively. However, I continue to be a skeptic about the term and its many meanings. With other advocates, I share a commitment to a positive goal of empowerment: for people (of all ages) to have a sense of autonomy, a feeling of being in control, and a confidence that they can and do make a difference. These qualities bring a sense of satisfaction, but seldom a feeling of power.

I prefer to approach the subject from the perspective of older persons who, living in the midst of a society in which stereotypes and certain realities diminish their feelings of being in control, seek to participate in the mainstream of life and not feel dependent or as persons without value. Then, having reviewed some of the forces that impinge on the participation of older persons in society, I will suggest ways in which we, as a society, can achieve the desired outcomes without focusing attention on the powerlessness of elders that adds to the burdens they already carry.

There are various ways by which the elders of society assume responsibility for their lives and remain in the mainstream of life. However, rather than an overt plan to empower older people to feel or act in powerful ways, we must remove the barriers that exclude older persons, and then get out of their way.

The reason empowerment seems attractive to advocates for older persons is that they sense that with long life there comes a certain purposelessness. The advocates notice that older people have lost their status, their work, their health, and need the intervention of advocates and advocacy organizations to help them overcome feelings of purposelessness and powerlessness. Advocates devise strategies to make older people feel competent again, to raise their spirits, and to destroy myths that cause them to feel useless, unable to make decisions important to their well-being.

Advocates advance the idea of productivity, suggesting that older people can be productive again. Those who find useful work and discover the sense of competence and self-worth that comes with it are a fortunate few. They have high levels of life satisfaction.

However, there are those whose poor health and personal histories offer little to raise their spirits. They know that someone who is not bedeviled by ill health, poverty, or isolation will have, in all probability, a good old age. But that status is closed to them, largely by a society that has taught young and old that to work is good and that to be healthy is to be "good," while to be ill is to be a burden to society, family, and taxpayers.

These folks do not need advocates to empower them, but a new definition of work that does not make a lack of work personally destructive. We need a new understanding of illness that does not leave the dependent person feeling not only like a burden but also diminished by a lack of health. We need to establish new values that center on the inherent worth of an individual and reject those values which—for those without work, health, or status—undermine their ability to feel in control, with value, and appreciated.

As members of the community, we should enable the elders of society through various strategies, including staying out of the way of self-directing older adults. These adults need to assume full responsibility for their lives, remain in the mainstream of life, act in personally satisfying and socially responsible ways, contribute according to their resources, and receive what they need to retain their dignity and a legitimate place in the family, neighborhood, community, and nation.

I have trouble with the idea that those who have power "empower" others to share their power. For too long the elders of America have accepted their "place" and a set of attitudes toward old age that diminish their worth and lessen their power.

Societies that place undue value on productivity, status, health, wealth, and independence find it difficult to accept—as persons of inalienable worth—those who are no longer independent, productive, healthy, and fully self-sufficient. The problem of undervaluing the elders of society cannot be solved by dispensing "power" as though it were available on demand. The problem is much more complex.

As we cannot dispense health to those suffering infirmities related to long life, so we cannot, by our action, empower people to have and use power without—in a sense—establishing a hierarchical relationship. When elders, and people of any age, feel they have the capacity to act responsibly, when they sense that they have value—without qualification by age, wealth or special status—they have a sense of autonomy and power that enables them to act in ways that are, for them, appropriate. When older people—and those of any age—develop within themselves the confidence that they have worth, a legitimate place in society, and something to share with others, they will take their rightful place in society's markets, businesses, governments, and social organizations. They do not lack the sense of personal power nor do they develop the added burden of feeling that they have status because someone has empowered them to act.

This concept is difficult for people with concern for others who want to lend a hand—to empower. At the same time, those who receive the helping hand want to show appreciation. Thus, in the act of empowering someone draws attention to the other's powerlessness, whether or not the older person, the "helpee" initially feels a lack of status or power. We need a different context for relationships that, without announced intention to empower, leave individuals feeling independent.

Given the conditions for growth, individuals will continue to develop, to fill a significant place in their families and communities, and to feel independent. Those conditions for growth require that people be received for who they are and not for what they do or did. Growth requires that individuals be free of unrealistic expectations or imposed judgment. When mature individuals feel that they have inherent value, personal relationships, and purpose, and when they reject stereotypical characterizations of old age that lead them to believe they have lost their status as productive members of society, then they have the autonomy they need to be confident, self-directing persons.

We can open doors. Older persons can be appointed to positions of responsibility. We can rhetorically develop the theme of empowerment. (Please note the underlying assumptions about *we* and *they*, and worry, if you will, about who comprise the "we" and who become a part of the great "they.") Our efforts will be largely ineffective if we focus on empowerment rather than on the resources someone can tap to develop autonomy.

This word "empowerment" symbolizes the delegation of authority, the assignment of responsibility, and an "authorization" for elders to assume new roles—often the same roles that society has systematically denied them.

In a democracy, power resides with the people. The people are the proper locus of power; those who govern derive their power from the people. In an ideal society, individuals are free to achieve their potential, neither restrained by barriers to their fulfillment nor assisted by those with the ability, authority, nor willingness to empower.

It is not easy to move from a concept of empowerment to a strategy that will enable society to acknowledge and use the talents, skills, and values of older persons. An appropriate role for individuals and organizations concerned about the quality of life for the nation's elder—and their own parents—is to create conditions in which people will flourish, unrestrained by stereotypes regarding their capacity to contribute and uncomplicated by the earnest efforts of some to empower others.

Colonial nations found, prior to their being thrown out of "their" colonies by democratic movements, power was neither theirs to give nor theirs to withhold from the people. After the revolutions, the people determined who should govern.

Those who were anointed with power by home office appointees who assumed power were called lackeys and recognized as holding a form of illegitimate authority. The authority was derived from powers who had neither the right to such power nor the right to dispense it.

In the light of this description of undervalued older people and a society that seems intent on burdening its elders with conditions that undermine their sense of self-worth, what's to be done? A song I recall includes these words, "Man, you've got to accentuate the positive, eliminate the negative."

First, we must eliminate the negative forces that leave an overwhelming number of older persons struggling to find meaning for their lives, despite illness; having no work to do and no place to go; and sensing the loss of dignity that comes with a loss of status.

We must redefine productivity and health and ascribe honored status to those who have contributed to so many over their lifetimes. We need to discover new roles and develop new opportunities for meaningful participation in various aspects of life in the mainstream. Those so engaged and unfettered by false values of productivity, competence, health and status will need very little from empowering advocates. On a more personal level, we must enable each person to feel accepted, unconditionally regarded, and without feeling judged about who they are and what they have to contribute.

To "accentuate the positive," we need to celebrate the achievements of older people. In so doing we will provide the nonjudgmental acceptance and empathetic understanding people of all ages need. They, and we, will flourish, for we will have properly focused the forces within our society that provide opportunities for growth, development, and recognition. The elders will have opportunities to give and a solid basis for receiving, without demeaning overtones of dependency.

These are the goals of advocates who wish to empower people, but by dealing with basic societal conditions we can do more than superficial efforts to counteract social forces that leave the elders of society without the affirmation they require to feel autonomous. As we move from strategies to empower the powerless to broadly based public education programs that enable persons, old and young, to feel good about who they are without qualification, we will move from a problem-solving effort to a developmental plan. This plan, when accomplished, assures future generations of older people that they may appreciate their achievements and spend little time worrying about their losses.

The source of the power will come from within individuals freed from the constraints of expectations and false values. That is an agenda for action that educators, advocates, opinion leaders, and politicians should agree to address.

Part 2

EMPOWERED ORGANIZATIONS

Chapter 4

Seniors' Organizations and Seniors' Empowerment: An International Perspective

Henry J. Pratt

Over the past quarter century, interest groups active on behalf of the elderly in the United States, and likewise in the other industrial democracies, have come to represent a major social phenomenon. As is well known, a handful of such groups have become extremely large, with one of their number, the American Association of Retired Persons (AARP), at 33 million members and $300 million in 1990 revenues now the largest, and probably the wealthiest, voluntary organization in the United States, and quite possibly in any country. AARP's approximate counterpart in the United Kingdom, namely, Age Concern, Ltd., with over a thousand local units, is likewise among that country's larger membership bodies. While systematic data relating to most of other countries are presently lacking, it is likely that similar observations would apply also in those cases. Moreover, there has been significant recent growth among smaller, more specialized aging organizations devoted to specific clienteles and particular problem areas.

And it is not alone their number and size that accounts for these groups' increasing level of social visibility and perceived importance. Another factor has been the public's growing awareness of senior citizens and generalized sympathy toward their needs and aspirations. To a large extent, the public has embraced the "compassionate stereotype," under which seniors are perceived as a group in deserving need—notwithstanding that the stereotype involves a distortion of reality in a manner potentially harmful to the specialized needs of various subsets of the elderly population (Binstock, 1983). Further adding to the perceived importance of seniors organizations has been population aging. Even though not an entirely new phenomenal—it actually became manifest in Sweden and France toward the end of the nineteenth century—population aging did not substantially impact the industrialized world in general until well into the twentieth century, and only recently has it become a "worldwide phenomenon that commands immediate attention . . ." (Myers, 1990, 20). As this trend has become generally recognized, the spokespersons for the elderly, including the leaders of seniors organizations, have been among the beneficiaries.

It is reasonable to assume, therefore, that voluntary organizations in aging can, and do, influence their own members' attitudes, values, and aspirations, and thereby indirectly exert an influence on their wider societies.

For the reasons given, aging organizations would qualify as worthy of serious attention even if they were not involved in the governmental process. Yet, it has been chiefly as a result of their increasing political activism that these associations have attracted the most attention, among both political elites and among voting electorates. There was a delay of a decade or more after these groups' initial involvement in the political process before they gained any appreciable measure of scholarly recognition. Yet, any disregard of these groups in the past has now largely been remedied, as social scientists have come to acknowledge their often significant governmental role.[1] Such enhanced interest has been especially apparent in sociology and political science, where several scholars have made the study of age-active interest groups a major part of their research agendas (Binstock, 1972; Pratt, 1976; Williamson, Evans, and Powell, 1982; Day, 1990).

Still, interesting and important questions remain to be addressed regarding these organizations, and it is unclear that these can be adequately treated through the single-country approach which has dominated this field to the virtual exclusion of cross-national comparison.[2] It becomes clear, upon reflection, that at least two difficulties confront the former of these approaches: first, single-nation analyses largely preclude one's controlling for idiosyncrasies of place and political setting; and second, the number of cases may fail to meet the minimum considered necessary from the standpoint of hypothesis testing.

Since the comparative approach has obvious appeal in terms of confronting these difficulties and at the same time enhancing basic understanding, the present paper will employ this approach, drawing in part upon the author's recent research into seniors organizations in Canada, Britain, and the United States.[3] My intent as a scholar concerned with the study of political interest groups is threefold: first, to describe how these aging organizations succeeded in initially forming themselves, bearing in mind the heavy odds against successful group formation; second, to consider a possible new basis for differentiating among seniors organizations; and third, to consider organizations from the standpoint of seniors' empowerment.

Group Formation

A useful point to bear in mind at the outset of this discussion is the inherently fraught and risky nature of mass-membership group formation and maintenance. Membership groups in any field represent a hazardous undertaking, confronting as they do numerous risks: the potential for debilitating member apathy and indifference (compounded by the distracting effects of television and other forms of mass entertainment); the possibilities for internal factionalism, discord, and cleavages; the threat of displacement of goals (i.e., away from the originally stated objectives and toward others neither formally acknowledged nor generally agreed upon), and so on. And additional risks apply especially to membership groups comprised of senior citizens—the limited life expectancy of the typical, newly recruited member (only 15 years or so beyond age 65); the reluctance to displace one's group affiliations of a lifetime in favor of senior-group status; the fact that membership eligibility often occurs at a time in one's life of declining personal income and consequent constraint in taking on new monetary commitments, including dues payment to a voluntary organization.

That the risks to age-group survival are real, not just imagined, is apparent from the historical record. The names of numerous organizations have appeared, only later on to disappear, from the listings given in successive editions of encyclopedias of associations published for various countries. While such organizational bankruptcies seem to have been especially common in the United States (Pratt, 1983, 247), the same applies also to Britain and Canada. And it is not merely the smaller, more obviously fragile organizations that have been at risk. One of the largest retiree/senior citizen organizations ever to arise, namely, the U.S.-based Townsend Movement, eventually succumbed, notwithstanding its early large base of members —in the hundreds of thousands—and seemingly secure finances (Holtzman, 1963). The special difficulties involved in forming a seniors organization, or indeed any association specific to the concerns of seniors, is implicit in the fact that the greatest wave of interest-group formation in U.S. history, namely, that occurring in the period from 1900 to 1920, of which it has been said that "there has never been anything like it before or since" (Wilson, 1973, 198), saw no effort to form a national organization on this particular basis.

This cannot be attributed to any lack of public acknowledgment of seniors as a distinct population grouping marked by special challenges and insecurities, since, as Andrew Achenbaum points out, senior citizens in the 1910s for the first time came to be recognized as "a national problem" (Achenbaum, 1978).

It can be taken as a given, therefore, that powerful external forces may be required in order for viable seniors organizations to emerge. What might these consist of? A clue may inhere in the tendency for such groups to originate in waves, or clusters, as opposed to random moments over time. This "clustering tendency," whose exact dimensions will be outlined below, appears not to have been remarked on previously in the literature. Moreover, it is not easily explainable on the basis of existing interest-group theory. While scholars have formulated hypotheses intended to account for the observable, wave-like patterns of group formation throughout American history, they do not entirely square with the observed pattern in aging. Thus, in his highly regarded theoretical work, *The Governmental Process*, David B. Truman (1951) develops the theme that the recurrent waves of new group formation are best understood as a response to environmental "disturbances" of one kind or another, especially technological innovation (resulting in economic disturbances) and war. Thus, in Truman's formulation an initial disturbance, resulting in the coalescence of a given group not previously organized, can easily end up creating a ripple effect, as other latent groups, threatened by the coalescence of the first, now proceed to organize in their own self-defense and in hopes of restoring the preexisting social balance (pp. 54–55). Writing some two decades after Truman, another leading political scientist, James Q. Wilson (1973, Chapter 10), offered fresh insight on this same point. This author observed that the tendency for interest groups to form in clusters often is reflective of a prevailing climate of "moral concern" which, from time to time, has surfaced throughout the course of American history. Given such an opinion climate, appeals made by organizers ("political entrepreneurs") to both present and potential group members are likely to achieve heightened credibility—above what might be expected in more normal times. The fledgling voluntary organization is therefore in a better position to survive its most vulnerable, fledgling stage and to evolve into a mature, stable organization.

While the formation of certain voluntary organizations in aging is explainable on the basis of one or the other of the above hypotheses, that does not seem applicable in general. It is true that the Townsend Movement could well serve as a textbook case of group formation stemming from a prior "disturbance," in this case the Great Depression of the 1930s. And the formation in 1970 of the "Gray Panthers"—a cross-generational interest group whose policy concerns encompass, but are not confined to, aging issues—was largely attributable to the heightened moral fervor of the 1960s, which contributed to this group's formation as it did also to other "movement" groups of the time. (Indeed, "Gray Panthers" represented a modification of "Black Panthers," the name used by a leading race-protest and self-help organization.)

Nevertheless, a survey of aging organizations formed sometime during this century, including ones in Britain and Canada as well as the United States, makes clear that the bulk of these were formed, not chiefly in response to some tangible "disturbance," or at a time of pronounced "moral fervor," but rather under quite different circumstances. Caution is warranted in making this point, since the motivations of the various group founders are not readily knowable, and one or the other element may have been present to some unsuspected degree. Yet, it is noteworthy that the waves of age-related organizational activity usually did not coincide with the forces or events specified in existing theory. Thus, for example, the two largest American age-membership groups, AARP and the National Council of Senior Citizens (NCSC), were both formed over a common three-year period, 1958–1961, as was also the National Council on the Aging (NCOA)—an association of professionals involved in this field. Notwithstanding the economic downturns of 1958 and 1961, this was a period of relative prosperity in the United States, and was in advance of the era of protest and activism that later on would mark the decade of the 1960s. The same point applies to the largest age-related organizations in Britain and Canada, those being, respectively, Age Concern, Ltd., and the National Pensioners and Senior Citizens Federation. The former of these was constituted in 1970—outgrowth of the existing National Old Peoples Welfare Council whose origins dated back some three decades—while the latter received its federal charter in 1954.[4] These were not especially stressful or exceptional moments in either British or Canadian history. In short, one is dealing here with interest-group coalescence occurring for the most part in periods of relative peace, social order, and economic good times.

It would appear, then, that some other factor, not specified in existing theory, was critically involved in the observed waves of organizational development. Before suggesting what the missing element might consist of, one should make clear what particular groups have comprised the various waves, and also the timing of their arrival.

Phase One: Foreign Models, Domestic Disseminators. In each of the countries covered in this research, an initial organizing wave in aging occurred at some point during the period from the late 1890s to the early 1920s. In Britain, it came rather earlier, and consisted of three groups, one dedicated to the cause of old age pensions particularly and two others which committed themselves at a critical point to a pro-pensions position.[5] The one was the National Committee of Organized Labor on Old Age Pensions, also referred to as the National Pension Committee (NPC), organized in 1898 by the social reformer Charles Booth and a few other industrialists-philanthropists such as the Cadburys. Chosen as its national director was Frederick Rodgers, a prominent trades unionist of that time. The two other groups consisted of the Trades Union Congress (TUC) and the National Conference of Friendly Societies. At their national conferences in 1899 and 1904, respectively, the two organizations approved resolutions supportive of government-funded, noncontributory pensions. (The 1904 vote by the Friendly Societies was especially significant, given that this organization had previously strongly opposed the public pensions concept.)

In the case of Canada, the wave of aging-related organizational activity at this time consisted not in the formation of any voluntary organization specific to pensions or aging, but rather in the willingness of two emergent social movements of the time to encompass support for old age pensions within their range of policy concerns. In 1905, Canada's Trades and Labor Congress, itself only recently formed, voted to endorse this concept, and two years later the Moral and Social Reform Council of Canada, formed by Protestant church leaders in 1907 as a major expression of the Social Gospel Movement, added its voice to the same demand.

With respect to the United States, the wave of interest-group organizing in aging lagged by almost two decades behind those in the other two countries. This can be explained on the basis of the liberalizations enacted by Congress in the Civil War veterans' pensions program, and the related abhorrence of public pensions on the part of Progressive Movement leaders, alarmed over widespread corruption in the administration of veterans' pension benefits. The liberalizations enacted by Congress in the 1880s and 1890s caused veterans' pension coverage to peak at just under one million beneficiaries in 1902, by which time the program encompassed some 30 percent of all men over age 65 and 56 percent of all native-born white males in the entire United States (Williamson and Pampel, forthcoming).

The above legislative developments contributed directly to the rejuvenation of the leading organization of Civil War veterans, the Grand Army of the Republic. At the time of its formation in the immediate aftermath of the Union victory of 1865, and for more than a decade thereafter, G. A. R. leaders remained indifferent to pensions, as enacted for the benefit of veterans with war-related injuries, even refusing to support the demands of pension agents. During the 1870s, the Grand Army struggled to survive, as membership fell alarmingly. But this was to change in the early 1880s, as the organization's newly elected national commander in chief, Paul Vandervoort, made pressure-group activity on behalf of pension reform a central theme in his campaign, substantially to increase G. A. R. membership. The new theme was successful. By 1884, in response to a rising clamor for pensions among rank-and-file members, the Grand Army had metamorphosed into a pressure group. And an emphasis on pensions issues from that point on remained central to the organization's incentive system, including the period after 1900 when membership was declining and the political influence of organized Union veterans was rapidly waning (Dearing, 1952, 213, 218, 270, 274, 496).

By the end of the decade of the 1910s, as death began claiming Civil War veterans in ever-increasing numbers, the United States was left without its earlier functional equivalent of a general pensions program. The same period also saw the decline of the Progressive Movement as a force in American society. Taken together, these developments can serve as explanation for why, in the immediate aftermath of World War I, a wave of interest-group organizing in aging, heretofore held in check, now made itself felt.

The wave consisted partly in a redirection of energies on the part of existing voluntary organizations, and partly in the formation of one new, age-specific organization. In 1919, two established social reform organizations, the Federal Council of Churches of Christ (counterpart to Canada's Moral and Social Reform Council) and the American Association for Labor Legislation (AALL), declared themselves strongly in favor of pensions coverage for all Americans (McKee, 1954). Three years later, a third group, the Fraternal Order of Eagles, under the leadership of its national director, Frank E. Hering, adopted a similar stance, and the Eagles then proceeded to spearhead a national movement aimed at securing old age pensions at the state level. Finally, in 1927, by which time the campaign led by the Eagles had lost its earlier momentum and direction, a new group was formed, the American Association for Old Age Security (AAOAS), under the astute leadership of a political entrepreneur, Abraham Epstein. (Epstein had been a former associate of Frank Hering's at the Eagles' national office.) Thus, from the 1927 point forward, up through and even slightly beyond the adoption of the 1935 Social Security Act, the pensions movement in the United States was jointly led by the

AAOAS and the AALL, acting in somewhat uneasy coalition (Pratt, 1976, Chapter 2).

The thread linking together all these various organizational beginnings was the common awareness among their elective leaders and senior-group activists in these countries of the public pension precedents recently set in various foreign countries, and the perceived applicability of those precedents to the conditions prevailing domestically. With ten European countries, in addition to Australia and New Zealand, having adopted public pensions for their citizens prior to 1900, social reform advocates in Canada, Britain,and the United States took it upon themselves to call attention to those models, and to educate the political elites in their countries regarding the possibilities in this field. A leading example of this role was the American intellectual and pensions propagandist, Isaac W. Rubinow. Rubinow's 1913 book, *Social Insurance with Special Reference to American Conditions* (Rubinow, 1913), pointedly called attention to the recent European initiatives, and argued that these should not be considered as alien schemes, but rather fit models for American adoption. Similar strong emphasis on the perceived appropriateness of foreign models is contained in the writings of Abraham Epstein (Epstein, 1922; Epstein, 1938).

Specially important in this effort to promote cross-border policy diffusion was the role performed by the more moderate and reformist (as opposed to the more doctrinaire) wing of the international socialist movement. Socialists of the former stripe had often been prominent participants in the European, Australian, and New Zealand campaigns leading up to old age pension adoptions, and at socialist international meetings and conferences public pensions became a frequent topic of discussion.

Although their numbers were never very large in absolute terms, socialists were often strategically placed and in position to press their viewpoints upon important elites, especially in the labor movement. Such efforts were largely successful with respect to labor in Britain and Canada, where union federations agreed early on to become involved in the public pensions cause. This did not apply to the United States, however, where the American Federation of Labor, under its long-time president, Samuel Gompers, consistently rejected proposals for labor endorsements in this area. Given the highly individualistic political culture in the United States, and widespread antipathy for socialist doctrine, socialists in this particular setting were forced to operate mostly behind the scenes, for example, by providing important encouragement and backing to pensions activists such as Abraham Epstein (Chambers, 1963, 165).

The forces here identified helped to influence public policy content, in addition to the formation of new groups and goal redefinitions on the part of groups already in existence. Conceivably, policy makers in Britain, Canada, and the United States might eventually have come to appreciate—on the basis of their own independent assessment of the situation—the need for old-age security legislation. Yet, there can be little doubt that legislative action in this field would have been longer in coming and weaker in content than eventually was the case, absent their awareness of foreign models of public pensions, as these were pressed on policy makers through pension movement propaganda and agitation. In other words, European models of governmental programs served as a major, if largely unacknowledged, input into early American, British, and Canadian decision making on pensions, and were likewise fundamental to the emergence in all three countries of the waves of pension-group formation.

Phase Two: The Dismal Years. Actions taken by governments on pensions and old age security continued to impact the formation of interest groups after adoption of initial public pensions legislation, but now the relevant actors became not foreign, but domestic governments, and the impacts no longer necessarily supportive and positive, but more often depressive and negative. Britain, Canada, and the United States adopted their initial public pensions legislation in 1908, 1927, and 1935, respectively. The newly adopted pensions legislation in all three countries had the potential to affect the elderly populations in at least three ways: first, by defining at least one segment of that population as separable, with eligibility for benefits typically made contingent upon one's first having retired; second, by sanctioning and making official a definition of the age at which "normal" retirement begins; and third, by calling attention to government's capacity to fund such programs, thereby redirecting attention away from more traditional sources of support for the indigent—the church, the local community, private charities.

Yet, in order for these potentially dramatic effects to have any tangible organizational impacts, the scope of pensions coverage would have to be fairly broad and the benefit levels at least minimally adequate. Neither of these conditions was in fact met in the initial pensions legislation as adopted. By far the most ambitious of these early measures was the American Social Security Act. Title I of this act, Old Age Assistance (OAA), authorized immediate relief to elderly persons deemed to be in acute need, while Title II, Old Age Insurance (OAI), made long-term provision for elderly persons under a contributory arrangement. Yet, the benefit levels provided in this legislation departed widely from what senior movement leaders had been demanding, for example, $200 per person per month under the Townsend Plan. The first benefits under OAI were originally not to begin until 1942 and would be a mere $10 per month for those who met the benefit criteria (Achenbaum, 1986, 203). And even as late as 1949, benefit levels under OAI lagged behind those paid by most states under the means-tested Old Age Assistance—$25 per month vs. $42 per month (Williamson and Pampel, forthcoming).

This meagerness of program benefits was a source of extreme frustration among pension movement leaders, Abraham Epstein in particular. But their voices from 1935 onward were little heeded; for example, there were virtually no senior movement leaders at the signing ceremony for the Social Security Act. Moreover, pension movement leaders were denied favorable access to the Social Security Board which, beginning in 1936, assumed responsibility for the new program (Pratt, 1976, 18).

The same point about the restricted coverage inherent in early old age pension measures applied also to Canada and Britain. British policy makers framed that country's 1908 Old Age Pension Act so as to restrict eligibility to men aged 70 and above, whose annual incomes from other sources did not exceed a very modest 21 pounds; pensions at reduced rates were also authorized for those earning more than this amount but not in excess of 31 pounds (Gilbert, 1970, 236). Other restrictions related to clients' perceived character, with the result that the overall program ended up being for the very old, the very poor, and the very respectable.

In regard to Canada, there was a fear among policy makers at the point of adoption of the 1927 Old Age Pensions Act that a universal system of old age benefits might disastrously impact the government's tax base and fiscal resources. Even though poverty among Canada's elderly at this time was acute, widespread and chronic, policy makers opted in favor of a system of low benefits and narrowly restricted scope. Parliament enacted a program that was based on the premise that an old person needed just over $1.00 a day to live on, notwithstanding that this was based upon an "empirically unverified assumption prevalent in government circles" (Bryden, 1974, 77).

Given the assumptions and resulting parameters of these initial public pensions programs, any indirect incentives arising from this source toward age-group formation were at best weak, and their real effect may have been more in the opposite direction. In symbolic terms, the involvement of government in the field of old age security may have been taken as a signal among erstwhile supporters of pension movements that the need in this area would now be taken care of.

Whatever the reasons, the result was apparent. In the United States, the two organizations which together had formed the core of the old age pensions movement of the 1920s and 1930s, namely, AAOAS (later renamed the American Association for Social Security) and AALL, both passed out of existence within seven years of the adoption of the Social Security Act. While the immediate cause of their demise was in each case the death of their long-time top leaders, Abraham Epstein and John B. Andrews, respectively, a more basic cause was probably their lack of favorable political access to the Roosevelt administration and the drifting away of many long-time supporters, now persuaded that Social Security was in the process of overcoming the old age insecurity problem. The picture in Canada was broadly similar: social reform organizations active nationally, in particular the Social Service Council (successor to the old Moral and Social Reform Council), now mostly drifted away from their earlier focused concern with pensions issues (Guest, 1980).

It would be misleading to suggest, however, that waves of pensioner-group formation were entirely absent from the Canadian and American scenes during this period. Despite the absence of any such development at the federal level, occasional waves of senior-group formation did occur among the Canadian provinces and American states. In 1932, the British Columbia Old Age Pensioners' Association was the first federation of community- based seniors groups to be formed anywhere, and this was followed by an Alberta federation in 1935 and one in Saskatchewan in 1939 (Gifford, 1990, 24–25). And in the United States, California proved itself highly congenial to the formation of seniors organizations during the 1940s, including the "Ham and Eggs Organization" and George McClain's "Citizens Committee for Old Age Pensions" (Putnam, 1970). The connecting link in these Canadian and American developments was the capacity of the provinces and the states, assuming the will to do so, to augment the base benefit provided by the two federal governments, in regard to both size and coverage, thereby bringing within the existing pensions system a larger number of elderly persons than was the case generally in that country.

Only in Britain does one find in this period a significant effort made nationally to form a seniors organization. While it would be unwarranted to characterize this single case as in any sense a "wave," this group still merits attention for what it reveals about the prevailing setting for pensions activism. At a meeting held in July 1916, eight years following the adoption by Parliament of the Old Age Pensions Act, a group calling itself the "National Conference on Old Age Pensions" voted itself into existence. The founding convention drew together representatives from a variety of existing organizations: trades unions, friendly societies, the cooperative movement, the "free" churches. The group was destined to endure for a time, and its activities included the formulation and presentation to Parliament of a set of pension-related demands. Yet, it did not survive long into the 1920s, and its objective of acquiring a mass base of senior citizen support was never to materialize (Thane, 1970).

In short, the political atmosphere created by the initial public pensions measures adopted in these countries involved little by way of incentives, and much by way of disincentives with respect to the maintenance of existing voluntary organizations, several of which now passed out of existence.

Phase Three: Universal Benefits, "Universal" Organizations. In 1925, 1950, and 1951 Britain, the United States, and Canada, respectively, adopted amendments to (or reformulations of) their original public pension enactments. These enactments authorized far more in the way of expanded coverage (i.e., their scope) than increased individual benefits, which were left decidedly low. Thus, Britain's 1925 Widows', Orphans', and Old Age Contributory Pension Act, introduced for the first time a contributory aspect into the public pension scheme, thereby providing for the extension of pensions coverage to essentially all regularly employed male workers. In the United States, the 1950 amendments to the Social Security Act, ones characterized by a leading scholar as the act's "third and final statutory founding" (Derthick, 1979, 273), enlarged by several million the number of workers covered under Social Security which, when combined with other expansions enacted over the next several years, resulted in Social Security coverage for 95 percent of the U.S. work force—up from 60 percent originally (Bernstein, 1988, 14). Canada's 1951 Old Age Security enactment eliminated the narrowly restrictive, mean-tested pension program of 1927, and replaced it with a universal "demogrant" covering all Canadians at age 70. (Subsequent legislation would lower the eligibility age to 65).

Yet, no such dramatic changes were authorized in benefit levels. This explains, for example, why in the United States the estimated poverty rate among persons 65 and above at the close of the 1950s remained a high 35 percent (U.S. House of Representatives, 1987, 5), and why in the United Kingdom as late as 1971, 42 percent of elderly persons were in the bottom range of family income. (U.K. Secretary of State for Social Services, 1985).

With millions of workers now newly entitled under government-administered old age pensions, yet still only poorly protected against economic insecurity, the situation became attractive to political entrepreneurs interested in the possibilities for age-group formation. It would not have been sufficient for such entrepreneurs to make their organizing appeals strictly on the basis of elderly peoples' shared political concerns relating to the pension levels, given the "free rider" problem under which rational, self-interested individuals can enjoy the fruits of organizational success whether they participate organizationally or not (Olson, 1965).

For this reason, any purely "political" voluntary organizations would probably have failed. Still, the possibilities were there, assuming that membership appeals could combine into a single package both an expressed resolve to lobby government on behalf of needed pension benefit increases and some additional basis for member affiliation. The additional element could consist, for example, in the offering of "tied sales," under which goods at cut-rate prices could be offered for sale on the condition of one's having first become a dues-paying member, thereby denying the goods to nonmembers. Or, alternatively, it could consist of local affiliates or clubs where members could find a sense of fellowship and solidarity not otherwise available. The group formation process could be enhanced, and the possibilities improved for ultimate success, if the fledgling organization could draw upon the resources of a sponsoring organization or "patron." And, in fact, the history of age-organizational efforts at this point is replete with examples of this. AARP, for example, in its formative years drew heavily on the expertise, money, and staff resources of the existing National Retired Teachers Association, which accounts for its long-time name, NRTA/AARP. And the National Council of Senior Citizens likewise benefited greatly from subsidies provided by some of the larger American industrial unions.

The policy developments described above were fundamentally important in the interest-group waves which occurred in all these countries beginning at a point about ten years after their reformulated pensions programs initially took effect. In Britain, the wave was somewhat slow arriving, following the adoption of the 1925 legislation. The delay most probably was the result of Britain's prolonged economic hardship of late 1920s and 1930s. Whatever the reason, toward the end of the 1930s two pensioner organizations were organized: the Scottish Pensioners Association and the National Federation of Old Age Pensions Associations (NFOAPA). The Scottish group survived for a time before disappearing, but the latter association, formed in March 1939, survives to the present time. In the United States, as previously mentioned, three organizations, AARP, NCOA, and NCSC, were all formed over the brief span between 1958 and 1961. The American wave also included the "Gray Panthers," formed in 1970. In Canada, finally, the wave occurred about a decade after the enactment of the 1951 Old Age Security Act. It comprised NP&SCF, now for the first time a "national" organization in fact as well as in name, and the United Senior Citizens of Ontario (USCO), formed in 1959 and expanding in the space of a decade to 300,000 membersby far the largest seniors organization in Canada (Gifford, 1990, 27-28). Formed a bit later, in 1969, but still part of the same Canadian wave, was Canadian Pensioners Concerned (Gifford, 1990, 46–47).

What is most noteworthy about these newly formed seniors organizations is their shared emphasis on seniors' commonality of interest, as opposed to differences of need and aspiration among various strata within the elderly community. The period was unique in terms of group formation on the mass-membership model—there has never been anything like it before or since. This can probably be explained on the basis that the existing benefit levels were experienced in roughly the same way by seniors in various social strata, large numbers of whom were either in poverty or else in low-income circumstances not far above a survival level. General membership organizations, each dedicated to the pursuit of political objectives on which seniors could unite (or already were united), would be congruent with such a social and economic setting.

Phase Four: Benefit Enhancement and the "Tidal Wave." A new wave of senior-group formation was to mark the 1970s and 1980s. As had been true in the earlier cases, it was closely associated with an altered public policy setting, as brought into being by reformulated public pension programs and—in one country—new public bureaucracies. To no small extent these policy shifts were made in response to pressure applied on government by the seniors organizations, as established during the third phase of policy formation. As will be shown, the new programs involved increases in average pension benefits (resulting from deliberate boosts in the pension coupled with automatic adjustments resulting from the indexation of benefits), and from an enhancement of pensions program visibility and perceived importance.

Despite differences regarding their particulars, the actions now taken by government in all three countries reveal certain basic similarities. The U.S. Congress, responding in part to pressure applied by the National Council of Senior Citizens (Pratt, 1976, Chapter 10), in 1972 adopted Social Security amendments which both indexed Social Security to the cost of living and boosted Social Security benefits by 20 percent—the highest single increase ever. This action, coupled with other benefit enhancements enacted in the years immediately previous, profoundly impacted the economic circumstances of Americans covered under Social Security. The poverty rate among persons 65 and above declined from 35 percent in 1959 to just 12.4 percent in the early 1980s (U.S. House of Representatives, 1987, 5).

In Canada, likewise, the period from the middle 1960s to the early 1970s was a period of substantial redirection in pensions policy. It began with the adoption in 1965 of the Canada and Quebec Pension Plans, under which the federal government shifted its earlier emphasis on mere survival to keeping up with lifetime living standards. The trend continued in 1966 with the Guaranteed Income Supplement (GIS), designed to assist the most poverty-stricken seniors, and included also Parliament's 1968 decision to index the basic OAS pension to the cost of living. (In the middle 1970s, it was decided likewise to index the GIS pension.) The period of policy reformulation ended in 1972, when Ottawa adopted the New Horizons program designed to assist seniors in forming their own community-based organizations. These several changes were responsive in no small degree to pressure applied on government by the National Pensioners and Senior Citizens Federation (Bryden, 1974, 194).

Finally, in Britain, the era of reformulation occurred over the period from 1968 to 1975. It began with the government's 1968 decision to merge the two existing ministries having primary responsibility for age-benefits administration, namely, Ministry of Health and the Ministry of Social Security, to form the Department of Health and Social Security. Placed in charge of this enlarged department, in a newly created post, was the Secretary of State for Social Services. The politicians who since have served in this post all have enjoyed higher levels of political visibility and stature than was true of their predecessors who had headed up either of the previously separate ministries. Britain's statutory change of greatest substantive impact at this time was the Social Security Pensions Act of 1975. This measure called for a much stronger, earnings-related component—referred to in the act as the Earning-related Pension Scheme (SERPS)—than that embraced in the more restricted and limited earnings-related pension scheme adopted by Parliament in 1959. And these years saw the continuation of a trend, dating from the 1952, toward enlargement of government outlays in the field of old age security (Pratt, 1993). Thus, as a proportion of gross domestic product (GDP), government spending in this field increased from 2.3 percent in 1950 to 6.7 percent in 1985, with no less than 30 percent of central government spending having now become social-security related (U.K., Secretary of State for Social Services, 1985, 99). These increased government outlays had major significance for personal income levels among the elderly. Whereas in 1971, 42 percent of all pensioners were in the bottom range of family incomes, by 1982 the proportion had fallen to just 23 percent, and, at the same time, the number of pensioners classified as low income had been slashed in half (U.K., Secretary of State for Social Services, 1985, 11).

One might have anticipated that the above program enlargements would lessen the willingness of seniors to make sacrifices toward the support of seniors organizations, given their presumed greater level of income security. Yet, no such deleterious effects actually occurred. Instead, the changes were associated in time with the emergence of substantial senior-group waves, possibly the largest such waves thus far in any of the countries here under discussion. After 1972, Canada saw a tide of voluntary-group formation in this field, both federally and at the provincial level. It is beyond the scope of this discussion to enumerate all the relevant organizations, but any such listing would include the Canadian Association on Gerontology (formed in 1971), Pensioners for Action Now (1972), the Canadian Council of Retirees (1975), the National Institute of Senior Centers (1977), the National Advisory Council on Ageing (1980), and One Voice Seniors Network (1987). Britain, likewise, was witness to an extraordinary wave of age-group formation. It consisted partially in the formation of new aging organizations, among them the National Pensioners Liaison Forum (organized in 1988) and the Pensioners Rights Campaign (1989), and also in redefinitions of goals—in more public-policy-aware and politically active directions—among all three of Britain's larger social welfare organizations in this field: Help the Aged, the National Old People's Welfare Council (which now renamed itself Age Concern, Ltd.), and the National Corporation for the Care of Old People (now renamed as the Center for Policy on Ageing). As it made itself felt in the United States, the same wave was no less exceptional. It consisted partially in the formation of new voluntary organizations. Thus, among the 27 groups that in 1981 comprised the Leadership Council on Aging Organizations, 14 had been established since 1971, just a decade earlier. And among the 23 aging groups having Washington-area headquarters, as listed in the 1990 edition of the *Encyclopedia of Associations* under the rubrics "aging," "senior citizens," and "retired persons," slightly over half (14) had been formed since the early 1970s. Involved as well were major enlargements in certain of the existing seniors groups, especially of AARP, whose membership in the two decades following 1972 ballooned by more than tenfold.

The scale on which newly formed aging groups at the national level sprang up during this period resulted in novel problems—and in novel solutions. Given the wide diversity of organizations competing for attention by both the general public and government, senior movement leaders came to recognize a need for some kind of coordinating and conflict-resolving apparatus. Such thinking led in the United States to the formation in 1978 of the Leadership Conference on Aging Organizations—a step taken under the auspices of Nelson Cruikshank, the White House Advisor on Aging in the Carter administration and one of the most prominent figures in the seniors movement from as far back as the early 1940s, when he was named Director of the Social Security Department in the American Federation of Labor. A similar need was felt in Canada where improved intergroup coordination was a primary objective behind the 1987 decision to form the One Voice Seniors Network.[6] In Britain, while no such leadership conference as such has been formed, the All Party Pensions Group in the House of Commons has functioned informally to foster heightened intergroup consensus.

In summary, the expanded benefits in aging, which now became widely available, coupled with elderly peoples' increasing financial dependency upon those benefits, provided strong indirect incentive toward the formation and maintenance of seniors organizationsboth newly formed and preexisting. And the increasing number and diversity of these newly formed groups in turn generated novel problems.

It should be pointed out also that the newly formed groups of the 1970s and 1980s were responsive not simply to the increased absolute size of government benefits but also to the form in which the benefits were allocated. As public policy came increasingly to emphasize the contributory principle, and "earned" entitlements as distinct from flat-rate benefits or "demogrants," there was increased tendency for senior citizens and retirees to fall into one or the other of two population subsets: the fairly advantaged elderly, consisting of families where the principal breadwinner had been regularly employed over a long period in a "covered" occupation, and the less advantaged, where the breadwinner has no such extended record of covered employment and consequently had little or nothing by way of pension accruals or earned entitlements.

In defining their political objectives, organizations in aging have come to reflect, to some degree, this increasing disparity. More so than previously, they have chosen to focus on the public policy concerns of one or the other of these subsets, resulting in an increased diversity among them. Even though united in their opposition to threatened reductions in existing aging benefits, such groups' non-crisis behavior is now perhaps less reflective of the commonalities, and more so of the disparities in policy outlooks and political aspirations. In contrast to the policy period immediately preceding, marked as it was by a commitment to shared political agendas and a perceived importance of erecting seniors organizations on the large-scale, mass-membership model, the groups newly formed in Phase Four have reflected the recent shift in policy outputs and a related tendency to form groups for somewhat more narrowly focused and specialized purposes.

Other Factors in Age-Group Formation. Before leaving the topic of age-group formation, one should at least mention two other factors that have facilitated this process in the past few decades.

Clearly, one has been the continuing, and in some countries accelerating, rate of population aging. While this demographic trend has been evident throughout this century, and even earlier, it has never been more apparent in the countries here under discussion than during the past three decades. In the United States, the proportion of elderly persons expanded only gradually over half a century after 1900—from 4.1 percent in 1900, to 5.4 percent in 1930, to 6.8 percent in 1940, and finally to 8.1 percent in 1950. After 1950, however, the rate accelerated, reaching 11.3 percent of the total in 1980. (In absolute terms, these figures reflected an increase in the elderly population over the period in question of more than 9 millionfrom 16.6 to 25.6 million.) (U.S. Bureau of the Census, 1990).

Canada showed a similar trend: relatively slow growth in the proportion of elderly (65 and above) from the turn of the century (1900) to mid-century—that is, an increase from 5.1 percent to 7.7 percent of the national total. This was followed by a surge in the numbers after 1951, such that by census year 1981 the nation was

9.6 percent elderly, representing, in absolute terms, a doubling in the number of elderly persons since 1951 (Statistics Canada, 1983).

In regard to the United Kingdom, the aging of the population first made itself felt rather earlier than in either of the North American countries. Britain's proportion of the population elderly (65 and above) was 4.7 percent in 1900, and this figure would very nearly double over the next 30 years, to reach 7.4 percent in 1931—a rate of expansion never quite equaled subsequently. Still, in the United Kingdom, as in the other two countries, the rate of increase over the past 30 years has been considerable, with the elderly's share of total population rising from 10.9 percent in 1950 to 14.8 percent in 1980 (Central Statistics Office, 1990). It is apparent, therefore, that expanding numbers of seniors in each country in recent decades have served as a basis upon which new organizations could be erected and existing ones potentially expanded.

The second factor relates to leadership. It would be misleading to suggest that the recent waves of senior-group formation have been entirely a result of external forces, including public policy outputs and demographic patterns. One should also bear in mind the important role played by various political entrepreneurs in aging, without whose involvement no amount of external incentive or stimulus would have resulted in group formation. The founders of the various organizations in aging have not generally been the same individuals who were later called upon to manage and administer them. The two roles normally require different talents and temperaments. Even though many formed groups ended up falling by the wayside, the senior movement was successful in finding capable and dedicated individuals capable of filling the required roles for the few groups which proved themselves viable.

The original leaders ("the founders") typically confronted a situation in which group survival demanded self-sacrifice and their long postponement of any hope of substantial tangible reward in the form of high salary. For there to be any hope of eventual success—whether measured in monetary terms or otherwise—the founders had to invest time, energy, and spirit toward a cause of uncertain and speculative outcome. They were a diverse lot in terms of occupation, background, and sex. Nathan Medd, founder of the National Pensioners and Senior Citizens Federation, Canada's first seniors organization nationally, was a retired trucking firm owner and real estate speculator in Saskatoon at the time of that group's inception in 1945. Medd was an amateur musician, who first became involved in the context of arranging social evenings for groups of seniors in his native Saskatchewan. In the United Kingdom, the Rev. W. W. Paton and the Hon. J. C. Birtles, who in the late 1930s and early 1940s together established the National Association of Retirement Pensions Associations (more commonly referred to as "Pensioners Voice"), were both strongly motivated by a sense of Christian charity. Paton was an ordained Presbyterian clergyman, who would perish in the London blitz less than two years after this organization was formed, whereas Birtles, a Manchester justice of the peace, was an active layman in the Church of England.

While little is know of Paton's activities, Birtles, in the early 1940s, traveled thousands of miles under difficult wartime conditions visiting cities and towns to help establish local pensioner associations affiliated with the national organization. In the Unites States, Dr. Ethel Percy Andrus, following a career in the Los Angeles public school system, where she had the distinction of becoming the first female high school principal in California, founded the National Retired Teachers' Association in 1947. On the thinnest of budgets, NRTA eked out an early existence, surviving in part on the basis of patronage provided by the California Teachers' Association and later the National Education Association. By 1955, the survival of NRTA was assured, having now achieved a membership of 20,000. Having accomplished this original organizational objective, Andrus was now in a position to undertake an even larger and more ambitious task of group formation. With the aid of a substantial investment of cash by a Poughkeepsie, New York, insurance agent, Leonard Davis, in 1958 she launched AARP. One observes here an important element of similarity between Birtles, Medd, and Andrus, notwithstanding the contrasts in national settings and group circumstances in which the three operated.

One final point to be made about the above leaders—and others whose names might be mentioned in the same context—is that the founding leaders were almost without exception beyond age 60 at the time of their group's formation. Thus, while those who are hired later to administer the organization might be, and often were, younger adults, the founders were in almost all cases seniors themselves. I know of but one exception to this among the membership groups presently active, and it is not among the more highly visible seniors groups.[7] The pattern of seniors serving as the founding leaders is probably of some significance from an empowerment of seniors standpoint.

Diversity Among Groups

The second question to be treated in this paper has to do with the basis for differing political behavior among senior organizations. The literature on aging contains treatments of the present array of aging organizations, with the groups clustered by category and discussed in terms of their policy objectives and distinctive styles (e.g., Lammers, 1983, 58–65). One point emphasized in these discussions is that the type of political organization specially emphasized in this paper, namely, the seniors mass-membership type, is but one among several. The other types include: professional organizations, service provider groups (both public and private), and various groups, such as women's and veterans' organizations, that frequently participate in age-policy struggles even though not themselves aging-based. It is important to bear in mind this diversity of types, and their varying significance for aging policy. Still, the groups classified as "senior mass-membership organizations" are probably the most highly visible and potentially influential, and it is therefore not unreasonable to focus upon them especially. The question for discussion, then, are what, if any, are the differing structural patterns and bases of political action among the mass-membership organizations?

Before directly confronting this question, it is helpful to take account of recent data indicating that in a global perspective it is the exception and not the rule for seniors organizations, or any type of voluntary organization in aging, to play an important role in government decision making. Required for an effective, organized expression for seniors in the political process are certain preconditions: minimal guarantees of civil liberties, especially the rights of freedom of speech and peaceable assembly; some societal tradition of voluntarism; and disposable personal income adequate to permit large-scale citizen support of voluntary organizations. While it may be possible to form nongovernmental organizations in aging, even in the absence of certain of these conditions, such groups are unlikely to possess much in the way of voice or autonomy. The above considerations apparently underlie the findings reported in a soon-to-be-published study, *Old Age Security in Comparative Perspective* by John B. Williamson of Boston College and Fred C. Pampel of the University of Colorado (Williamson and Pampel, forthcoming). This study compares seven countries—four in the developed world (Britain, Sweden, the United States, and Germany) and three in the developing world (Brazil, Nigeria, and India). Although not concerned with seniors organizations primarily, Williamson and Pampel do reference such groups in evaluating the relevance of the "neo-pluralism model."

Two findings reported in this study are of interest in the present context. First, among the three developing nations, nongovernmental aging organizations in no case have been significant actors in regard to old age security policy. The authors explain this in terms of several factors: these countries' authoritarian traditions of government, prevailing low literacy levels, and extreme ethnic and/or tribal diversity that results in generally low levels of national consensus. Second, even though senior citizen mass-membership organizations exist in all four of the industrially developed countries, they have acted independently, in a highly visible pressure-group role, only in the two countries characterized by "liberal" political cultures, namely, Great Britain and the United States.

In Germany and Sweden, voluntary organizations in aging likewise have not been especially important, yet for a different set of reasons. Both these countries have embraced, since World War II, the principles of democratic corporatism under which various class-based interests—urban workers, farmers, employers are legitimated, and their representatives made part of the decision-making process. The elderly represent a nonclass (or cross-class) interest, and are therefore accorded little standing under corporatist principles. Their representatives, even though consulted from time to time by government ministers, are not perceived as a highly legitimate external source of policy input. The tendency for them not to be included in the governmental process has worked a hardship on these groups' efforts to achieve major societal stature.

For the reasons given, it would appear that senior citizen organizations represent an independent source of policy input and realized political influence in only a handful of countries—ranked low in terms of corporatist assumptions and high in terms of the legitimacy accorded to interest-group activity. Prominent in any listing of such countries would be Canada, Britain, and the United States.

Yet, even in the three "liberal" countries mentioned, not all organizations involved in aging have been alike in terms of their emphasis placed on public policy and lobbying. Whereas some organizations have been "political" in a very elemental sense, others, even though encompassing a political and public policy aspect, have been more business- and/or social-welfare oriented. The distinction made here is a subtle one, and ought not to be driven too far lest it end up becoming a distortion. Still, it appears pertinent. Some sense of it is implicit in the fact that at least 40 percent of the members of AARP join for the benefits, but only 14 percent to support its lobbying activities, and moreover, that of AARP's 30-million-plus membership only 400,000 are considered "active" in any real sense (Novack, 1991). While precise comparative figures are not available for the more politicized organizations, it is highly probable that data on, for example, the National Council of Senior Citizens—the origins of which trace back to the Senior Citizens for Kennedy effort in the 1960 presidential election—would reveal "activists" to represent a larger proportion of the group total, and that membership commitment to "lobbying activities" to be far higher than AARP's 14 percent.

In each of the three countries examined, one finds at least one mass-membership group whose origins trace back to some public policy campaign, or crusade, which served initially as part of its basic appeal for member support—in the United States, the crusade for national Medicare legislation, in both Britain and Canada the decades-long struggle to achieve a more adequate and "liveable" public pension benefit. At the same time, one finds other mass membership organizations whose origins were unrelated to any such national effort or cause, and whose involvement in government came about only gradually, and as a "by-product" of what were initially nonpolitical sets of objectives.[8]

None of the three countries has lacked for at least one organization of the former type. In Canada, there are at least three presently active: the NP&SCF, Canadian Pensioners Concerned, and Pensioners for Action Now. The United States also has at least three: the NCSC, the National Association of Retired Federal Employees, and the "Gray Panthers."[9] Britain, on the other hand, for almost a half century had but one, namely, the National Federation of Old Age Pensions Associations (reconstituted in 1983 by the substitution of "Retirement" for "Old Age" in its official name). Even though Britain saw the emergence in the 1980s of several groups of the "political" type, their stability over time has yet to be demonstrated.

The reorientations in public policy occurring in the 1970s and 1980s were evidently not particularly congenial in terms of the maintenance needs of the more highly politicized aging organizations. With the exception of the Retired Federal Employees group in the United States, which expanded considerably, all now struggle simply to maintain their existing support bases and to prevent serious slippage in membership and income.

In contrast, the pattern among the less highly-policitized aging organizations has tended to be one of substantial growth. This applies especially to AARP, whose rate of expansion was nothing short of phenomenal, and also to Age Concern England, Britain's leading association of volunteers in the aging field. And it may apply as well to the Canada's One Voice Seniors Network, even though this group's recency of formation makes for some uncertainty in assessing its current situation. It bears mentioning that One Voice, formed in 1987, was in large degree an outgrowth of the Samuel and Saidye Bronfman Foundation's long-standing involvement in the aging and social welfare fields. With strong Foundation backing, One Voice sprang into existence fully fledged and polished as a lobbying force.[10]

It is unclear, exactly, why the recent past has proved relatively difficult for the more politicized seniors organizations. One possible explanation is that their stated goals are now seen as less compatible than in earlier years with the concerns and aspirations of an increasingly middle-class- oriented and financially secure elderly population. Elders may no longer be preoccupied to the large-scale extent as before with the policy concerns identified by these groups as chiefly important: the adequacy of the base-level pension, affordable health care, subsidized seniors' housing, and so on. If this be true, then the more politicized organizations find themselves in the ironic situation of having become in some degree the victims of their earlier lobbying successes, given that their own political activism contributed importantly to the public policy setting now in place.

Yet, these more overtly political organizations have not lost their earlier potential for lobbying effectiveness, nor have they been pushed entirely to the margins by other political actors in aging. On several occasions over the past two decades groups of this type have spoken with remarkable vigor and directness, including some situations where their larger counterparts have chosen the path of caution and circumspection. An example of this occurred in connection with the 1981–83 struggle over reform of the U.S. Social Security system. Despite the obvious importance of the changes then under consideration on Capitol Hill and in the Executive Branch, AARP was unable to wield much by way of political influence, notwithstanding its huge membership, complete team of lobbyists, and $41 million budget, whereas the much smaller, yet more highly politicized, NCSC wielded no small amount of power in the course of this controversy. This is explainable on the basis that the leaders of NCSC "had no doubt about the organization's political agenda . . . [which] meant that [as compared to AARP it] had more lobbying weapons" (Light, 1985, 76). Similarly, in 1985 Canada's NP&SCF, despite a minuscule budget, was able to spearhead a campaign that ended up compelling the government of Brian Mulroney to reverse itself on an announced plan to de-index the Old Age Security pension, for reasons of cost containment, and to withdraw the plan entirely (*Toronto Star*, June 6 and June 16, 1985). Likewise, Britain's NFRAPA, having coalesced with the Trade Union Congress (TUC) to help form the National Pensioners Convention, played a role in thwarting efforts by the Thatcher government in the middle 1980s to drastically scale back certain of the public pension benefits mandated under SERPS. None of this should be taken as suggesting that the more highly politicized organizations are in all cases primary, or even necessarily secondary actors in various age political struggles. What it does suggest is their considerable potential for political effectiveness in cases of perceived frontal attack upon established public pension programs.

The large size of seniors organizations on the model of AARP entails an increased risk of internal cleavage and factional strife as compared to their smaller, more cohesive counterparts. Yet, in circumstances where the former type of organizations manage to reach internal consensus, their capacity to influence the governmental process can be very considerable. A case in point was the protracted struggle in the United States over mandatory retirement legislation, which went on in various venues—White House Conferences on Aging, congressional committees, the Executive Branch—over a quarter century beginning in 1961. In combination with sympathetic members of the House and Senate, AARP, having come to regard this legislation as justifying the full mobilization of its legislative arsenal and other resources, made itself a driving force behind its eventual adoption. There is every reason to believe that, absent backing of AARP, neither the 1978 legislation outlawing mandatory retirement at age 70 nor the 1986 legislation outlawing the practice altogether would have been adopted when they were, or in such clear, unambiguous form (Ford, 1978–79; Pratt, 1989, 27).

In summary, in political terms not all mass-membership organizations in aging are alike. Such groups vary both in terms of their particular legislative goals and in terms of their degree of central emphasis on political activism, seen as an element in their basic incentive systems.

Seniors' Empowerment

The third concern to be treated in this paper relates directly to the topic of this symposium, namely, the empowerment of seniors. There are, I believe, at least two valid ways of defining "empowerment." The first emphasizes the capacity for direct control by seniors of the voluntary organizations of which they comprise the nominal constituency. A corollary to this definition is the possibility of oligarchy and goals displacement. A voluntary organization may become dominated by an unrepresentative minority, or ruling oligarchy, consisting not of seniors in the main but of others—professional staff, funding sources, and so on—who are chiefly concerned for their own personal enhancement and job security. Through this essentially undemocratic process, the groups can end up losing touch with the expressed wishes and interests of senior citizens. Unfortunately, I am unable to deal with this possibility in a seniors organization context, given the information available to me. My studies of senior-citizen and other aging organizations over the past 20 years have not been concerned, except perhaps incidentally, with group internal dynamics—neither from a "seniors' empowerment" standpoint, nor from any other. Moreover, the published literature provides little by way of enlightenment.[11]

Yet, there exists a second possible definition of "empowerment," and in regard to that I can perhaps offer some useful insight. It conceptualizes empowerment as the mobilization of seniors' political strength through organizations that act upon government in a pressure-group capacity. While skepticism is warranted concerning the claims sometimes made for "senior power"—a phrase popular among seniors activists and employed chiefly for its intimidating effect upon politicians, but without any necessary empirical substance—one can apply the term "power" with some validly in the present context. As revealed in a number of studies, some of them mentioned previously in this essay and also as summed up in a U.S. context by Christine Day (Day, 1990, Chapter 5), seniors' mass-membership groups have earned a reputation for considerable political influence. Although the senior groups seldom if ever act entirely alone in these situations, and more typically join hands with other individuals and groups, various analysts have rated their contribution as occasionally quite significant, not only in regard to policy struggles occurring in American national government, but also in the Canadian (Bryden, 1974, 194–195; Gifford, 1990). Yet, it also is true that seniors organizations do not always prevail in situations where their political strength is put to the test. Setbacks from their standpoint are by no means rare, as was illustrated by the 1988–1989 defeat of AARP in the course of the struggle on Capitol Hill over Catastrophic Health Care.

This raises the obvious question: what factors have served to determine whether seniors organizations in a particular instance can be successful in the governmental process? Stated differently, given the potential for seniors' political empowerment, what factors may determine the extent to which such potential becomes actualized?

One should begin by summarizing the several factors which have contributed positively to senior organizations' present reputation for political influence.[12] Such reputation is explainable essentially in terms of five factors: (1) typically large memberships, including substantial numbers of regular voters; (2) considerable wealth and related organizational infrastructures; (3) capable and dedicated national leaderships; (4) generally high levels of internal cohesiveness and absence of debilitating factionalism; and (5) the prevailing public view of old people as a group in legitimate need and deserving of public attention, and the consequent legitimacy accorded their organizational representatives. While seniors organizations are not unique among national interest groups in terms of large size, financial resources, and leadership capacity, the other groups occupying this category—for example, organized medicine and organized labor—typically must deal with entrenched opposition in the course of their political interventions. In regard to senior-citizen groups, however, the demands put forward tend not to confront such predictable, organized opposition, although caution is called for in making this statement, given the recent political backlash against the elderly (Day, 1990, 107).

Among the several factors mentioned here, none is more deserving of emphasis than elderly persons as voters, and the related awareness among elective office-holders that many of these same individuals hold membership in one or more of advocacy organizations in aging. Studies reveal that the elderly disproportionately regard voting as the only way they can have a say about how government runs things. For this and other reasons, elderly voters have steadily increased as a proportion of the American electorate.[13]

The striving for seniors empowerment, as defined in governmental terms, is nevertheless seriously constrained. The constraint consists, in the most fundamental sense, in the very concept of a seniors' "interest," which upon critical examination can be shown to lack any high degree of precision. The resulting ambiguity makes itself felt both internally within seniors organizations, and also in regard to the demands made upon government.

As suggested above in commenting on AARP, the views espoused by the active minority in a seniors organization may not always reflect adequately the thinking of its full membership. Apathy in the ranks appears to be more of a problem for mass-membership organizations of seniors than is true of their counterparts in most other fields. The literature on political socialization indicates that, while a certain amount of resocialization can occur in middle or old age, the strongest group attachments and political affects tend to be formed in adolescence or in early adulthood (Greenstein, 1968). Most people reach old age with their primary affiliations—to family, ethnic group, neighborhood, church, political party, occupation—already firmly fixed. It is true that events occasionally occur that serve to intensify older people's attachment to old age organizations, with a resulting potential for dramatic surges of political self-consciousness and awareness. (Such a surge occurred in connection with the Townsend Movement in 1934–1935.) Still, given that primary attachments are mostly formed early in life, and that age-related political concerns are typically overlaid on those attachments, surges in senior-group sentiment at one point are prone to later abrupt fading, as was illustrated by the Townsend Movement's marked decline, beginning in 1937. In no sense is this meant to suggest that senior organizations are wholly lacking in rank-and-file support for their public policy stands and, indeed, several striking cases of fairly unified senior-group sentiment on a given issue have been documented in the literature. It is rather to suggest that such support tends to vary widely, more so than might be encountered in organizations composed of younger persons, and with only occasional positions having widespread and intense internal backing.

One consideration that comes to the fore in defining a "seniors interest" is the extremely wide scope of potential senior citizen political concern, and the resulting difficulty in concentrating seniors' political resources in a manner likely to generate influence over public policy choices. Unlike most other reputedly influential interests in national government, seniors organizations feel some obligation to cover, to the best of their ability, essentially the entire domestic policy landscape. Clear focus is often difficult to achieve, more so than would be true of groups active in other fields. For example, the National Rifle Association in the field of gun legislation, has a clear advantage stemming from its narrow focus and resulting capacity to concentrate political resources on a couple of key standing committees— essentially one each in the U.S. House of Representatives and the Senate. In striking contrast, in the early 1980s, senior staff personnel in the National Council of Senior

Citizens responded to an interviewer's question by stating that the works of no fewer than 22 standing committees in the House and Senate and 59 subcommittees are considered of "high interest" from their standpoint. And likewise, AARP staff personnel manifested similarly "high interest" in the works of no fewer than 31 standing committees and 36 subcommittees. And not only were there more committees and subcommittees to keep track of, but these committees were, broadly speaking, much less likely to be considered as "friendly" to the seniors' interest than was the case for the committees regarded as highly important by the National Rifle Association.

This is not a circumstance that admits of any easy remedy. Any serious attempt on the part of seniors organizations to narrow sharply their scope of public concern—in hopes of realizing a more pronounced political impact—would risk overlooking certain of the compelling concerns that exist within the elderly population. It is quite probable, in fact, that one of the factors contributing to the "tidal wave" of senior-group formation of recent years has been the near-impossibility of any one group's adequately addressing the vast scope of relevant elderly concerns, and the perceived need to form new organizations of narrower scope and more specialized mandates in part, at least, to ensure that no policy concerns are overlooked or underemphasized.

But the very existence of the expanding number of groups has created a new set of problems from the standpoint of political representation, as was earlier discussed.

CONCLUSION

Questions relating to the empowerment of seniors in an organizational context admit of no easy answers. The explanation for why this is so consists partly in the fact that the required research, relating to group internal dynamics, has yet to be undertaken, at least with respect to organizations currently active. A second reason for the problematic character of seniors' empowerment consists in the unusual nature of the "seniors interest." Power, by definition, denotes a capacity to shape outcomes in the face of opposition; it is relational, referring to the control of specified objects with respect to specified purposes. In that sense, seniors' empowerment confronts the difficulty of the ambiguous nature of the relevant objectives. What governmental and political decisions are ultimately important from a seniors' standpoint? To what decision makers in government is it most essential to gain access? Opinions differ, often sharply, among seniors themselves and among their organizational representatives.

The findings presented in this paper, while leaving certain questions open, do perhaps offer an increased element of understanding. As revealed in the section on senior-group formation, the issue of empowerment was of little moment so long as national governments were uninvolved in old-age security, or else (as became the case early in this century in each of the countries referred to) involved marginally, but not in ways affecting elderly persons generally. This situation later would change, as governments acted first to expand social security/public pension coverage to include essentially all workers and their dependents, and then later on by enlarging pension benefit levels while at the same time adding new benefits, for example, medical care for the elderly under the U.S. Social Security system. In the process, the elderly became increasingly dependent on government income-security programs, and such programs therefore served as a critical indirect source of incentives toward the formation of aging organizations—initially on a limited scale, later on much more extensively. "Empowerment" emerged as an issue as the stakes were raised, and as control of older peoples' destiny was moved further away from their own direct control.

Even though seniors organizations became, in some cases, large, well funded, and professionally managed, it has been shown that no exact correspondence exists between their large resource base and any realized level of political power and influence. Paradoxically, large size has proved simultaneously an advantage and a disadvantage; an advantage from the standpoint of favorable access to government, a disadvantage from the standpoint of cohesion, given that seniors of widely diverse backgrounds and personal circumstances must now confront one another in common organizational frameworks. Cross-pressures within voluntary organizations are probably more apparent today than at any time in the past.

On the basis of the growing numbers of elders presently on the scene, and the expected increases in those numbers well into the twenty-first century, observers occasionally have predicted a continuing increase in the realized political power of senior citizens. One should be cautious in accepting such predictions. In the first place, advocates for the elderly, including the aging organizations, long have faced, and will likely continue to do so, difficulties in simply maintaining their policy concerns securely on governmental agendas. A leading study (Elder and Cobb, 1984) makes clear the ease with which their particular policy concerns can be displaced by competing priorities. And second, the findings reported in this paper are supportive of the view that past increases in apparent empowerment among seniors have almost inevitably been accompanied by new elements of vulnerability and potential weakness. The present period is no exception. While this is not to suggest that the political momentum on behalf of seniors will be impossible to maintain, it is to suggest that achieving such an objective will likely prove both arduous and challenging.

The present study also points up the existence of a fairly wide field for needed further research. As suggested at the outset, the study of voluntary organizations in aging, viewed in cross-national perspective, is still in its infancy. Future studies could usefully explore the extent to which the findings of the present research may be generalizable to other countries, in both developed and developing nations. It appears highly plausible, for example, that the close interdependency shown here between seniors' organizations and public policy outputs also may apply in other nations. Yet, one suspects that in those settings the concrete manifestations of the linkage will be quite different, given the absence in most nations of "activist" political culture, which typifies Canada, Britain, and the United States. An exploratory effort at most, the present study has scarcely scratched the surface of this highly important social phenomenon.

NOTES

1. Illustrative of the recognition presently accorded such political organizations by students of government is the current content of college-level American government textbooks. The author recently examined the contents of 11 such texts, sent to his department by their publishers, including all the leading books of this type currently available. The survey revealed that seven of the 11 referenced AARP—well above what might have been expected, considering that these texts devote but limited treatment to interest groups and typically name only a handful. It is quite likely that a similar collection of American government texts from as recently as the mid-1970s would not have mentioned AARP, or any other aging organization. This surmise cannot be easily tested, since no texts from that or any other earlier period are readily available. Yet, three books devoted explicitly to interest groups and published in the 1970s contained not a single reference to AARP or to any other seniors organization. The books are: James Q. Wilson, *Political Organizations* (New York: Basic Books, 1973); L. Harmon Zeigler and Wayne Peak, *Interest Groups in American Politics* (Englewood Cliffs, New Jersey: Prentice-Hall, Second Edition, 1972); Carol Greenwald, *Group Power* (New York: Praeger, 1977).

2. An exception to this statement is C. G. Gifford's illuminating book, *Canada's Fighting Seniors* (Gifford, 1990), which treats aging organizations in Canada, the United States, Britain, and several of the European countries. Although an indispensable source of data and interpretation on its country of main interest, namely Canada, its non-Canadian references are fairly limited, and the sections devoted to non-Canadian organizations do not formulate and test scientific hypotheses.

3. The data for this paper draw in part on my recently published book, *Gray Agendas: Interest Groups and Aging Policy in Canada, Britain and the United States.*

4. The founding year for this organization was 1945. Yet, for several years it functioned more as a regional movement than a national one, with its member units being entirely drawn from Canada's four western provinces. Only in the 1950s did it achieve genuine presence at the national capital in Ottawa.

5. I have elected here to disregard an early British pension reform group, the National Providence League, organized in 1882 by the clergyman William Blackley. As discussed by Ashford (1986), this group was not only short-lived—it did not survive the decade of the 1880s—but it had little impact on the course of political events.

6. Gifford observes that One Voice has succeeded in involving a fairly wide array of seniors' organizations, at both the federal and provincial levels and in both English and French Canada, but that it still falls short of reaching some of the largest organizations as well as involving the grassroots groups (Gifford, 1990, 253).

7. The group is the National Alliance of Senior Citizens, founded in 1974 by the 27-year-old C. C. Clinkscales (see Day, 1990). Clinkscales died in 1990, and consequently some doubt exists as to this group's continued viability.

8. Of the two types of groups described here, the latter, "initially nonpolitical" type, fits the model outlined in Mancur Olson, *The Logic of Collective Action*, in the section on "By-Product Theory of Large Pressure Groups" (Olson, 1965, 132–141). However, the former, or initially "politicized type" appears unreconcilable with Olson's "Logic."

9. Some question may be raised over designation of the "Gray Panthers" as an "aging organization," given its self-defined character as a transgenerational movement. The designation appears justified on the basis of this group's sustained concern over policy issues in the aging field, and related political activity.

10. The Samuel and Saidye Bronfman Foundation ranks tenth in size among Canada's philanthropic foundations, with assets of roughly $50 million. With support from this source, One Voice was in a position to lease office space in a modern high-rise office structure in central Ottawa, situated close to the various ministries of government.

11. One exception is a thoughtful essay dealing with the "Gray Panthers": Jacobs and Hess, 1978. For studies treating the internal dynamics of seniors' organizations of earlier times see: Pinner, Jacobs, and Selznick, 1959; Holtzman, 1963.

12. The following discussion is based in part on my essay, "National Interest Groups Among the Elderly: Consolidation and Constraint" (Pratt, 1983).

13. Bruce Jacobs, "Aging and Politics," in Robert Binstock and Linda George (eds.), *Handbook of Aging and the Social Sciences*. 3d ed. New York: Academic Press, 1990, p. 350.

REFERENCES

Achenbaum, W. Andrew. 1978. *Old Age in the New Land: The American Experience Since 1790*. Baltimore: Johns Hopkins University Press.

———. 1986. *Social Security: Visions and Revisions*. Cambridge: Cambridge University Press.

Ashford, Douglas. 1986. *The Emergence of the Welfare States*. New York: Blackwell.

Bernstein, Merton C., and Joan Broadshaug Bernstein. 1988. *Social Security: The System That Works*. New York: Basic Books.

Binstock, Robert. 1972. "Interest-Group Liberalism and the Politics of Aging." *Gerontologist* 12: 265–280.

———. 1983. "The Aged as Scapegoat." *Gerontologist* 23: 136–143.

Bryden, Kenneth. 1974. *Old Age Pensions and Policy-Making in Canada*. Montreal: McGill/Queens University Press.

Central Statistical Office. 1990. Annual Abstract of Statistics. Great Britain.

Chambers, Clark. 1963. *Seedtime of Reform: American Social Service and Social Action, 1918–1933*. Minneapolis: University of Minnesota Press.

Day, Christine L. 1990. What Older Americans Think: Interest Groups and Aging Policy. Princeton: Princeton University Press.

Dearing, Mary R. 1952. *Veterans in Politics: The Story of the G. A. R.* Baton Rouge: Louisiana State University Press.

Derthick, Martha. 1979. *Policymaking for Social Security*. Washington, DC: Brookings Institution.

Elder, Charles, and Roger Cobb. 1984. "Agenda-Building and the Politics of Aging." *Policy Studies Journal* 13: 115–130.

Epstein, Abraham. 1922. *Facing Old Age: A Study of Old Age Dependency in the United States and Old Age Pensions*. New York: Alfred A. Knopf.

———. 1938. *Insecurity, A Challenge to America: A Study of Social Insurance in the United States and Abroad*. 2d rev. ed. New York: Random House.

Ford, Laura C. 1978–79. "The Implications of the Age Discrimination in Employment Act Amendments of 1978 for Colleges and Universities." *Journal of College and University Law* 3: 161–209.

Gifford, C. G.. 1990. *Canada's Fighting Seniors.* Toronto: James Loriner, Inc.

Gilbert, Bentley B. 1970. *British Social Policy, 1914–1939.* Ithaca, NY: Cornell University Press.

Greenstein, Fred I. 1968. "Political Socialization." *International Encyclopedia of the Social Sciences* 14: 551–555.

Greenwald, Carol S. 1977. Group Power: Lobbying and Public Policy. New York: Praeger.

Guest, Dennis. 1980. *The Emergence of Social Security in Canada.* Vancouver, B.C.: University of British Columbia Press.

Holtzman, Abraham. 1963. *The Townsend Movement.* New York: Bookman Associates.

Jacobs, Bruce. 1990. "Aging and Politics," in Robert Binstock and Linda George (eds.), *Handbook of Aging and the Social Sciences.* New York: Academic Press, 3d ed. 350–361.

Jacobs, Ruth, and Beth Hess. 1978. "Panther Power: Symbols and Substance," *Long-term Care and Health Services Administration Quarterly* 2, 238–244.

Lammers, William W. 1983. *Public Policy and the Aging.* Washington, DC: Congressional Quarterly Press.

Light, Paul. 1985. *Artful Work: The Politics of Social Security Reform.* New York: Random House.

McKee, William Finley. 1954. "The Attitude of the Federal Council of the Churches of Christ in America to the New Deal: A Study in Social Christianity." Unpublished M.A. thesis (History), University of Wisconsin. (Available in U.W. Memorial Library, Madison).

Myers, George C. 1990. "Demography of Aging," in Robert Binstock and Linda K. George (eds.), *Handbook of Aging and the Social Sciences.* 3d ed. New York: Academic Press.

Novack, Janet. 1991. "Strength from its Gray Roots: The American Association of Retired Persons." *Forbes Magazine*, November 25.

Olson, Mancur, Jr. 1965. *The Logic of Collective Action.* Cambridge, MA: Harvard University Press.

Pinner, Frank A., Paul Jacobs, and Philip Selznick. 1959. *Old Age and Political Behavior: A Case Study.* Berkeley: University of California Press.

Pratt, Henry J. 1976. *The Gray Lobby.* Chicago: University of Chicago Press.

———. 1983. "National Interest Groups Among the Elderly: Consolidation and Constraint," in William P. Browne and Laura Olson (eds.), *Aging and Public Policy: The Politics of Growing Old in America.* Westport, CT: Greenwood Press.

———. 1989. "Uncapping Mandatory Retirement: The Lobbyists' Influence," in K. C. Holden and W. L. Hansen (eds.), *The End of Mandatory Retirement: Effects on Higher Education.* San Francisco: Jossey-Bass.

———. 1993. *Gray Agendas: Interest Groups and Public Pensions in Canada, Britain and the United States.* Ann Arbor: University of Michigan Press.

Putnam, Jackson K. 1970. *Old Age Politics in California: From Richardson to Reagan.* Stanford, CA: Stanford University Press.

Rubinow, Isaac. 1913. *Social Insurance: With Special Reference to American Conditions.* New York: Henry Holt.

Statistics Canada. 1983. Historical Statistics of Canada. Ottawa.

Thane, Pat. 1970. "The Development of Old Age Pensions in the U.K., 1880s–1925." Unpublished Ph.D. dissertation, University of London.

Toronto Star, June 6 and June 16, 1985.

Truman, David B. 1951. *The Governmental Process.* New York: Knopf.

U.K., Secretary of State for Social Services. 1985. *Reform of Social Security, Background Papers* 3: no. 1.

U.S. Bureau of the Census. 1990. Statistical Abstracts of the U.S. 110th ed. Washington, DC: Government Printing Office.

U.S. House of Representatives, Committee on the Budget. 1987. *Hearings Before the Task Force on Income Security.* 100th Cong., 1st Sess. Washington, DC: Government Printing Office.

Williamson, John B., Linda Evans, and Lawrence A. Powell. 1982. *The Politics of Aging: Power and Policy.* Springfield, IL: Charles C. Thomas.

Williamson, John B., and Fred Pampel. Forthcoming. *Old Age Security in Comparative Perspective.* Oxford University Press.

Wilson, James Q. 1973. *Political Organizations.* New York: Basic Books.

Zeigler, W. Harmon, and Wayne Peak. 1972. *Interest Groups in American Politics.* 2d ed. Englewood Cliffs, NJ: Prentice-Hall.

Chapter 5

Empowering Older Persons Through Organizations: A Case Study

Heather McKenzie

I intend to analyze the organization of which I was chief executive officer, to determine how closely it approximates the observations and conclusions delineated by Henry Pratt in his paper, included in this volume, "Seniors' Organizations and Seniors' Empowerment: An International Perspective," and to demonstrate that midlife/seniors' empowerment can have a very definite impact on social and public policy.

My analysis will examine the following: the variables that led to the formation of the organization; its objectives (both articulated and unarticulated mission statements); its structure, operations, and early achievements; how the impact of changing demographic patterns led the organization to expand its objectives; and its later achievements. Finally, I will make some recommendations that should increase the empowerment potential of future midlife/senior organizations.

VARIABLES LEADING TO THE ESTABLISHMENT OF THE ORGANIZATION

First to Pratt's "confluence of variables" that led to the formation of the parent organization, the National Council for the Single Woman and her Dependants (NCSWD). Were there "powerful, external forces" that enabled the group to emerge? Yes. There were three: (a) the demographic pattern of rapid population aging; (b) convention (historically, families had provided care for their frail, disabled elderly. Ninety-five percent of the elderly were cared for in the community by family members. It was common for families to relegate the primary caring responsibility to the never-having-been-married women in the family.); (c) the presence of an unprecedented number of never-having-been-married women.

(The bulge in these numbers was due to the savage erosion of eligible, marriageable males from 1939 to 1945 by World War II.)

The forces were in place, but to coalesce, they needed a catalyzing agent. That agent was to be the Reverend Mary Webster; middle-aged, unmarried, an ordained minister of religion and carer of her own elderly parents. She had observed that single women were conspicuously absent from her congregation. On investigation, she found that many of these women were at home caring for elderly frail or disabled parents; she resolved to change the status quo.

As a first step, Mary Webster obtained funding to carry out a survey of households within her own local authority area. The survey showed that single women carers were often severely socially isolated and subject to serious financial hardship. The reasons for the financial hardship were multiple. If single women stayed home to provide care, their standard of living fell in the short term, due to immediate loss of earnings; longer term, their occupational and state pensions were seriously eroded along with any nest egg (which would be presumed to be relatively small, bearing in mind that on the economic remuneration scale, women were paid significantly below the norm for men).

These single women did not have an advocate. Mary Webster resolved to become that advocate. She was the model leader, devoting her time, energy and expertise toward a cause which almost certainly was neither of "uncertain nor speculative outcome," as Henry Pratt writes in the previous chapter. Additionally and importantly, she invoked the support of eminent individuals as patrons; clergy—among whom was the Archbishop of Canterbury, parliamentarians, and academics. Enlisting such influential support would later prove invaluable in helping the organization identify sources of funding and achieve its goals.

THE LAUNCH

A group with particular characteristics had been identified in a country that had what Pratt describes as a strong "societal tradition for voluntarism." An association was to be formed to protect the interests of and to advocate on behalf of this group. The first challenge was to publicize the concept and to reach potential members. Two powerful strategies—the involvement of an interested media and the selection of a highly respected, national venue—were deployed.

The evocative themes—compassion, morality, and guilt of other family members— were certainly among elements that aroused the interest of leading women journalists. They wrote a series of articles on the plight of single women carers and publicized information on the venue of the proposed meeting at which that plight would be addressed publicly for the first time. Through the auspices of a member of parliament, the inaugural meeting was held in a revered venue: the Grand Committee Room of the House of Commons.

These elements unquestionably set the stage for a successful launching of this new, voluntary organization, which was prima facie, an organization for single women carers. Second and perhaps as important to its initial successes, it was the first organization for the segment of society defined as never-having-been-married women! Women from all socioeconomic backgrounds were represented and became founding members. A majority of those women were later shown to be middle-aged and therefore directly relevant to the population under discussion in this paper.

And so in 1963, the first organization for the narrowly focused purpose of meeting the needs of single women carers was set up. It was the first of its type in the world. The organization was established as a registered company, to protect its independence, and as a registered charity.

FUNDING

The group's eminent patrons identified sources of funding through private foundations. (Not being dependent on government funding, the organization could remain independent of government influence in developing its agenda). With reliable sources of funding available, organizational membership dues could be kept at a nominal fee so financial hardship would not preclude any qualified member from joining. Later, bequests left by former members would become an important source of revenue. It was not until the 1980s that the organization became the recipient of any government money.

STRUCTURE AND GOVERNMENT

NCSWD was set up as a membership organization with both at-large members and members associated with a local branch or chapter. These branches were established within geographic regions where there was a sufficient concentration of members.

The governing body was called the Committee of Management. It was comprised predominantly of representatives from branches, although it included some at-large members. Representatives from other relevant organizations were also members and helped gain lobbying support from their organizations for NCSWD initiatives.

NCSWD staff reported to the Executive Committee, which was appointed from those serving on the Committee of Management. The staff report was then presented to the entire Committee of Management, which was responsible for the main business of the organization. Therefore, a defined segment of the membership, predominantly from among the branches, had a definite voice in the government of the organization.

ORGANIZATIONAL OBJECTIVES

The company's charter spelled out a wide spectrum of objectives for the head office. Its two fundamental roles were to make policy recommendations to the

Committee of Management and to implement adopted recommendations within the parameters of available financial and staff resources.

Its service and program functions, also clearly spelled out in the charter, included:

- to respond to questions from individual members and make referrals where indicated to governmental and other relevant voluntary agencies;
- to act as an advocate on behalf of never-having-married women carers in all issues related to home care and long-term care in institutional settings;
- to make grants to members in destitute financial circumstances;
- to collect annual dues, including branch membership dues, and keep membership records (branch treasurers were entitled to collect dues but could retain only a specific sum for branch use);
- to set up branches, advise on strategy, and supervise branch activities;
- to publicize the organization as a resource for single women carers through activities such as National Carers' Week (a mechanism that has been adopted in the United States with National Family Caregivers' Week);
- to produce a newsletter that informed members, branches, government departments, and other relevant voluntary organizations about initiatives of the national office and branch activities;
- to commission substantive research studies on relevant issues and publish findings and reports;
- to identify issues, collect data, and prepare lobbying strategies (there was no doubt from the organization's inception that it would function as a pressure group. The *whole* membership *in fact* participated in lobbying activities. Sample lobbying letters for use by membership were included in the newsletter publication);
- to hold at least one, and usually two conferences annually;
- to discuss and formulate future policy; and,
- to build special-needs housing, which would enable caregivers to remain longer in the workforce.

THE ROLE OF BRANCHES

A director of development was responsible for establishing branches. The process deployed in setting up a branch was to work initially through a steering committee, comprised of social workers, nurses, and identified carers in the targeted area. The headquarters provided seed money and direction to newly formed branches.

Branches were financially autonomous; officers were volunteers. Branches served as the eyes and ears of the organization at the grass roots. Their role was to be supportive of single women carers and to identify deficiencies in health services and personal social services at local levels. The data they fed back supplemented headquarters data in making substantive cases for change at the legislative level. Branches were required to implement strategies and policies developed by the central Committee of Management.

EARLY ACHIEVEMENTS

Successes with legislation and with the provision of services and programs were among the early achievements of the organization.

In the 1970s, NCSWD worked with other organizations in a successful campaign for the introduction of the Attendance Allowance, which was a milestone in the area of financial benefits for the very frail and/or disabled. Qualifying conditions were stringent. The benefit provided two rates of allowance; a lower one for those who required constant care and attention by day or night, and a higher one for those who required constant care and attention by day and night. It was a non-means-tested and nontaxable benefit.

Next, NCSWD succeeded in achieving the introduction of a tax allowance for single women carers. Then the organization convinced many local authorities to change their housing policies as they affected surviving carers.

The organization's formidable success came with the introduction of the Invalid Care Allowance, a noncontributory benefit that was not means-tested but was taxable. Typical of government benefits, the amount payable was based upon Pratt's "empirically unverified assumption," that carer benefits were not required to match unemployment benefits. Importantly, however, carer benefits protected pension rights of the recipient. To qualify, the carer had to be a man under age 65 or a single woman under age 60, who was unemployed because of the need to provide care 35 hours a week for a relative in receipt of the Attendance Allowance. This allowance changed the financial profile of single women (and men) carers by providing some remuneration for loss of income due to having to give up work to provide care. And it was significant in that it protected the state pension rights of those who received it. Married women were excluded from qualifying.

Several forces combined to enable the Attendance Allowance to be enacted. First, the organization made optimal use of data contained in queries and specially designed questionnaires sent to members. Information was accumulated as to which services carers took up, which they resisted, why they resisted them, what gaps existed in service and program provision, and which services they perceived as relevant to their most pressing needs. Second, the organization—by now a highly visible, nonpartisan pressure group—had campaigned unrelentingly. Third, it had had the support of formidable parliamentarians. Fourth, and very importantly, the political climate was favorable. Pratt describes this as a time when "Britain's statutory change of greatest substantive impact . . . was the Social Security Pensions Act of 1975." Therefore, it could be said that the campaign for the Invalid

Care Allowance was perfectly timed, fitting into the government's mind-set of the day.

Success with programs and services was also achieved early in the history of NCSWD. Its advisory and referral service became a reference point, not only for individual carers but also for professionals. Expert advice across a wide spectrum of issues was provided. More than 40 branches were set up in England, Ireland, Scotland, and Wales. Substantive research to identify many of the social, financial, housing, and support needs of carers was undertaken. Undoubtedly, some of this research led to wider interest on the part of academics and policy makers in the needs of familial carers. Some research results were published in eminent professional and academic journals, including *The Lancet*. An internally brokered respite system was set up.

A WIDER POTENTIAL CLIENTELE BECAME
INCREASINGLY APPARENT

NCSWD had been successful in drawing attention to the plight of single women carers and in having changes introduced that gave them greater recognition and support. It became increasingly apparent, however, that there were other carers who also desperately needed support.

Over time, inquiries came increasingly from carers who were outside the organization's officially stated scope, as well as from professionals concerned with them.

This was in part due to the organization's "lobbying successes and associated activism," as Pratt has described it. Parallel to the above development, the executive director had several books on caring published (three of them addressing the needs of all carers). The publicity generated by these publications produced an avalanche of queries from familial carers of all socioeconomic levels and marital status.

Additionally, demographic trends were beginning to change the category of women who constituted the status of single women. There were more divorcees and separated women, who along with a growing number of married women, were entering the labor market. Caring was increasingly taking its toll on these other women.

At the same time, the government had announced its intention of making care in the community an integral part of its social policy. All indications were that NCSWD should expand the focus of its work.

However, despite a pressing argument that a wider constituency would lead to greater lobbying power, the membership strongly resisted. Lengthy debate ensued. After months of exhaustive argument, a referendum was held and the decision was reached to include all family carers of the disabled and or infirm elderly within the purview of the organization's objectives.

THE NEW ORGANIZATION

The organization became known as the National Council for Carers and Their Elderly Dependants (NCCED). The public's response was overwhelming. Queries poured in. Almost immediately, the impact of long-term care on family carers became a prominent issue of public debate.

The membership at the branch level also reacted strongly. When branches were first formed, only active carers had joined. In time, however, the membership comprised large numbers of former carers. (Many retained membership because of the single woman status of the members and the socializing element.) The needs of the currently active carers and former carers were disparate. With the development of the expanded organization, many former carers, unhappy about the extended function of the organization, resigned.

NCCED'S ACHIEVEMENTS

The staff of the new organization designed a more comprehensive range of materials to support carers, including *A Carers' Guide*, that explained available support services. Every avenue for publicity was assiduously pursued in an effort to bring information on financial benefits and other services to a wider public. NCCED's advisory service responded to thousands of queries annually. Approximately one-eighth of these queries came from prospective carers; this was regarded as a formidable achievement.

The group expanded its educational efforts. With guidance from the national office, the branches developed seminars on coping measures for the active carers among their membership; special seminars were designed for professionals in a position to help educate carers. Seminars on the needs of employed carers were given to human resource personnel.

In a legislative victory, the category of eligible dependants under the Invalid Care Allowance was expanded to include carers who are friends as well as those who are family members.

The organization built two housing projects for carers and their dependants (one in conjunction with a housing association). Both schemes were highly acclaimed.

NCCED gained international recognition when the Executive Director was invited to Australia to help set up the New South Wales Carers' Association. Professionals from developed and developing countries consulted NCCED on the needs of carers.

The government made a grant available to expand the organization, with the promise of a very large grant to follow.

Probably the most important achievement of the organization was that the many and varied needs of a group in society, which had previously been ignored, were now at the forefront of social and public policy.

The development and successes of the organization supports the concept of empowerment defined by Pratt as "the mobilization of middle lifers' political strength, through an organization, which acted upon government, in a pressure group capacity."

SOME RECOMMENDATIONS

The strategies deployed by this organization that led to its successes may well be emulated by embryonic organizations. Among those strategies are the following: (a) define and target a specific population; (b) carefully orchestrate support across a wide spectrum of influential religious, political, and academic personages (as relevant); (c) clearly define objectives; (d) identify reliable sources of funding; (e) ensure that research is substantive; (f) concentrate on achieving one objective at a time; (g) develop short- and long-term agendas; (h) where relevant, use newsletters, not only as sources of information but as instruments for unifying the membership and campaigning for additional members; (i) if it is a membership organization, ensure that members are proportionately represented in the governing body and be cognizant that there is a right time for every political maneuver.

Voluntary organizations do, as Pratt said, "influence values and aspirations of members and therefore exert their influence over a wider society."

Chapter 6

Tradition Impedes Organizational Empowerment in Japan

Takako Sodei

Empowerment as a concept is rather foreign to Japan, not only for elders but for the populace at large. Until the end of World War II, freedom of assembly and of association was denied by the Maintenance of the Public Order Act under the military government. If more than three persons got together, there was a danger of being arrested by the police or the secret police. It was only after the war that the Japanese obtained freedom of speech, of assembly, and of association. Until the beginning of the cold war, the American occupation forces were rather generous to mass movements like the labor movement and the student movement led by communists and socialists. They were politically oriented movements, some of which aimed at overthrowing the government and establishing a people's government. There was also a massive demonstration by housewives asking for more rice in the marketplace.

These radical movements lost momentum around 1950, as the American occupation forces changed their policy and looked to the Japanese government to become a responsible member of the Western alliance. In June 1950, the Korean War started, and 24 members of the central committee of the Japan Communist Party were quickly purged. The Japanese government began to put more emphasis on economic recovery than political issues, and people's interests were redirected from politics to the economy.

Senior movements started around the middle of the 1960s, a period of high economic growth. Up until that time, problems of the aged were usually dealt with at home by the family. With the decline of agriculture and the increased mobility of adult children, particularly the eldest son on whom parents traditionally relied in their old age, having their own source of income became both a necessity and a priority for older persons. When the National Pension System started in 1961, payments were not enough to live on and were jokingly referred to as "pocket money to buy candy bars for the grandchildren."

In 1964, the All Japan Free Workers Union, a communist-oriented federation of day laborers, organized the first big rally of elderly people, demanding old age guarantees such as opportunities for work, income maintenance, medical services, and housing. One of the great successes of the old age security movement was to obtain free medical services, for the elderly. As a result of pressure from the All Japan Free Workers Union, the Democratic Doctors' association, some chapters of senior citizens' clubs, and several labor unions, the Tokyo metropolitan government started to subsidize medical expenses of those age 70-plus in 1965. At first, the central government strongly opposed this step, but it changed its stance and started a similar system in 1973. In the same year, the Tokyo metropolitan government, under a socialist governor, lowered the age of eligibility for free health care from 70 to 65.

In 1972, the Tokyo Council for Promoting Old Age Security was organized, consisting of the Tokyo chapter of All Japan Free Workers Union, some chapters of the Tokyo Metropolitan Government Employees Union and some chapters of senior citizens' clubs, most of them under the influence of the Japanese communist party. They organized mass rallies and held sit-ins in front of the Ministry of Finance and the Ministry of Health and Welfare, asking for better pension and medical services, more work opportunities, and the construction of housing for the elderly and homes for the aged. Although these movements were partly successful, they failed to attract a large following because many old people remained opposed to communist-oriented movements. Moreover, with the improvement of economic conditions, the number of day laborers who played a major role in the movement decreased, and those who remained became old and frail.

The 1970s saw an improvement in the economic conditions of the elderly. Thanks to high economic growth, pensions improved and work opportunities increased. According to a survey of retirees by the Ministry of Labor, the number saying they could not support themselves if they did not work dropped from almost 71 percent in 1974 to slightly more than 41 percent in 1979. With the increase in the number of healthier, more prosperous elders came a shift in interest from financial issues to health and meaningful lifestyles. Since the middle of the 1970s, many groups oriented toward leisure activities have emerged.

SENIORS' ORGANIZATIONS

There are now two types of seniors' organizations in Japan: the "top down" type, such as the senior citizens' club, and the "grassroots" type, such as the Women's Group for Improvement of an Aging Society (WGIAS).

The Senior Citizens' Club

Senior citizens' clubs had been organized since the early part of the 1950s as voluntary associations. In 1954, the first nationwide survey of senior citizens' clubs was conducted by the National Council of Social Welfare. There were then 112 chapters. In 1962, the Japan Federation of Senior Citizens' Clubs (FSCC) was organized and, with the National Council of Social Welfare, held a conference for the enactment of the *Law for the Welfare of the Aged*. The law was enacted in 1963, and the Ministry of Health and Welfare began to subsidize senior citizens' clubs having more than 50 members. Each club now annually receives a total of 57,600 Yen (U.S.$500) contributed in equal measure by national, prefectural, and municipal governments. In addition, financial aid is available for activities such as training leaders (especially female leaders), intergenerational activities, membership drives, and helping the frail elderly in the community.

This financial aid had both a positive and a negative impact. The positive effect was financial stability, which enabled the clubs to expand their activities. The negative effect was becoming more dependent on the government and losing interest in political issues.

Since financial aid started, the government's control has grown. All the important posts in FSCC are occupied by a former Minister of Health and Welfare and other high-ranked officials of the Ministry of Health and Welfare. Thus, members are expected to vote at elections for a given candidate who usually belongs to the Liberal Democratic Party, the party in power. As recipients of financial aid from the government, it is difficult for these clubs to act as pressure groups or to organize antigovernment movements. For instance, when the government tried to reduce medical subsidies for the elderly and to abolish the free medical expense system in 1975, senior citizens' clubs did not act as a pressure group in opposition.

Today, the number of local chapters is 131,653 with a total of 8,520,590 members. Although membership is still increasing, the participation rate is declining. When people reach age 60, they receive an invitation from their local government to join. Bearing in mind that the average life expectancy in Japan is 76 for males and 82 for females, 60 is by no means elderly. Many of the 60-year-olds simply ignore the letter; some become angry because they do not think they are old.

The three most popular activities at senior citizens' clubs—singing, folk dancing, and playing gateball—are hardly attractive activities for the well-educated "young old" living in cities, who tend to organize around interests like sports and hobbies, regardless of age. Or they simply prefer to socialize with younger people. In addition to the decrease in new participants, younger members tend to leave because of gerontocracy in the senior citizens' clubs themselves, where leaders average around age 80.

Although two-thirds of club members are female, leadership is always in the hands of men. There are few female presidents; at the prefectural level there are almost none. The Ministry of Health and Welfare is now giving financial aid to clubs that try to increase female leadership. To attract new members, many clubs are now trying to expand to include volunteer activities, intergenerational and international activities, and educational programs.

The Women's Group for Improvement of
an Aging Society (WGIAS)

In September 1982, the first "Women's Symposium on the Problems of Aging" was held in Tokyo. It was the first time that women had organized a conference on aging, and 600 attended. The uniqueness of this event was that women without any political party, labor union, or company affiliation had organized the symposium. The organizers were professional women in their 40s and 50s who were themselves facing conflict between work and eldercare, or were afraid of losing their jobs in order to take care of their parents or parents-in-law. The leader, Keiko Higuchi, then a freelance writer in her late 40s who later became a college professor, had just lost her mother after a long and difficult time of caring.

Three topics dealt with at the first meeting were elder care at home, community support for elder care, and poverty of older women. Since the conference organizers were middle-aged, professional women (including myself), the major concern was the compatibility of work and elder care—that is how to take care of elderly parents without giving up work, so that the caretakers would not have to face poverty in their own old age.

In Japan as well as other countries, including the United States, elder care is traditionally the role of women. Nearly 90 percent of caregivers are women in their 40s and 50s (one-third are over 60). From one-fourth to one-third of working caregivers quit their jobs. (This figure is comparable to the American experience.) Many people, including women themselves, have long believed that it is a woman's fate to take care of parents or parents-in-law. The women's symposium was the first time that women in Japan spoke out to challenge this assumption, asking why only women had to be responsible for elder care.

At first there were no plans to organize a group, but the symposium convinced many that it was a good idea. WGIAS was officially formed in March 1983. Since then, we have held a conference every September attracting 1,500 to 3,000 participants. In addition, we hold a conference in a city outside Tokyo every other year, with the help of local chapters and financial aid from the local governments. In 1983, when WGIAS was formed, individual members numbered 298 and group members 11. In 1991, these numbers were 901 and 77, respectively.

We try to be politically neutral to attract a wide variety of people. Thus, our members range from supporters of the Japanese communist party to the Liberal Democratic party. Because of this neutrality, we have been able to bring together a Minister of Health and Welfare, a socialist governor, government bureaucrats, company executives, and labor leaders at our symposium. These are people who rarely sit at the same table.

In addition to a large annual conference, we hold seminars on such topics as long-term care, women and financial stability, housing for the elderly, and medical services. We have also conducted surveys on caregiving, on attitudes of students toward aging, and on the opinions of female local politicians toward aging. In addition, WGIAS has published books and organized visits to nursing homes and hospices.

We often submit proposals on such issues as pensions, long-term care, community care, and medical services from the woman's viewpoint to the Ministry of Health and Welfare, as well as to the Tokyo metropolitan government. It is not easy to measure the impact of our activities, but the recent white paper on health and welfare distinctly mentioned that it has become impossible to put the whole burden of elder care on women's shoulders, and the time has come for men to share the burden. This has been our position for the last ten years. Also, we proposed in 1985 that an adult day-care center be built in every elementary school district, so that even frail elders could go there by themselves or with little help from the family. In 1989, when the Ministry of Health and Welfare issued the "10-year strategy for health and welfare" (known as the "Gold Plan"), it promised to build an adult day-care center in every junior high school district, an area somewhat larger than an elementary school district.

Although family caregiving has always been a major concern, we have gradually broadened our scope to include participation in politics, intergenerational relationships, and gerontological education. Without taking part in politics, it is difficult to realize our goals. Two years ago, we ran a 70-year-old woman candidate in a local election. Some members joined her campaign. Last year, we held a symposium for local female politicians on aging issues in the community. Regardless of her political affiliation and constituency, every female politician is deeply concerned with health and welfare services for the elderly. It is not so easy for women to be elected at the national level in Japan, where national politics are still dominated by men, big money, and strong ties to a powerful political boss. It is rather easy, however, for women to be elected at the local level, where people are more interested in issues concerning everyday life. We are planning to hold a two-day seminar for female politicians and candidates in the fall of 1993.

Women's liberation has not been successful in Japan because neither men nor women supported the movement. The women's movement for improving an aging society, however, represents a new type of endeavor, one to liberate women from the burden of caregiving. Inasmuch as this woman's group succeeds in bringing about change through its own initiative, free of government interference, it reflects a new direction for seniors' organizations in Japan.

THE DIFFICULTY OF MOBILIZING OLDER JAPANESE

Some of the reasons it is difficult to mobilize older Japanese through their organizations can be found in any society, but others may be unique to Japan.

The Status of the Elderly

As is quite common in any industrial society, the status of the elderly is not high in Japan. Although the seniority system is still observed in the workplace, it can be maintained only as long as people are employed. Thus, some older politicians and business men can enjoy enormous power, but ordinary people lose their influence once they retire.

Attitudes of the Elderly

In contrast to the United States, where people are encouraged to be active throughout their lives, disengagement from society has traditionally been regarded as the ideal of aging in Japan. Politicians and businessmen who wield considerable influence use their power behind the scene, a practice seen often not only in Japan, but also in China.

Government Initiatives

The heavy involvement of government in supporting seniors organizations and promoting activities for seniors serves to dampen the initiative of the older people. There are two main reasons why the government is so eager to encourage social participation by the elderly: (1) the hope that their participation as volunteers can help reduce social service costs, especially for the frail elderly; and (2) the hope that an expected beneficial impact on their health may reduce government medical expenses.

As a result, virtually every government ministry currently sponsors activities for older people, including but not limited to senior citizens' clubs, traditional arts and crafts, sports festivals, gardening, and raising cattle. Although some of these government programs help to organize or increase the size of seniors' groups, their efforts almost never lead to greater involvement by the individual members, who tend to depend on the government policy or on the initiative of a professional staff paid by the government. Many groups are expected to cooperate in the campaigns of bureaucrats running for elected office. Although these politicians depend on older voters, they do not necessarily work for them. Dependent on government money, these groups find it difficult to exert pressure, and many of them prohibit political activities by their members except during elections.

This individual passivity in the face of government activism reflects the fact that, traditionally, the government has tended to intervene in the lives of Japanese people. Although many do not necessarily welcome such interference, it is rarely resisted due, in part, to a long history of feudalism and military government.

Gender Differences

Many seniors' organizations controlled by men tend to be under the umbrella of the establishment. Organizations for former labor union members are often controlled by the active union members. There are many groups for former employees of large companies, but they focus on leisure activities and socializing. Here again, both companies and labor unions support their activities financially and often interfere with (or according to them, "advise" on) the retirees' activities.

Japanese men, especially those who are employed, work very hard and very long. They even spend their holidays with the company. Therefore, they are isolated from the communities where they live and where most activities are in the hands of women.

On the female side, there are new moves to organize groups for protecting or expanding their own interests. Consumer cooperatives, which have been quite active since the postwar baby boomers started their own families, have served as a base for many women running for elected office at the local level. Japanese women are interested in the problems of aging because they are now faced with providing care for their parents or parents-in-law, at the same time realizing that it will be difficult or even impossible to depend on their own children in old age. While men can rely on their wives for care, women generally cannot rely on their husbands. Some women have organized mutual help groups for caregiving, as have some consumer cooperatives on behalf of their members.

Organizations of women have difficulty in obtaining government support because they often lack connections with people in power. This deficiency, however, is rather helpful in creating an independent power base. Some local governments have recently begun to subsidize female groups, a tendency that may weaken their effectiveness and reduce the voice of women against government power.

CONCLUSION

Although the number of organizations for the elderly are increasing and there is general social interest in elder issues, it is extremely difficult for elder organizations to exert pressure on existing government policy.

At the risk of sounding pessimistic, elders may never be able to influence government policy at the national level. However, as organizations grow and become more diverse, and as women take on a more active role, older people should at least become more vocal and capable of influencing the context of their day-to-day lives.

Chapter 7

Establishing a Seniors' Organization in Denmark

Bjarne Hastrup

There is a long-standing tradition in Denmark for people to set up groups, associations, and clubs of various kinds. Danish farmers formed a cooperative over 100 years ago, allowing their agricultural sector to become the only one in the world to not merely survive the agricultural crisis at that time but to emerge strengthened from it. During the course of the ensuing century, other strong, popular movements have followed in the wake of Denmark's farmers, including various labor organizations and—even later—organizations for interests as diverse as the environment and cancer research.

When then 75-year-old Ensomme Gamles Værn (EGV), a society for the care of lonely old people, decided to initiate a restructuring process to make the society better prepared to meet the challenges of the new millennium, the most important proposal was to establish a new national association. EGV had already built old people's homes, pensioners' accommodations, day-care centers and clubs, and had organized many activities throughout Denmark. Despite there being over a million elderly people in the country, EGV only had contact with some 12,000 of them. Although much was done for this group, the organization needed a national scope.

Therefore, the Landsforeningen Ældre Sagen (the DaneAge Association) was launched in 1987 with a huge, nationwide campaign. Since then, approximately 260,000 people have become members of DaneAge, a fourth of the population group within only seven years. As a result, DaneAge has entered the *Guinness Book of Records* as the fastest growing membership organization in history.

One novel idea of the association is that its membership should also include young people. About 10 percent of the association's members are between ages 18 and 60. This process is enabling DaneAge, for many reasons, to take a giant step toward the twenty-first century. First, we avoided the possibility of a generation gap occurring by allowing anyone over 18 to be eligible for membership. Old age comes to us all, so DaneAge wants both young and old people involved in the organization. Second, the association has made it very clear that it is the elderly themselves who must tell politicians and the world at large their hopes, wishes, and dreams for both now and the future. The fact that a considerable percentage of the younger members are between 50 and 60 means that the association is forward-looking and listening to the opinions of tomorrow's senior citizens.

The association has chosen to emphasize the role of the 161 local committees, so that elderly people are responsible for organizing and taking action themselves. This social aspect of the association's work is an important one, even in a welfare society such as that found in Denmark, where by far the greatest amount of care and pension schemes are paid by the state.

Another DaneAge strategy is to formulate specific political points of view, so that the association can maintain a strong position both locally and nationally within those spheres of the political debate that affect the elderly. And finally, senior citizens are directly involved in the development of their local area, for example, through DaneAge's active participation in local planning projects and so on.

This is just the start. Through the DaneAge organization, a number of senior citizens have received training aimed at improving their organizational and political abilities so that they are capable of active involvement in many fields. But it is just as important that the organization has a nationwide network, to ensure that grassroots opinions can be heard directly. The association, for example, set up a political committee charged with the task of gathering the political viewpoints of senior citizens throughout the country, so that these ideas can quickly be heard in the Danish parliament, the Folketing. The fact that DaneAge has so many members meant, too, that both the government and the Folketing were quick to take a positive attitude toward DaneAge and negotiate with the association.

Through DaneAge's meetings of delegates and via the work done in the association, each member has a real influence through his or her representative on how the organization should be run. This is mirrored by the fact that an important element when establishing the association has been placing of demographic principles at the very center of the organization. This especially Danish, and to a certain extent, Scandinavian phenomenon will hopefully inspire others to follow suit elsewhere in the world.

Today, the association also has an office in Brussels and thus has considerable influence on how the European Union's policies for the elderly will be formulated in the years to come. The European Commission has supplied the association with several grants aimed at, among other things, an exchange of information, project information, and similar schemes between Denmark and other member countries.

But the most important factor for the association is that it remains future-oriented. An example is its work with Ældre Fonden (Senior Citizen Fund), with whom it has founded a research council the purpose of which is to conduct research and analysis in areas that have not yet received the attention they deserve.

In this way, we hope to obtain a sensible balance between, on the one hand, demographic principles so that senior citizens can be heard in the political debate, and on the other, specialists and researchers to document the points of view that are prevalent, including the dismissal of various myths that are neither relevant for elderly people nor tell the truth about them.

The main question looming on the horizon is whether an organization such as DaneAge can cope with all its elements. During the first seven years the answer has been yes, and the organization has been a dynamic one. There are great expectations that this flexible, indeed resilient, organizational structure will also continue well into the new millennium.

Part 3

THE
EMPOWERED
INDIVIDUAL

Chapter 8

Hearts and Minds: Elder Empowerment and Cultural Revolution

Julia Tavares de Alvarez

I think that any discussion of empowering the elderly must begin with this assumption: The phenomenon of aging is now producing something new under the sun—an alteration in the fundamental character of this planet's human population. Such a basic social change will require a parallel shift in social consciousness. Without it, nothing else we might plan for will ultimately be effective.

Thus, to truly empower the elderly, we must reexamine nothing less than the intellectual and moral infrastructure that supports our efforts to deal effectively with world aging. We must focus on the ultimate source of all potency in human affairs: consciousness, will, and belief.

On one level, we are well on our way to exploring and developing the political and economic means of empowering older persons. The Plan of Action on Aging, the idea of productive aging, and the new recognition of the importance and talents of older women are a few developments that have begun to point the way.

But we are not paying enough attention to that aspect of empowerment that ought to precede these developments, and without which political and economic progress will stall. Summoning the political will to cope with global aging in the coming decades also will require a revolution in thought and feeling. There must be a change in what everyone perceives and believes to be the place of elders in the social fabric.

We must distinguish between the instruments through which older people everywhere might be empowered, and the political and personal will in whose absence the implements of empowerment will lie unused.

When we say "power," what are we talking about? Some words that come to mind are "ability," "capacity," "forcefulness," "authority," and "influence." These words share a striking similarity: They all imply a context of interaction. In a social context, power is about the interaction of the self and others; one is empowered when others believe in and acknowledge it.

It amazes me how much the negative attitudes associated with old age are a result of social definitions. Too many people in our youth-oriented societies view aging as an unmitigated process of decline. They think that old age is necessarily a story of illness, poverty, isolation, desolation, and depression. Such attitudes lead people to accept as inevitable a circumscribed role in later life. They make growing old an exercise in failure. The young cannot imagine that they too will age. Therefore, they have little empathy for their elders. Indeed, for those who revere youth, age is something to be feared. There can be no true and lasting empowerment of the elderly under these circumstances. Such attitudes must change.

Power also comes from within. You must be able to imagine yourself as having power. You must feel entitled to be powerful. You must believe that others will accept your empowerment. You must regard it as something natural and right, appropriate in the scheme of things.

Those who would speak of empowering the elderly must ask themselves: How do we get older people to believe in the potential for their empowerment? How can we generate the force that must work from the inside out? How do we begin to effect this global change of attitudes, outlook, expectations—this massive change of mind, if you will? If we are to think globally, the United Nations must of course play a role.

To that end, many of us worked hard to secure the passage of the United Nations Principles for Older Persons last year. Basic changes in society must be certified by the social institutions that count. Social relationships will not change permanently unless the changes are imbedded and recognized universally in the social matrix. The UN Principles were an essential step in that direction.

The UN Principles begin to provide the moral and social underpinnings for our struggle. They affirm and authenticate our goals. In getting them passed, no money was appropriated, no commission created, no projects announced. Not one bureaucrat was hired. The product of our effort was words, but they were far from mere words. They were the beginnings of social commitment, the creation of a universal standard of decent treatment of and respect for older people.

But we must reach deeper. Our goals must be—literally—sanctified. These changes in consciousness must become ingrained, second nature to us all. They must begin to take hold on the most fundamental way we relate to the world. If we are to ask people to act differently in basic ways, they will first have to think and feel differently than they do now.

What else, then, do we need to provide this sea change in human consciousness? They say that the pen is mightier than the sword, But the images and symbols by which we relate to the universal and eternal are mightier still. I believe that if we are truly to empower the elderly, we will need to do more than we have done to enlist the religious institutions of the world in the transformation of consciousness we so desperately need.

Religion speaks to first things, and the first thing we must fight when empowering the elderly is despair. Despair is the great enervator. At its worst, life becomes a process in which there is nothing but the darkness closing in, with abilities and possibilities progressively foreclosed. Then one may feel more or less demoralized, but certainly not empowered. In this state of mind, a person does little but wait for life to write "The End."

Religious institutions are also uniquely qualified to define authoritatively the position of elders in society. Are elders created any less in the image of God than everyone else? One might think so. You can't empower what you can't see. In many parts of the world, the elderly are almost invisible—figuratively and literally. Aging must take on a human face if the elderly are to be empowered in this world. A blank mask won't do.

Empowering elders means including them again in the human family as full, functioning members. Churches, temples, mosques, and synagogues must play a role in effecting this change. The aging of populations will make new and unique demands on us. Humanity will need a new outlook, frame of reference, and value structure. We really need to see the elderly differently than we have in the past. We need a new ideology, not just new ideas.

Here's a specific example of what I mean. Ten years ago, following the World Assembly on Aging, the World Council of Churches published *The Church and the Aging in a Changing World*. In it they said: "Nothing is as natural to the human experience as the fact of aging. . . . Aging is, therefore, an integral part of creation. . . . In God's sight, all human beings have dignity because they are made in his image." The Council then went on to apply these principles systematically to every aspect of aging, and thus provided a vision and then embodied it in the worldly tasks that face us.

We do not hear enough about the ideas that were expressed in this publication of the World Council of Churches. Nor do we tap sufficiently the potential resources for changes in consciousness that exist in other religions. Judaism, for example, is rich in this potential. Jewish communities are known for their care of their elder members. Just as important, this religion has a tradition of respecting the abilities and importance of older people. The Ten Commandments' admonition to honor thy mother and thy father does not have a cutoff date at age 65. Here is the definition of "elders" from *The New Standard Jewish Encyclopedia*: "In biblical times, a member of the authoritative group of the nation. The elders were influential in shaping the form of government and served as judges and chief representatives of the people. . . ."

Islamic clergy are often men of advanced age. And it would not surprise me if virtually every other religion offers examples of the way in which age is honored in both practice and principle.

A Roman Catholic myself and an ambassador from a Catholic country, I am keenly aware of the role that the Church might play in this area. We don't know exactly how many Roman Catholics there are—estimates run as high as 980 million people. At the very least, they make up an eighth of the world's population, much of it in our developing nations. Headed by a 72-year-old Pope, the Church is an institution whose size, authority, and tradition of social action makes it exceptionally—one could say, uniquely—well situated to put a human face on aging.

In fact, many issues that are central to problems generated by the aging of the world's population are already key concerns of the Church. The family is an obvious one. The Church has focused its attention on the relationship of parents to children, which is understandable. But the explosive growth in the number of older family members also demands consideration.

The breakdown of the extended family in our developing nations, with which I am sure my readers are familiar, is stranding many of the elderly in rural villages. It also often places new demands on them without honoring or supporting their efforts. Although mired in poverty, many must care for their grandchildren because their children have left for the cities to find work.

In refugee communities, older people have often served as surrogate parents to children orphaned by the turmoil of politics. In its booklet, the World Council of Churches advocates organizing "intentional family communities" for support and sustenance when such social upheaval has rent the bonds of traditional family ties. Because of its size, the Roman Catholic Church needs to be in the forefront of providing a new moral, ideological, and social direction to societies that will have to call on older people to take such active roles. The moral, psychological, and social ties across generations need to be bolstered. What institution is better equipped to act so universally than the Roman Catholic Church? Where will the Church be in the impending crisis of aging if it does not provide this leadership? The Church itself, after all, is beginning to face a crisis caused by the aging and forced retirement of its priests and nuns, especially in the industrialized world.

Theology and institutional policies always respond to social changes. Here is indeed a challenge to the world's largest religious body.

Related to these issues and the role of the elderly in society is the broader question of intergenerational relationships. In the West, there has been much talk of conflict—even war—between generations over access to society's limited resources. More generally, with the new phenomenon of global aging, we will need to reexamine and reinvigorate the ties between the generations with respect to such issues as responsibility and dependence.

Earlier, I said that we have to see power in context. Another way of putting this is to say that power is always connected to something, that it never exists in isolation. But the isolation of elders is exactly what blocks their empowerment. The rest of society defines them as separate kinds of beings and then can't identify with them. Often economically separated from society when they pass a certain age, elders are physically separated by modernization and urbanization in our Third World, and by the creation of old-age retirement ghettos in the developed nations. Out of sight, out of mind.

We need to change our minds about all this. And we need religious institutions as active, enthusiastic allies in our cause. It is not enough that they get behind individual projects. They need to be out in front providing active moral leadership. World religious leaders and institutions need to be heard from. We can't do it without them. Specific social, economic, and political measures aimed at empowering the elderly are techniques and tools. But before we can empower the hands, we must first fortify the mind and the heart.

Chapter 9

The Psychological Basis for Empowerment

Jane Myers

Empowerment may be defined as a process of helping people gain, regain, or maintain personal power or control over their lives, a sense that they can influence the people and organizations which affect them. The processes of aging combine to make older persons particularly vulnerable to perceived or actual losses of power, resulting in a need for empowerment.

The ultimate goal of empowerment is to enable persons to live in a manner that maximizes their ability to develop independent, positive, satisfying lifestyles. This goal can be reached through a focus on two sets of factors, those external to the individual and those internal. The external perspective—empowerment through groups, agencies, organizations, and governmental policies—is addressed in other chapters in this book. It is critically important, as the factors that combine to make older people vulnerable to a loss of power affect all members of the older population. At the same time, the processes of aging have their initial impact on individual older people. If groups and societies are to benefit from the contributions of independent older persons, individual approaches to empowerment are needed. Hence, the focus of this chapter is on the internal psychological factors which affect perceptions of empowerment among older individuals.

Individual empowerment is a complex, multidimensional, psychological process. It is best understood through consideration of individual psychological factors which, when combined with societal and environmental changes in response to aging, can lead to a lack of empowerment in a previously independent person. The interaction between individual and societal changes in later life sets the stage for a negative, self-perpetuating cycle of "disempowerment" and, at the same time, reveals implications for reversing this negative spiral downturn upwards toward a positive spiral of "reempowerment."

PSYCHOLOGIAL CONCOMITANTS OF
EMPOWERMENT IN LATER LIFE

Psychologically and socially, the older population is extremely heterogeneous and diverse. One of the major things that older people have in common is their ability to cope with the challenges and changes of later life and to adapt successfully to their varied life circumstances. In fact, most older people adjust successfully to the processes of aging and experience a sense of life satisfaction in their later years. Factors that correlate with a feeling of morale, or high life satisfaction, in later life include the presence of a spouse or children, a satisfying social support network, adequate income, good physical health, adequate housing, access to transportation, and independence. Even in the absence of these factors, many older individuals experience a sense of contentment.

At the same time, it is clear that some older persons do not experience satisfaction or contentment, and that their internal emotional reactions are unrelated to their objective life circumstances. What differs for these older people are their attitudes toward their life situation. These attitudes, in turn, are affected by psychological factors related to empowerment, such as locus of control, self-efficacy, and self-concept.

Locus of control refers to how a person evaluates personal responsibility for events in his or her life. Those with an internal locus of control perceive themselves as responsible for or in control of the events in their lives, while those with an external locus of control see themselves as having little or no control over external circumstances or forces which seem to determine the events in their lives. Younger persons often experience a sense of personal power as they make decisions which lead them in desired directions. As people age, on the other hand, they are apt to experience changes over which they have less control and which lead them in undesired directions. For example, older persons may experience a loss of health, income, spouse, or friends, all losses they did not choose yet have to endure. Consequently, their locus of control may move from internal to increasingly external as they objectively reevaluate their ability to influence major events in their lives.

Albert Bandura (1982) proposed the concept of self-efficacy as an explanation of behavior and behavior change. People avoid activities they believe exceed their coping abilities and undertake those they consider themselves capable of handling. Efficacy expectations influence the decision to attempt a behavior, the length of time it will be attempted, and the effort involved. Low-efficacy expectations in the face of obstacles will result in persons experiencing serious doubts or giving up, while high-efficacy expectations will result in greater efforts being extended to achieve desired results. Some older widows, for example, are active in civic activities, social affairs, or travel. Others are largely isolated and uninvolved with life. Objective circumstances and resources may be similar for all widows; however, some experience a high sense of self-efficacy while others do not.

Many persons reach their later years with a high sense of self-efficacy, having learned throughout their lives that they were capable individuals whose efforts would be rewarded. Yet, the circumstances and multiple losses of later life, over which they have no control, may lead to a low sense of self-efficacy, even among persons who felt otherwise when younger. In addition, older persons with an already low sense of self-efficacy may be expected to react to the losses of later life by giving up more easily and withdrawing.

As they experience a decreased sense of personal power, older persons may question their own self-worth, leading to a decline in their sense of self-esteem or self-concept. They "learn" a new sense of self, often one that is less positive than was the case earlier in life. A process of social breakdown sets the stage for and contributes to a self-perpetuating loss of personal power.

AGING AND LOSS OF POWER:
THE SOCIAL BREAKDOWN SYNDROME

Even older persons who cope successfully with aging may find, at some point, that coping strategies once successful in helping them maintain independence may be unsuccessful in helping them meet the demands of later life. As an example, consider a man in his 40s who experiences difficulty in reading, the result of normal, age-related changes in visual acuity. He "learns" that a visit to an opthalmologist and the purchase of glasses corrects the problem. Over the next 30 years, the identical sequence of events occurs each time difficulty is experienced with reading. A visit to a physician and a new prescription for lenses corrects the problem. At age 75, he is diagnosed as having macular degeneration, a progressive disease that will eventually result in blindness and is not correctable with eye glasses. He is given a pamphlet by the physician explaining the condition. He refuses to read it, considers the new, younger physician to be the source of the problem (after all, the eye doctor he had for 30 years *always* corrected his problem), and tells everyone who will listen that the doctor "ruined" his eyes with eyedrops. He continues to seek additional opinions, certain that the "right" doctor will not only agree with him but will prescribe new glasses so he can again read. His solution "worked" for many years, but his changed circumstances now cause that solution to be ineffective.

This example is not uncommon, and it reflects the disruption in healthy functioning that often occurs as new coping behaviors are attempted. Older persons who experience a high sense of self-efficacy and an internal locus of control will be much more likely to attempt new and innovative solutions to their life problems, while those with an external locus of control will increasingly expect those around them, agencies and organizations to resolve their problems. They may become angry when help is not forthcoming, blaming others for their problems and expecting others to find solutions. When such older persons are encountered, it is important to recall that their feelings may be a reaction to the changes and losses of aging. Further, their reactions likely will follow a typical pattern of behavior described by John Kuypers and Vern Bengtson as "social breakdown" (1973).

The social breakdown syndrome depicts the process by which vital, active, older persons experience negative adjustments in later life. It describes the process of disempowerment, at least as it occurs in Western societies. It defines the relationship between social inputs and self-concept that results in a self-perpetuating cycle of negative psychological functioning. The process involves four stages that repeat in an increasingly negative pattern.

Stage One

In the first stage of social breakdown, older persons experience a precondition of vulnerability, often as a result of pervasive negative attitudes toward aging. In general, societal attitudes toward older persons are negative, and often older persons internalize these negative societal perceptions as self-descriptions. For many older people, declining physical strength and health cause doubts as to one's ability to continue living independently. The loss of social status that accompanies retirement is another example of a phenomenon that can create doubts as to one's actual abilities and capabilities.

Stage Two

When one person or a group of people express doubt about an older person's capabilities, Stage Two begins. Frequently, family members and friends innocently initiate this stage when they encourage an older person to relinquish some of their activities, hopes, or dreams. When employers or co-workers suggest retirement, when physicians advise that favored activities be discontinued, or when unkind drivers express impatience at one's slower pace, the older person begins to hear a message that he or she is no longer the independent, respected person of younger years. As trusted friends and society in general provide messages that one is less capable, the older individual is increasingly likely to question his or her abilities.

Stage Three

At this point in the breakdown cycle, the older person is inducted into the sick role, which is synonymous with illness and dependence rather than health and independence. The sick role can be desirable for younger people, as it is temporary and provides relief from responsibilities for a more or less finite length of time. For older persons, however, the time out from work tasks or dysfunctional relationships until one is "well" again are secondary gains that may not be realized, as they may not regain their health. The older person is expected to accommodate to the sick role, and, as this occurs, skills for independent living may atrophy or disappear as a result of disuse.

Stage Four

In the fourth and final stage of social breakdown, older persons continue to experience the atrophy of independent skills and behaviors, and increasingly view themselves as sick and incapable. They internalize a new self-perception as inadequate and incapable of continued independence. As self-efficacy is increasingly impaired, they experience few expectations of successful outcomes of independence.

The fourth stage sets the cycle to repeat, with a different starting point. The older individual is now even more susceptible to the negative evaluations of others, and is even more vulnerable than previously to the internalization of new roles and new, more negative self-perceptions. The breakdown cycle gains momentum and becomes a downward spiral. It will eventually lead to incapacity and death, in the absence of interventions. Because of the salience of psychological factors, psychological interventions are required.

PSYCHOLOGICAL CONCOMITANTS
OF BREAKDOWN

Older persons can become vulnerable to social breakdown in many ways. Certainly, changes in perceptions of control from internal to external, decreased self-efficacy, and a lowered self-concept are primary factors. In addition, psychological reactions that can, singly or in combination, contribute to breakdown may be the result of depression, discouragement, or learned helplessness.

Depression is common among older persons, and when it is severe it can become self-perpetuating. It is often a "normal" reaction to loss, accompanied by feelings of sadness and immobility, feelings of low self-esteem and worthlessness, hopelessness, and powerlessness. Older persons who are depressed may become lethargic, withdrawn, and incommunicative.

Persons who are discouraged truly do not believe themselves capable of solving their own problems. They have no confidence in their abilities and are likely to give up rather than attempt to overcome obstacles. They assume themselves to be inadequate and are pessimistic about their future.

When placed in situations where they have no control and where nothing they do can effect a positive outcome, people can "learn" that they are helpless. Whether they actually can affect their circumstances is relatively unimportant; what matters is that they truly believe they can do nothing to change their problem. Learned helplessness is a serious psychological condition which is exceptionally difficult to treat or reverse; people who experience it are reluctant even to try to take action on their own behalf. They are often apathetic, listless, depressed, and unmotivated. An example is an older person placed involuntarily in an institution, who learns that he or she is helpless in the face of major life decisions. The learned helplessness may generalize to any and all decisions, including such minor issues as what to eat, what television program to watch, or what to wear on a given day.

The various psychological concomitants of breakdown may occur in isolation or in combination, the latter situations being the most difficult to treat. Under most circumstances, however, it is possible to slow down, stop, or even reverse the breakdown cycle. The most effective means of accomplishing these objectives requires attention to the underlying cause of social breakdown: a perceived and/or actual loss of personal power.

EMPOWERMENT THROUGH SOCIAL
RECONSTRUCTION: REVERSING BREAKDOWN

The Social Reconstruction Syndrome (SRS) is a model of interventions designed to offset the negative effects of social breakdown (Kuypers and Bengtson 1973). The underlying assumption is that the cyclical nature of breakdown can be interrupted, slowed, or reversed through inputs at any level of the cycle. This could include societal, environmental, and psychological interventions at any point in the process. Interventions that occur early and that are consistent have the most potential for being successful.

Societal inputs include the need to change ageist stereotypes and beliefs and develop valued roles for older persons during their retirement years. In societies where older persons fill valued roles, the susceptibility to social breakdown which occurs in Stage One does not exist. Many activities and roles can be meaningful for older people if valued by society. These include kin-keeping, grandparenting, and providing volunteer or community service. Whatever roles contribute to a sense of meaning and purpose for older people will serve as barriers against social breakdown.

Environmental interventions are aimed at improving the adaptability of older persons through improving the nature of and access to social services. These services are what is meant by external empowerment. Many older persons could remain living independently if they had assistance with housekeeping, preparation of meals, or transportation for needed trips to hospitals, physicians' offices, and shopping centers. Living independently will, in and of itself, foster feelings of self-worth among older individuals.

The encouragement of self-efficacy through empowerment is a vital strategy for interrupting and reversing the breakdown cycle. By helping older persons experience a sense of control in the management of their lives, and by promoting older persons as capable and self-determined, a sense of empowerment can be fostered. This may require significant modifications in the environment as well as individual perceptions. For example, one way to empower persons is to provide a means of involvement that promotes a sense of ownership and control. Advisory boards and resident panels are examples of strategies for involving older persons in decision making on their own behalf. Educational interventions can help older persons under-stand and adapt to the aging process. Family members as well as older persons are likely to develop a sense of efficacy when included in decision making.

In general, consumers placed in the role of passive recipient, such as occurs when the medical model is predominant, tend to become and remain disempowered. Sometimes it will be necessary to structure an environment where the older person can be allowed and even encouraged to make independent choices. Through deliberate encouragement, through a focus on developing a new psychological perspective as a capable individual, empowerment and social reconstruction may be promoted.

EMPOWERMENT THROUGH WELLNESS: PREVENTING OR POSTPONING BREAKDOWN

The negative cycle of social breakdown can have a positive corollary. It is possible to reverse the cycle, so that it may be self-perpetuating in a positive direction. From a societal perspective, this will require a change in the pervasive negative attitudes toward aging. Policy and decision makers need to reexamine the philosophy of doing things to and for older people, rather than deliberately creating environments in which they can do things for themselves. Personal involvement in the decisions that affect one's life can lead to a sense of empowerment. And, importantly, empowerment is self-perpetuating. Older persons can become increasingly empowered as they continue to make decisions that affect their lives in a positive direction.

Viewing social breakdown from the perspective of prevention as well as reversal leads to an emphasis on wellness. Wellness focuses on self-responsibility, on the need to be assertive in creating the life you want rather than passive in just reacting to circumstances. Through an emphasis on freedom of choice, wellness approaches increase the responsibility of individuals for their self-care. Wellness is essentially an empowering philosophy that has a goal of helping individuals identify areas of their lives over which they have control, and assisting them to make healthy lifestyle choices which enhance their physical and emotional well-being, as well as their continued ability to make even more healthy choices.

A useful model of wellness to employ in helping older persons experience a sense of empowerment was defined recently by Melvin Witmer and Tom Sweeney (1992). These authors presented a holistic model for wellness and prevention symbolized in a wheel of wellness. Spirituality is the core of the wheel and one of five major life tasks that empirical data support as important. The four additional tasks are self-regulation, work, love, and friendship. This model incorporates research and theoretical concepts from a variety of disciplines, including anthropology, education, medicine, psychology, religion, and sociology. It provides an integrated paradigm that can serve as a basis for theory building, clinical interventions, education, advocacy, and consciousness raising.

The five life tasks exemplify the characteristics of a healthy person, and interact dynamically with several life forces: family, community, religion, education, government, media, and business/industry. The life forces and life tasks interact with and are affected by global events, both natural and human, positive as well as negative. In a healthy person, all life tasks are interconnected and interact for the well-being or detriment of the individual.

Persons planning wellness interventions must conduct needs assessments and design interventions to address holistic functioning in each area identified in the model. Positive changes may be facilitated through creating a positive, healthy environment, in which helpers communicate a sincere belief in the capability of individuals to assume responsibility for their own total well-being. Such an environment is inherently empowering.

As we grow older, the cumulative effect of lifestyle choices becomes increasingly significant. Although the negative impact of unhealthy choices becomes increasingly evident, the good news is that it is never too late to change. Positive, healthy lifestyle choices can enhance the quality of life, across the life span, beginning whenever they are implemented. A philosophy that emphasizes wellness across the life span is one way to respond to the challenge of creating a world where empowerment is the norm for all persons, regardless of their life circumstances.

CULTURE: A MEDIATOR FOR
INDIVIDUAL EMPOWERMENT

Social definitions of aging and psychological reactions to aging are defined by and differ according to culture. Thus, the social breakdown model, social reconstruction, and individual empowerment will be viewed and implemented differently in different societies. As presented in this chapter, social breakdown is an accurate description of what is commonly experienced by older persons in Western societies. Care providers in these societies can use the strategies outlined here for fostering empowerment of older individuals.

On the other hand, the models presented in this chapter may be ineffective or not useful in explaining and predicting adjustment to old age in societies that define the social value of older persons as positive and worthy of respect. For example, it is traditional in Eastern cultures that older people are respected or even venerated by virtue of their age. Thus, an important precondition of Stage One of the social breakdown model—the susceptibility to breakdown resulting from pervasive negative societal views of older persons—is not met in these cultures. The next stages may not occur or may not occur in sequence. To enter Stage Two, older persons must begin to question their worth; and while this may still occur, the manner in which they are treated by others in some societies may serve to mitigate self-doubts. Taking on the "sick role" may not lead to the social breakdown of Stage Three but rather to socialization in the form of care being provided by younger family members, especially daughters or daughthers-in-law.

Although older persons may become increasingly dependent in these societies, they still can maintain the respect of family members and society at large, as they have roles to fill which others value. In such societies, the circumstances of later life do not directly or necessarily lead to social breakdown, nor is the individual disempowered in the sense that this occurs in Western societies.

In African-American cultures, among others, the expectation is that older family members will be cared for within the family. Again, social breakdown is less of an issue, becoming a factor in individual adjustment if and when family members are unable to provide needed support; in such cases, the older person must depend on social institutions to meet his or her basic needs.

Moreover, what is seen as disempowered and unhealthy in one society may be viewed as both healthy and desirable from other cultural perspectives. In Buddhist cultures, for example, emotional detachment from life is viewed as desirable, even as a state of advancement to a higher level of functioning. Within these cultures, detachment is a sign of healthy functioning. In Western societies, the same behaviors would usually be viewed as unhealthy and a sign of the beginning of a social breakdown cycle.

Many more examples could be given of cultural variation in relation to the social and psychological definitions of older people. Empowerment of older persons will, similarly, be defined differently in different cultures. Empowerment as defined in Western cultures could actually be counterproductive in Eastern cultures. Empowerment from a wellness perspective, a viable concept in Western society, may be useful regardless of culture so long as cultural definitions of wellness behaviors are used as the basis for implementing wellness interventions. Attention to physical, emotional, and spiritual wellness seem to be universal aspects of all cultures. Older persons who experience wellness are, by definition, those who meet the highest standards and expectations of the culture in which they live. They are able to experience a sense of empowerment regardless of their circumstances.

In summary, a cross-cultural perspective on individual psychological empowerment may best be achieved through a wellness philosophy. Social breakdown may occur in all societies; however, the definition of the stages and preconditions may vary considerably. Clearly, all societies need to examine healthy roles and behaviors for older people, and to foster these roles in order to enhance the quality of life for all persons across the life span.

REFERENCES

Bandura, Albert. 1982. "Self-Efficacy: Mechanism in Human Agency." *American Psychologist* 37(2): 122–147.

Kuypers, John, and Vern Bengtson. 1973. "Competence and Social Breakdown: A Social-Psychological View of Aging." *Human Development* 16(2): 37–49.

Witmer, J. Melvin, and Thomas Sweeney. 1992. "A Holistic Model for Wellness and Prevention Over the Lifespan." *Journal of Counseling and Development* 71(2): 140–148.

Chapter 10

Empowering Older Mexicans Through Study and Action

Celia Ruiz

VEMEA, an acronym for Vejez en Mexico, Estudio y Acción (Aging in Mexico, Study and Action), is a center for the study of aging and the empowerment of the elderly, located in the city of Cuernavaca. It is a place for the old, managed by the old.

The urgent task VEMEA has set for itself is to acquire knowledge about the reality of the final stages of life and to find ways of having a more humane old age. To this end, the center is dedicated to helping older persons directly and to enabling them to help themselves. The center follows principles that call for instilling respect for the elderly—both by those who are already elderly and by those who have not yet reached this stage—as persons capable of assuming responsibility for and taking charge of their own lives. In addition, VEMEA promotes consciousness raising on the issues of aging among all classes of people and at all levels of society. To understand the center, it is necessary to understand the principles that drive it and its founder and director, Betsie Hollants.

Ms. Hollants, now 88 years old, came to Mexico from Belgium 33 years ago and grew to be a part of her adopted homeland. Her work with the elderly began about ten years ago when she was forced to retire, solely because of her age, from a position running another center she had set up. That first center provided assistance to the women of the large farming population in the state of Morelos. Although she had been told that, as a foreigner, she could not succeed in that project, the center she started not only still exists but has a branch in Mexico City.

With the bulk of her retirement money, Ms. Hollants bought a large house in Cuernavaca, a resort town in the state of Morelos, 60 miles south of Mexico City. That house is now the headquarters of VEMEA. With the remainder of the money, Ms. Hollants bought books on aging.

Those books were the start of what is now the Center for Information and Documentation on Aging, the only library of its kind in Mexico, containing publications exclusively on the subject of aging. The collection includes newspaper and magazine clippings, periodicals, leaflets, university theses, and a variety of books and other texts. VEMEA maintains contact with institutions worldwide that contribute literature on the aged in different languages, though most is in English. The center receives researchers and students from the nation's universities and other institutions and occasionally provides volunteers who translate material into Spanish from other languages.

The very existence of this library is a source of pride for VEMEA's members, who see it as an affirmation of their own status, a symbol of their position as publicly recognized citizens.

VEMEA grew out of a series of informal gatherings. Betsie Hollants invited all sorts of people to talk about aging and death. She served coffee, tea, and cookies to those who came: architects, social workers, anthropologists, directors of homes for the aged (of which in the early 1980s there were just a few), nurses, caregivers of older family members, and others who simply wanted to hear about old age. She neglected to invite doctors, however, perhaps because she was proposing that aging is a normal stage of life. Doctors became interested, however, and started coming to the talks about aging and death, as the meetings were known. Little by little, older people from the community started coming, too. As these were the people VEMEA wanted to serve, it was important to let them talk. Plenty of time was set aside for them to exchange ideas as Ms. Hollants and her colleagues listened carefully to what was said.

DEATH IN MEXICAN CULTURE

Dying was among the subjects they discussed. Death is very much a part of Mexican culture. On the Day of the Dead, graves are adorned with flowers and food put on altars so that the dead may return and eat. On this holiday, periodicals publish satirical or humorous verses called *calaveras*, or skeletons, about the living, commenting on their improprieties or virtues as if they had already gone off to the netherworld. Ingrained in the culture is a belief in continuity after death. Mexicans talk to their dead. So it is easier for them to talk about death.

Despite the visibility of death in their culture, the tendency among older Mexicans to avoid facing old age and dying remains strong. The elderly participants in the early salons, however, became interested in discussing how old age is, among other things, a preparation for the end of life. They introduced the declaration that "aging is not a disease but a normal state in the life cycle." While illness certainly exists in old age, it is a subject to be talked about more with doctors and nurses than with friends and family, and illness must never be the only reason for contacting and interacting with others.

The participants in VEMEA's salons expressed two other strong desires: to continue working and being occupied and to stay close to their families. They insisted on selling their wares, vegetables, fruits, and other products at the market, no matter how little money they made.

THE ROLE OF WOMEN

In the early days of the discussion groups, older women remained quiet or spoke very little. So gatherings for women only were arranged, in which they were encouraged to talk. The organizers figured this was important, since women are the "natural" caretakers of the old. Able to express themselves freely, women began raising their awareness of aging. Little by little, after many gatherings, they began to form cohesive groups and construct their own group history on aging.

The tradition and history of Mexico makes women the supporters and maintainers of the family group. Since the public manifestations of a society—rituals, institutions, and so on—are the creation of men, and the conquest of Mexico by Hernan Cortez in 1532 destroyed all such overt expressions of native Aztec tradition, men were left out of the new Spanish culture. But since women's culture is a private one, neither public nor written down but passed on by word and by deed, women remain to this day a strong, cohesive force. They serve as the transmitters of the ways of our indigenous ancestors.

Thus, it became apparent that VEMEA had to count heavily on women for carrying out its work. Of course, men are also included, but they come in smaller numbers, and the major share of transmitting VEMEA principles of the rights and responsibilities of the old is done by women.

ANCIANOS Y SUS AMIGOS

Out of the experiences of the seminars and talks, out of the poverty of the people, out of the groups that got together developed the idea of starting a day-care center.

VEMEA obtained financing from international organizations that fund projects in developing countries. It purchased a large house and founded ANSAM— Ancianos y sus Amigos (Older Persons and theirFriends). Open Monday through Friday from 9:00 A.M. to 5:00 P.M., this center offers meeting rooms, a large kitchen, bathrooms, showers, and a garden. Fifty older people belong to the center; about three-fourths of them show up every day. Anybody who is old enough and willing to cooperate can participate in the center's life. Volunteers of all ages are welcome to help with the work of the community. The staff consists of a director, who is a physician, his assistant, a social worker, a psychologist for the aged, a nurse, and several volunteer physicians.

Daily life in the center revolves around the members, who tend the vegetable garden, cook their own meals, wash dishes, and clean the kitchen. They do physical exercise, sometimes on stationary bicycles and sometimes in their wheelchairs; watch television; listen to the radio; sing as a chorus; act out sociodramas on themes they developed, usually referring to their personal problems; and welcome guests invited for lunch. They have an opportunity to take training courses in subjects such as health, nutrition, personal care, manual skills, and so on. They organize parties and dancing, and sometimes drink a little wine and eat chocolates. They visit Betsie and bring her gifts of candy. A local factory has given them boxes and cards to paint. Most importantly, they talk about all matters that concern them.

The elderly who come to the center have begun to participate in managing it. Planting a vegetable garden was their idea, and later on they insisted on firing the cook so they could prepare their own meals.

Twice a month, ANSAM's elderly members distribute basic supplies to their colleagues in need of such assistance who cannot come to the center. The food baskets contain staples such as rice and beans, sugar, cooking oil, and pasta. Toilet paper, soap, and medicines are also routinely included among the supplies provided.

As transportation is a major problem in Cuernavaca, ANSAM owns two station wagons. These vehicles take center members to visit their colleagues who are ill, older friends in the community, or on excursions to nearby towns. When a member of the center dies, those who wish to attend the burial, visit the family and follow the rituals.

OUTREACH TO THE COMMUNITY

Although successful and efficiently run, VEMEA still serves only a small segment of the older population. Two steps have been taken in the last four years to reach more people:

1. Comprehensive, three-day workshops have been organized on the subject of women, aging, and death. Professionals in different fields conducted these sessions, with each approaching the theme from the perspective of his or her specialty: biology, medicine, psychology, psychoanalysis, sociology, history, religion, economics, politics, anthropology, body work, sexuality, meditation, and group work. Emphasis was put on preparing for old age and death beginning with childhood.

The workshops attracted attendees from several states in the country, including professionals working in the care of the elderly, interested people of all ages, and older persons concerned with their own aging process. A desire for group commitment developed, a few small groups were formed, and volunteers were attracted.

One such group is Las Reinas (Queens), older women who have met for the past seven years to explore aging and compare their experiences with growing older. The group gives workshops open to women of all ages.

2. The formation of CABHComunidad de Ancianos Buen Hogar (Community Outreach to the Elderly). To reach people not necessarily interested in belonging to ANSAM, VEMEA decided to motivate those members familiar with its principles to give talks wherever old persons normally gatherin the market, the church and

the dispensary. Small groups of about 15 are formed. Each group meets once a week on its own, and once every other week with other groups to exchange ideas. They assign tasks among themselves. For example, a group in the dispensary arranged to seek donations and funding to buy medicines that they distribute free to poor, sick people.

As a result of CABH's work in the market, a space was purchased there and a permanent stand built offering legal services to the elders at very low cost or free of charge, thanks to the work of volunteer attorneys. This project is independent of CABH or VEMEA.

Since VEMEA's principles are consistent with Christian teaching, the church has also welcomed CABH members. Churchgoers have proved willing to listen and explore the process of aging.

While VEMEA heads both ANSAM and CABH, each is an independent project and each offers support to the other whenever possible. For example, VEMEA helps CABH with stationery and photocopying. ANSAM helps CABH with transportation.

OBSTACLES TO EMPOWERMENT

The progress Cuernavaca's elderly have made toward empowering themselves has not come easily. They have faced, and still face, significant obstacles, some of which are external. One such hurdle has been the heavy workload of women and the tradition that they should stay inside the home. Another is the tendency to resent and reject those who care for them, forgetting that caregiving can be unpleasant, not only because it is strenuous work but also because it forces younger people to confront their own aging process and eventual death.

In addition, VEMEA's work is impeded by a lack of government support. It is only lately that retired people have begun to organize and exercise political pressure to obtain higher retirement pay. (The legal retirement age in Mexico is 60.) Poverty and lack of experience with formal organizations also hampers efforts to organize the elderly. The percentage of older persons who have worked in structured corporations where they learned the discipline of organizations is small. Most Mexicans of this age group have been self-employed, either in agriculture or as artisans, a work history that implies low income and makes for dependence on the family rather than on public social cohesion. VEMEA encourages the elderly to seek support outside the family within the community of the elderly. Whenever they cannot go out, they are encouraged to use the telephone to communicate with each other, and in this way have created a supportive network.

HOW TO FACE A SHORT FUTURE

In addition to external obstacles, the elderly in Cuernavaca must deal with the internal, psychological dimension of empowerment. Like people around the world,

Mexicans are both indifferent to and afraid of talking about aging and death. They often face this stage of their lives with silence, even though it is a highly vulnerable time that finds most of them with less money, more physical pains, a higher risk of becoming ill, and the loss of family members and friends. In addition, they have to face cultural stereotypes that devalue older people. Old people do not always recognize the consequences of what is happening to them, often simply because they have nobody to discuss their circumstances with. They work off many of their problems through complaints and thus lose their energies to do something constructive.

Given the chance, they can face their fears of deterioration and death, of the burden that they may place on others, of their loneliness and isolation. Longevity has given them a great deal of experience in coping with crises and difficulties.

The very fact of survival is a strength. Reaching old age is something to be proud of. It shows that one has come a long way, through experiences rich in variety and content. Not only have most older people acquired emotional strength, they have also acquired skills in performing tasks and in relating to many types of people. All these strengths can be drawn on to facilitate the empowerment process.

However, in the last stage of life, the fear of physical deterioration and death can be devastating. The person who negates these fears risks emotional illness. Although painful, confronting the fears lowers anxiety, anger, and depression. Facing them may mean that the older person mourns the loss of youth and of past relationships, when physical and intellectual abilities were formidable, when productivity and self-esteem were high, and when one was surrounded by loved ones, colleagues, and community. By going through a mourning period, older persons can avail themselves of their inner strengths and become aware that the resilience required to reach old age is contained within. Armed with this knowledge, they can learn new ways of enjoyment, of dealing with pain, and frustration, and of accepting themselves and others.

VEMEA's goals and principles, arrived at after many hours of discussion on the nature of aging, dying, and death, are meant to help older people come to grips with the fact that their own futures are growing short.

GOALS AND PRINCIPLES

VEMEA seeks to engage in study of the aging process and to raise awareness of its findings among people of all ages. The purpose of this study is the well-being and dignity of the elderly.

VEMEA seeks to train those who care for the aged by instilling the VEMEA principles, which also serve to make the caregivers aware of their own aging process.

VEMEA tries to educate people of all ages about the aging process while eliminating stereotypes on aging. It promotes the idea that aging starts early in life and, since cultural and family beliefs about aging are instilled in childhood, corrective measures should be taken then. It has proposed that the national department of education include instruction on aging and the life cycle from primary school on.

VEMEA shares its knowledge about working with older people with other groups and learns from them as well. It has established relations with organizations and individuals dedicated to the elderly and helps in the creation and the operation of such groups.

VEMEA tries to make families and caregivers aware of the fact that older persons wish to remain at home, if at all possible, and be an integral part of the family.

At the public level, VEMEA supports organizations advocating for favorable legislation for the elderly.

VEMEA attributes its success to these principles:

1. Respect for the elderly and a strong belief that they are important and have the potential to remain active and in charge of their own aging process. This creates trust and acceptance in the older persons and in the family and friends around them.

2. Understanding the ways of the elderly and the meaning that their behavior and attitudes have for them at this stage of life. At deeper levels of the personality these have to do with fear, negation, or acceptance of deterioration and death.

3. Understanding the ways in which the culture deals in a social way with the expression of aging, dying, and death.

4. Understanding the ways the culture survives and promoting those whenever they lead constructively to the group's interest. In the case of VEMEA, promoting women to be active in transmitting VEMEA principles and the care of the elderly; respecting festivals and rituals that have meaning for the people.

5. Promoting group cohesion by following these principles and creating a sense of purpose for the elderly that motivates them to help themselves and help other older persons.

6. Confronting middle age or younger people with their own aging process and motivating them to do work with the old. Such work can be a meaningful experience that can change a personal relationship to aging and death.

Part 4

IN DEVELOPING COUNTRIES

Chapter 11

Older Persons: Issues Concerning Their Empowerment and Participation in Development

Mukunda Rao

Issues related to participation, self-reliance and, to a much lesser extent, empowerment have been subjects for debate for a very long time. While they cannot be exactly equated to motherhood and apple pie (as Americans would term them), their importance and need is rarely questioned, and it is even rarer that any major global policy document in the development field does not have some reference to participation and self-reliance. At the international level, the post-World War II developments leading to the end of colonialism and the emergence of newly independent countries are clearly seen as vindication of the right of people to make their own political decisions and to chart the course of their political, economic, and social development. After the implosion of centrally planned economies in Europe as well as rest of the world, issues of participation and self-reliance are being debated in the significantly different contexts of global economic recession, increased global interdependence, privatization, and decentralization. Political considerations continue to influence perceptions of and possibilities for participation, self-reliance, and the empowerment of people for their own development, although development literature concentrates primarily on social and economic aspects. While participation and self-reliance seem to attract almost universal approval, one wonders as to how firm the actual commitment is, viewed in the context of the formidable obstacles that people, especially the weaker and more vulnerable groups, face in the practical arena of implementation.

Participation issues concern real or perceived notions of self-worth and self-esteem as well as a future orientation and the ability to take risks. They also include questions related to social, economic, and cultural parameters and the different sources of stimuli for participation, whether it is the state, local organizations, or the professionals in the helping fields. Participation issues also deal with areas of conflict and strategies to enhance participation. Participation, self-reliance, and empowerment are complementary but not synonymous themes. They will be explored in this paper with reference to older persons and in the context of recent global policy developments concerning the relatively disadvantaged population groups.

PARTICIPATION AS A GLOBAL THEME

Citizen participation in development received significant global attention through the adoption in 1969 by the United Nations General Assembly of the landmark Declaration on Social Progress and Development. Among other matters, it called on member states to encourage citizen participation in the preparation and execution of national plans and programs of economic and social development. A year before, in 1968, the first International Conference of Ministers Responsible for Social Welfare recommended that the importance of the human factor in development should be fully recognized, as well as the involvement of people in their own and the society's betterment, in order to promote social progress and basic social reforms. Parenthetically, it should be noted that this landmark conference is the first to elaborate the concept of developmental social welfare in which popular participation is a key component (United Nations, 1969b). Later, in 1975, the Economic and Social Council called upon member states to adopt popular participation as a basic strategy for national development; encourage the widest possible active participation of all individuals and national, nongovernmental organizations in the development process in setting goals, formulating policies, and implementing plans; and include popular participation as an integral element in local, regional, and national development plans and programs. At the international level, the Council recommended that the United Nations development program and other related agencies consider popular participation as a distinct category for technical cooperation (United Nations, 1975).

A few years later, popular participation figured prominently in the international development strategy for the third United Nations development decade, which began in 1981. It affirmed that "the ultimate aim of development is the constant improvement of the well-being of the entire population on the basis of its full participation in the process of development and a fair distribution of the benefits therefrom ... full and effective participation by the entire population at all stages of the development process should be ensured" (United Nations, 1981).

An international seminar, convened in 1982 by the United Nations in Yugoslavia on popular participation, attracted over 35 representatives of governments and explored in much depth various aspects of this theme including: How is popular participation influenced by political ideologies; by bureaucratic and administrative structures; by religious and cultural values? How is popular participation influenced by planning approaches? What are the ways of stimulating participation? What role do motivation and incentives play in this regard? What are the special features of popular participation in the contexts of rural areas and urban slums? Interestingly, the seminar included in its recommendations to the General Assembly "The right to popular participation, including worker's participation in management and self-management, as an important factor in development and its human rights aspects" (United Naions, 1985). It is perhaps the first time that this theme is promoted as a human right.

More recently, the Guiding Principles for Developmental Social Welfare Policies and Programs in the Near Future, adopted by the General Assembly in 1987, identified participation as an area of concern (United Nations, 1987a). "A trend of special importance to social welfare is the growing prominence of the concept of participation as both an aim and a means of social development." Full and free participation on equal terms in all social, political, and economic activities underlies the corpus of international instruments adopted by the United Nations and is emphasized in strategies adopted in recent international conferences, notably the Nairobi Forward-Looking Strategies for the Advancement of Women and strategies concerning the situation of specific population groups, including disabled persons, youth and the aged. "A basic principle and objective of social welfare policy is to promote the widest possible participation of all individuals and groups, and greater emphasis needs to be placed on translating this principle into practice. This may be achieved through new partnerships in the field of social welfare policy, providing opportunities for a greater involvement of beneficiaries, individually and collectively, in decisions concerning their needs and in the implementation of programs, including community based programs" (United Nations, 1987b).

These "snapshots" of policy evolution on popular participation over a period of 20 years show the concern of the international community on its need and importance within the broader context of development. The resulting global policy instruments reveal the gradual comprehension of the crucial and, at the same time, complex facets of participation as a concept and as a policy priority in its implementation at national levels.

Participation has consistently occupied a central place in the evolution of development approaches, at a conceptual as well as policy level. In the formulation of the strategies for the three development decades, and in the outcomes of global events described earlier, there has been a gradual shift from the treatment of participation as a desirable and necessary ingredient for the success of governmental programs to viewing it as a right and as an end in itself. As is the case with the problem of finding a global consensus on approaches to development, formulations on participation tended to be rather general, exhortatory, and avoided the thorny questions of power, hierarchy, and control of key resources—that is, until one looks at another quite separate set of global developments specifically focused on specific population groups, variously described as vulnerable, weaker, or relatively disadvantaged.

PARTICIPATION: WOMEN, DISABLED PERSONS, YOUTH, AND OLDER PERSONS

The first among these to claim global attention are women, although they cannot be rightly termed as a group, constituting, as they do, a majority in the world's population. Beginning with the International Women's Year (1975), through the Copenhagen World Conference (1980) and the Nairobi World Conference (1985), participation was viewed through a quite a different set of lenses. Unequal opportunities for participation, overt discrimination, economic exploitation, and oppression experienced at family, community, and national levels lent a much sharper edge to the participation debate. The Nairobi Forward-Looking Strategies for the Advancement of Women (FLS), adopted by the Nairobi Conference, explicitly address the basic questions of obstacles to equality in social participation, in political participation and decision making, as well as "areas of special concern" such as urban poor women, elderly women, abused women, and migrant women. FLS postulates that "The effective participation of women in development and in the strengthening of peace, as well as the promotion of the equality of women and men, require concerted multi-dimensional strategies and measures that should be people-oriented. Such strategies will require continual upgrading and the productive utilization of human resources with a view to promoting equality and producing sustained, endogenous development of societies and groups of individuals" (United Nations, 1985). Thus, participation is seen not only as an end unto itself, but as a means to attain equality, to redress problems, and to maximize one's own potential.

FLS is first among the many global policy statements on popular participation to express a degree of frankness and specificity that has not been attempted before. Participation of women, or rather their nonparticipation and "underparticipation" in areas such as employment, health, education, industry, trade, science, and technology are elaborated in terms of existing obstacles and overcoming them at national levels.

The process that was set in motion by women and FLS was further accelerated by the global events (international years, decades, global conferences) associated with the elderly, disabled persons, and youth. An important development in this process is the larger role that the particular group (be they women, disabled persons, or elderly) has assumed in speaking for its own problems and needs. An example is the change from initial designation of International Year *for* Disabled Persons to International Year *of* Disabled Persons. This 1981 event, which was followed by the UN Decade of Disabled Persons, was accompanied by the emergence and active functioning of organizations in which disabled persons themselves assumed leadership roles. The world program of action concerning disabled persons has as its purpose the realization of full participation of disabled persons in social life and development and of full equality (United Nations, 1983b).

Participation of disabled persons in decision making is emphasized, but what is of special significance is the articulation of participation in the context of equalization of opportunities. Disability is not accepted as an inherent impediment and disabled persons should not have to "adjust" themselves to a physical and social environment that is inappropriate to their condition. Equalization of opportunities for disabled persons means that discriminatory practices with respect to disability have to be eliminated so that access to physical environment, income maintenance and social security, education and training, and other related areas are made possible and easier. In this task, the obligations of disabled persons are also recognized, but the onus is on the societal institutions to make the necessary alterations in their functioning so as to make the full participation of disabled persons in development possible and meaningful.

As reflected in the basic needs strategy that was put forth at the 1976 World Employment Conference, equalization of opportunities and the positing of participation as a social right alludes to the need for a basic structural transformation involving redistribution of economic and social power, especially from the viewpoint of so-called vulnerable and disadvantaged groups. Vulnerability, disability, or disadvantage are seen more as results of discriminatory social constructs than as due to some inherent and unalterable individual or group failings.

Participation has also figured very prominently with the global spotlight on youth questions in the period preceding and following the 1985 International Youth Year. It is also one of the three major themes undergirding the year, the other two being development and peace. At the global and national levels, youth are also included (while they constitute one-fifth of the total population) as a "specific" or a disadvantaged group needing special attention. From a societal viewpoint, their full participation or integration is seen from one perspective, as an answer to marginalization, delinquency, crime, deviant behavior, and social unrest.

While this perception is rarely made explicit, another perception of youth participation in development features far more prominently in the global dialogue and policy instruments relating to youth. This perception is reflected in more positive terms and in the context of benefits to be derived by the whole society through improved participation of youth in their societies.

"A central question is the degree to which young people participate in development. The four forms of participation—political, economic, social, cultural—often overlap and are frequently interdependent. Political participation, a crucial element in the structure of society, is a controversial area because it concerns the distribution of power. Consequently, it is as difficult to quantify as it is to analyze. Further, the lines between political participation and political mobilization have become increasingly blurred. Young people, particularly students, have often been deeply involved in this form of participation and have sometimes articulated the need for more political participation" (United Nations, 1985a).

The Guidelines for Further Planning and Suitable Follow-up in the Field of Youth is the principal policy outcome of the International Youth Year. At the outset, it states that participation means the recognition throughout society that each person has the potential for judging and deciding matters that concern his or her life and has every opportunity of doing so. It requires also that each person is aware of this opportunity, has access to the means necessary for utilizing it, and feels satisfied that his or her contribution has been effective and recognized as such. Full participation of youth in the life of the nation is important to the achievement of the objectives of national development. At the same time, youth cannot participate meaningfully where they are the objects of any form of exploitation.

The priorities identified in the guidelines were reiterated in a recent report. "The overriding need for fuller and more effective participation by youth in society is now more widely recognized. Such participation can be real only if the young are seen not only as objects of social development process but also as its subjects, not solely as resources for development, but as partners in decision making. They should have the right to participate in economic, social and political life and, the right to expect that their participation has purpose and is taken seriously. Thus, participation of youth is both a goal in itself and a means of improving prospects for the attainment of peace" (United Nations, 1991b).

The 1982 World Assembly on Aging and the Resulting Vienna International Plan of Action on Aging (VIPAA) is the first and still the most comprehensive global policy instrument directed toward older persons. To this must be added the recent "United Nations Principles for Older Persons" adopted by the General Assembly in 1991. In a somewhat surprising contrast to the global instruments concerned with women, disabled persons, and youth, VIPAA does not contain many explicit references to participation of older persons in the development process. Participation is not treated as a major theme, although one of the specific objectives is to propose and stimulate action-oriented policies and programs aimed at guaranteeing social and economic security for the elderly, as well as providing opportunities for them to contribute to and share in the benefits of development.

In the statement on principles, it affirms the general position that "The aim of development is to improve the well-being of the entire population on the basis of its full participation in the process of development and an equitable distribution of the benefits therefrom. The development process must enhance human dignity and ensure equity among age groups in the sharing of society's resources, rights and responsibilities" (United Nations, 1983a). Another principle states that the aging should be active participants in the formulation and implementation of policies, including those specially affecting them. A recommendation related to health services refers to their participation in them, as does also another recommendation dealing with economic aspects. In general, references to older persons' participation are not very prominent, leading one to wonder as to the reasons for the lesser importance given to this matter as compared to other global plans of action. Could it be that participation is primarily seen in an economic framework, in which older persons can make little or no contribution?

A distinguishing feature of VIPAA, as well as the rest of the global policy documents concerning older persons dating back to 1982, is the distinction that is often drawn between the developmental and humanitarian aspects of aging. While developmental aspects deal with macro-societal-level questions of population aging, humanitarian aspects are those that are concerned with improving the conditions of individual older persons. Implicitly and often explicitly, humanitarian aspects are treated as more important relative to developmental aspects, which call for more basic structural modifications. Participation, even in its broadest conception, is intimately associated with people and their interaction with their environment. One can only speculate whether this association of participation with humanitarian aspects of aging has any bearing on its low priority in the policy documents. The succeeding ten years, however, have seen a change. The United Nations Principles for Older Persons, adopted by the General Assembly in 1991, include three principles under the rubric of participation. They state that "Older persons should remain integrated in society, should participate actively in the formulation and implementation of policies that directly affect their well-being, and should share their knowledge and skills with younger generations; older persons should be able to seek and develop opportunities for service to the community and to serve as volunteers in positions appropriate to their interests and capabilities, older persons should be able to form movements of associations of older persons" (United Nations, 1991a). The Declaration on the Rights and Responsibilities of Older Persons (adopted earlier by the International Federation on Ageing) also includes very similar statements on the participation of older persons, with the important difference that they are couched in terms of "rights" rather than principles (International Federation on Ageing, 1991).

Vulnerability or relative disadvantage of older persons, women, disabled persons, and youth is not an inherent or unalterable condition, as stated earlier. However, treating them as such over a long period of time has made even the persons and groups affected believe and sometimes behave as if it were a fact. In addition to the groups mentioned so far, one could add other groups to the ranks of the vulnerable refugees, migrants, children, minorities, indigenous people, and so on. If added together, they would certainly constitute a large majority, each group distinguished by a special badge of discrimination, disadvantage, or exclusion. The groups, of course, often overlap each other, as in the case of older women, older refugees and the disabled old. Add yet other factors, such as poverty and residence in rural areas and urban slums, and vulnerability and disadvantage are magnified correspondingly and their impact even more intense. In such a situation of escalating disadvantage, the stage is set for competition among these many groups for the scarce resources that are available to them.

OLDER PERSONS: SELF-RELIANCE
AND EMPOWERMENT

Thus far, the discussion has almost entirely focused on questions of participation as they concern vulnerable groups. This reflects more or less correctly the global priorities accorded to participation. In a parallel development, self-reliance as a concept and as an objective in developmental policies gained higher profile in the late 1970s and 1980s. On a broader level, collective self-reliance of developing countries was identified as a desirable goal in the strategy for the Third Development Decade. To what extent self-reliance at the national level is feasible or even desirable in an increasingly interdependent world is debatable. Also, this increased emphasis on self-reliance and its particular timing—coming as it did during the divisive debates on global economic and trade imbalances and the disenchantment with the "welfare states"—leads one to wonder as to the motivations for this emphasis. National self-reliance and efforts toward achieving it do not substitute for efforts toward attaining greater equity and justice in the global economic domain.

Similarly, within countries, vulnerable groups, including older persons, when faced with the question of self-reliance, are compelled to look closely at several factors. What does self-reliance imply? How is it related to existing or future external supports? What meaning does self-reliance have for groups that have so much less to begin with?

Self-reliance cannot mean self-isolation or a substitution for the mutual social support system that exists and that needs to be constantly reinforced. Self-reliance, as encompassing social, psychological, and economic aspects, involves for older persons retention and development of a sense of control and autonomy over their own lives. Further, very much like participation, self-reliance is a process which might be valued for its own sake, but in which different individuals and groups become involved at different paces, depending on many attendant circumstances.

The evolution of developmental social welfare on the global level has also seen increasing emphasis on self-reliance alongside popular participation. The 1968 International Conference of Ministers Responsible for Social Welfare and the recent 1987 Interregional Consultation on Developmental Social Welfare Policies and Programs, as well as other global meetings held between these dates, have identified the promotion of self-reliance and the maximum utilization of people's potentials as higher priorities relative to remedial and curative approaches.

For older persons, self-reliance involves a process of discovering and identifying their innate and potential strengths, and a growing sense of self-worth and self-confidence that it is possible to bring about changes in their personal lives, as well as in the conditions that affect them. In addition, it also includes the development of abilities to identify the internal and external resources available to them, to learn to stand up on their own, to tolerate failures, and to move at their own pace. Interestingly, increasing self-reliance is often associated with greater willingness to cooperate and collaborate and learn from others. While self-reliance should work toward reduction of dependency, it also works well within a context of inter-dependency—a context in which one group does not try to control the other, but utilizes it as a growth-producing resource. Self-reliance for older persons or for any other disadvantaged group needs to be institutionalized and acquire a firm base of social power. Development of an organizational base with concomitant productive assets, financial resources, knowledge and skills, social networks, and information are key ingredients in this context. As informal networks of older persons develop into self-reliant and more formal organizations, they will be better able to interact with external organizations, be they governmental or otherwise.

This is particularly important in times of economic constraints, when there is a need to ensure that older persons are not pushed into marginal and dependent roles because they are in need or in receipt of services. During the recent years of reductions in social expenditures and social services, there has been an increasing pressure to transfer responsibility for some of these services to the family, the community, and nongovernmental organizations. Such a transfer, especially when it is not accompanied by corresponding resources and corresponding devolution of power, cannot promote self-reliant organizations and cannot promote meaningful participation of people in activities that are of concern to them.

An analysis of characteristics and indicators of self-reliance identifies the following: (1) high degree of autonomy in decision making, (2) activities that are progressively self-sustaining, (3) activities in which vital inputs are internal rather than external, (4) ability to relate to outside groups as equals and partners—rather than as receivers, givers, or patrons, and (5) a strong sense of purpose and clear identity (International Council on Social Welfare, 1976).

As applied to organizations, development of self-reliance, has to be seen as a process that needs to be nurtured and facilitated first by the members of these organizations, aided as needed and appropriate from the outside.

Compared to self-reliance, empowerment figures even less prominently in global themes. Without searching far and wide for definitions, empowerment as a concept and a goal clearly refers to the process of acquiring greater strength and ability by mobilizing internal as well as external resources (Lloyd, 1991). As the key ingredients of development process, participation, self-reliance, and empowerment are closely interrelated and overlap each other.

It is not easy to explain the low visibility of empowerment in the global developmental strategies, including those specifically dealing with vulnerable groups. The predominant roles of governments in the formulation of these strategies might be a reason. Governments, representing as they do the status quo and the established order in their countries, could not be expected to support the possible destabilization that might result from empowerment. Another reason could be that empowerment implies the possibility of increased demands on the state and establishment, as well as potential confrontation.

It might be useful to view participation, self-reliance, and empowerment as a continuum. Participation of individuals and groups, including those on the peripheries, contributes to increased self-reliance to undertake more difficult and complex tasks and this in turn leads to their empowerment. Obviously, this progression cannot be automatic, smooth, or complete, because a great deal depends on the obstacles encountered along the way, as well as on the strength of the internal drive of the people concerned and their capacity to move ahead.

PARTICIPATION AND EMPOWERMENT:
RELEVANT PARAMETERS

Ideally, greater participation and empowerment of groups such as the older persons would only depend on their desire and strength to improve their situation. It would not encounter any resistance from other groups and might even attract their support, especially considering their state of disadvantage or disability. There would not be any clash of interests and there would be strong support from the state and its administrative machinery for participatory and empowerment activities, in line with the various national and global policy instruments. Not surprisingly, this is hardly the case.

Political parameters clearly influence and even determine the nature, direction, and extent of participation and empowerment. Even under authoritarian and dictatorial regimes, participation is possible as long as it is in line with the dictates from above, as long as it does not disturb the status quo, and as long as it does not involve any substantial redistribution of power, authority, or resources. Empowerment, in the sense that was described earlier, is out of the question. As one progresses along the political continuum from authoritarian to democratic states, one would assume that the path toward participation and empowerment would be easier and smoother. Perhaps this is so, until one takes a closer look at what is being asked and demanded, what is at stake, what vested interests are threatened and, again, how much redistribution of power and resources is involved. Power certainly is a major political parameter. Authentic participation and empowerment has to be concerned with redistribution of power and control of productive resources.

National bureaucratic and administrative machineries also constitute a major factor in the political parameters for participation. The power of bureaucracy is formidable in any country in allocating resources, in interpreting regulations and in abrogating a large share of the benefits of development for themselves. In poorer countries, in countries where the educational disparities are large and where there are close alignments between bureaucracy and the national elites, participation parameters for older persons are very much constrained. Participation other than of consultative, advisory, or similar passive nature, runs into the danger of threatening the interests of bureaucracy. Of course, where the bureaucrats, technocrats, and the administration, especially at the local levels, are truly committed to participatory development, are able to restrain their impulse to self-advancement, and are honest and efficient, the corresponding political parameters are that much wider and receptive. Goals and strategies for participation and empowerment of older people have to necessarily plan for the type of political (including bureaucratic) environment that exists in a given situation.

The economic parameters for the participation of older persons, as well as other population groups, are very much influenced by the international recession, dating back to the early 1980s. At the macro level, the series of oil crises, declines in growth rates, growth of inflation, problems related to balance of payments and, most importantly, the burden of foreign debt have had profound effects on national economies. Combined with the structural adjustment policies and their negative social impact, these developments translate into harsh repercussions in terms of escalating underemployment, unemployment, and poverty for older persons, and particularly those residing in the developing countries.

Older persons striving to increase or even to retain, their participation in the economic sphere need to contend with the near universal perception of their diminished economic capacities and diminished economic contribution to national development. In addition, in the industrialized world and in the formal sectors of the developing world, enforced and mandatory retirement as early as age 55 constitutes a major hurdle. For those in rural areas and in most of the developing countries, control of land, water, and other productive resources is vital for economic participation. The poor and landless among older persons have to contend with this problem for eking out even a bare existence.

In regard to social and cultural parameters, the situation varies even more from region to region, one religious group to the other, one social class to the next, between men and women, and between many other variables. On the positive side, older persons are accorded respect, carry prestige, and even authority in many countries. They are valued for their experience and participate actively in key areas such as the settlement of disputes and serving in a leadership capacity in secular as well as social areas. Marriages, separations, property settlements, religious rituals are some examples of occasions where older persons play important roles (Margolies, 1990).

On the other hand, there is the expectation not only in the so-called traditional societies, that older persons should not be too active, should slowly withdraw from active life and volunteer to provide their services, with little or no remuneration. In between these positive, and not so positive, extremes are to be found infinite variations that influence the type, extent, and areas of participation in the social context.

While, for analytical purposes, political, economic, and social parameters are being treated in a discrete manner, in reality, they overlap and interact with each other, resulting in a constantly changing and dynamic flux. Whether and how individual older persons or groups and organizations grasp these dynamics, and exploit them for their own and the larger society's betterment, constitutes a key factor in the unfolding and elaboration of their participation and empowerment strategies.

Another major element in this configuration of strategies is the potential and the real possibility of conflict at many different levels and with diverse groups. Even among older persons, it is unlikely that there would be uniformity of interests. Seeds of conflict exist in all stages of participation and empowerment. Related strategies must address questions of conflict and ways and means of understanding it, neutralizing, and managing it so as to advance further with minimum friction.

PARTICIPATION AND EMPOWERMENT OF OLDER PERSONS: OBSTACLES AND OPPORTUNITIES

A discussion on obstacles and opportunities concerning the participation and empowerment of older persons has to take into consideration their heterogeneity. This heterogeneity has to contend with the major problem of defining or even describing when a person becomes a member of this group. There are serious questions about using a chronological age, a practice restricted to the formal employment and pension practices in industrialized countries and to a similar but a very small segment in developing countries. Other indicators, such as having grand children or being dependent economically, are also flawed because of the varied demographic and economic conditions in different parts of the world.

Even when one accepts the criterion of age 60 and older as a general guideline, several factors intrinsic and extrinsic to older persons influence their participation and empowerment. Among the intrinsic factors are their own economic standing, social status, health condition, gender, and religious affiliation. Extrinsic factors include rural or urban residence, political system, pattern of control of productive resources, and overall values concerning aging and the roles and functions of older persons. Further, their participation and empowerment is also related to the extent of solidarity that they have or are willing to develop with others, as well as their specific targets and objectives. The fact is that older persons are almost as heterogeneous as their national societies. The commonalities between the "young old," "old old" (over 80), older women, minority old, rural old, old landless peasants, older refugees, and migrants are not easy to delineate. Conflicts of interests between these subgroups pose problems as well as challenges for the design of participation and empowerment strategies.

The nature and degree of obstacles encountered are also closely related to the particular arenas and objectives of participation and to what stakes are involved and what vested interests are threatened. For example, participation by a middle-class urban group in an advisory council will have little resemblance to the participation of an organized group of landless, older peasants. Another example is the participation of older women in a traditional Islamic country, as compared to a similar group in a Nordic country. Participation of older persons, notwithstanding their membership in any one of the subgroups identified earlier, if it is geared toward economic objectives, has to contend with the prevailing economic situation. First, there is the continuing and deepening global recession, the high degree of unemployment and underemployment, the cessation of global dialogue (if it ever existed) on North-South economic imbalances, the declining level of multilateral and bilateral assistance for nonmilitary aid, and the decreasing attention to distributive questions, including social justice and equity. These factors also translate at national levels into diminishing social expenditures and keener competition among the various needy and disadvantaged groups for the available resources. As for social security systems, there is little support for their expansion where they exist (United Nations, 1991c). In the developing countries, where their coverage is sparse, there are no prospects for new initiatives as they struggle with overwhelming economic crises. Much the same can be said for social services and other supportive measures for the older persons, especially the more vulnerable and needy among them.

All these and other obstacles in the economic sphere need not necessarily be seen as insurmountable or even negative. They might be viewed as challenges requiring appropriate changes in the nature of participation objectives, strategies, and processes. Concentration on small-scale projects, self-help efforts based on a clear identification of available but underutilized resources, participation in supplementary income projects, learning of new skills, the organization of easier credit schemes, production and marketing cooperatives, the aggressive seeking out of information and other resources are examples of participation and empowerment. Successful projects which have survived and stood the test of time are functioning in all areas of the world under governmental and, more often, under private auspices. Activities focused on improved economic capabilities of older persons and their increased participation in the economic life of their countries are to be found in many parts of the world (Tout, 1989). While they are innovative and even pathbreaking, many questions remain concerning the expansion of their coverage and expansion of their resource base so as to include most if not all of those in need.

Another cluster of obstacles in the related area of work and employment is the actual or potential competition with youth, women, disabled persons, and others also seeking to increase their economic participation. The severity of such competition will naturally be more intense in economically depressed areas, calling for different participation strategies based on building coalitions and cooperating on the delineation of discrete areas of economic activity that complement rather than compete with each other. Lack of self-confidence and fear of alienating those in power also serves as an important obstacle to participation by older persons, especially those located further down in the hierarchy of vulnerability and disadvantage. Paradoxically, those in greatest need are also least able and least willing to take the risks inherent in participatory initiatives.

Earlier in this paper, we dealt with the question of close linkage of participation and empowerment of older persons to the sharing of resources, power, and authority with other groups. While this might be viewed as an obstacle, older persons possess many attributes and strengths to overcome these obstacles with minimum friction and conflict. They possess life experiences rich in variety and content. The very fact of survival and longevity, experiences of interacting, coping and succeeding in difficult life situations, occupational skills acquired over a long time, home management and child-rearing skills, skills in relating to different individuals and groups, as well as other inherent strengths could be tapped and harnessed to facilitate participation and empowerment processes.

Side-by-side with expanding democratization processes are the moves toward greater privatization and stress on voluntary initiatives. While there are many hidden traps and pitfalls in these moves, opportunities also abound which could be successfully exploited to enhance participation of older persons in small-scale projects, in assuming active advisory or even decision-making roles in relevant service settings and, in general, in taking full advantage of the prevailing trends toward more democracy, private initiative, and a different "welfare mix."

The organizational realm offers another broad cluster of opportunities for widening participation and empowerment of older persons. Older persons with common or similar needs, problems, and aspirations benefit from the structure and discipline that only organizations can offer. Organizations, even in the process of their initiation and development, enable older persons to define objectives, identify resources, articulate their viewpoints, resolve differences, and arrive at consensus. Organizations of older people can serve as "spokespersons," negotiate on behalf of their membership, and provide protection to their members from possible reprisals.

Organizations of older persons or those representing their interests have increased in number and strength, even in areas where aging is not perceived as a priority issue. A handbook, issued by the United Nations in 1988, lists 270 such organizations and institutions from all over the world (United Nations, 1988). In their functions, a number of these organizations list advocacy as their major function. Most of them operate under voluntary auspices, although many receive support from their national governments. Several of these are also linked to international organizations and benefit from advice, finances, and technical expertise, as well as the solidarity such linkage implies.

International organizations concerned with aging and older persons play key roles in influencing global policy on aging. They were instrumental in the convening of the World Assembly in 1982 and in the Forum of NGOs that preceded it, as well as in the formulation of the final report. Through their advocacy and representational roles at various intergovernmental meetings, they serve the cause of participation and empowerment of older persons. However, it is at the national and local levels that the greatest need for organizational development is to be found. Particularly in poorer developing countries, and in the pockets of poverty in industrialized countries, the need is acute. Against this background of continuing need, one can also learn from the successes of organizations like HelpAge (India), ProVida (Colombia) in the developing world, and that of the American Association of Retired Persons (U.S.). They have been remarkably successful in expanding their scope and coverage from a modest base, in becoming financially self-reliant in a short period, in providing their membership many opportunities for self-advancement, and in serving as effective "spokespersons" of older persons in their countries.

Obstacles and opportunities for participation and empowerment do not neatly balance each other. Obstacles to the participation and empowerment of older persons are formidable in several countries, but they are also surmountable. Opportunities in this context are fewer, but they are amenable for expansion and exploitation by older persons themselves, by those acting in their behalf, as well as by coalitions of people across age, class, and other lines.

MEASURES TO ENHANCE PARTICIPATION AND EMPOWERMENT: SOME ISSUES

As noted earlier, there is a widespread global consensus at the policy level that participation of people is an important element and even a prerequisite for development. This has been further reinforced in regard to the participation of specific population groups. Although most of these policy statements are directed toward governments, reports of their implementation at the national level indicate that the results fall far short of the targets originally envisaged. For older persons, the report of the Secretary-General on the second review and appraisal of the implementation of the VIPAA concludes that, while there has been increased awareness concerning the aging of populations, little progress was made in instituting responsive policies and programs. The report then goes on to make as many as 18 recommendations on as many themes, in order to prod on the process of implementation (United Nations, 1989).

More recently, global targets were proposed by the United Nations for the decade beginning in 1992, including matters such as a review of existing social security systems, the establishment of training and research centers and, on a broader level, "to integrate aging in mainstream development in the 1990s to ensure support for developing countries in adjusting their institutions, policies and programs to the aging of their populations" (United Nations, 1991d).

The key ingredient in translating these global policies, even partially, at the national level into relevant legislative and administrative measures, is vigorous participation by and on behalf of older persons. Such participation, in turn, requires an awareness of political processes, the ability to build coalitions and, most importantly, to operate from sound organizational bases. Older persons are by no means a uniform or homogeneous group. The better educated and more affluent elderly could take the initiatives needed to start such organizations but keep them open to include the less advantaged old.

While participation is needed and necessary to implement pro-aging policies, legislative measures are also needed to promote participation in a meaningful way. In many countries, the economic arena is crucial for many older persons and their participation in it is inhibited by many factors such as age discrimination, mandatory retirement, lack of training and retraining opportunities, and the mismatch of employment market with the situation of older workers. Legislative and administrative measures aimed at enhancing economic participation of older persons, by eliminating existing barriers and opening new avenues, will also contribute to the overall development effort. In all countries, and especially in the developing world, it is important for older persons and their organizations not only to work toward advancing their particular interests, but also to participate actively in the improvement of the family, community, and national contexts in which they operate. How this balance is to be achieved is an issue that should be constantly addressed, if empowerment and participation of older persons is to be viewed as an integral element of everyone's participation in development.

Knowledge is empowering even in small measures. Educational measures also have a role in rearranging societal priorities concerning older persons. In many parts of the world, they are accorded a lower priority relative to the needs of children, women, or the disabled. "This may be because of low visibility of the growing gap between societal norms of care for the aging in the family and the actual ability of families to conform to the norm. . . . the elderly continue to be considered as a dependent, helpless category needing care rather than as able citizens with a number of purposeful life ahead of them" (Bose, 1989).

Education in a broader sense needs also to be directed toward trade unions, employer's organizations, cooperatives, and other organized groups, so as to inform them to take positive interest in questions concerning older persons whose ranks their members will join at some time in the future. Also, educational measures focused on communities and specific target groups, such as employers, could focus on the potential benefits that participation of older persons can bring. Measures of this kind related to disabled persons have achieved considerable degree of success in altering public images and impressions.

Education of older persons to enable them to become aware of their civic rights, of their entitlements, as well as the manner in which political and administrative structures affect them, is also an important aspect of their empowerment.

Decision makers, community influentials, and political leaders are unlikely to pay heed to the concerns of older persons unless and until their voices are heard and their strength felt through organized and systematic efforts. As self-help efforts contribute to greater self-reliance and self-confidence, they will also serve as good bases for participation on more and more meaningful matters. As this process progresses and organizations of older persons acquire greater skills in negotiation, confrontation, and coalition building, they will be able to function more effectively in many arenas, including the political. After all, the asset that is uniquely associated with aging is experience, and it is this asset that can best serve to advance the participation and empowerment of older persons.

Measures to enhance the participation and empowerment of older persons need to be tailored to suit the strengths and weaknesses of the particular subsets of older persons. Retired civil servants or executives obviously operate from a different basis as compared to older rural women or the "old old" in institutions. The more vulnerable, the more disadvantaged, and the less active old require greater support from outside, more modest objectives, and quite a different set of participation and empowerment strategies. In many developing countries, older persons' organizations are primarily urban-based and draw their membership from better educated middle classes. It is difficult to currently estimate what degree of solidarity exists between these various subgroups of older persons. But in improving the situation of the more disadvantaged elderly, the importance of harnessing the strengths and skills of better situated older persons cannot be overemphasized. An issue for consideration here is the question of solidarity of the old on the lines of global "sisterhood." Is it desirable to work toward such a solidarity? Is it feasible?

Another question is related to who initiates participatory and empowerment processes, particularly in the case of the vulnerable and more disadvantaged elderly. External agents, if they are government sponsored, are most likely to steer participation to the ends that the government favors, which may or may not coincide with the desires or interests of the older persons. Their concept of participation could translate into people making contributions or joining in predetermined programs. External agents, if they are sponsored by private or voluntary organizations, are likely to influence the course of participation by their own preferences and expertise in strategies and approaches that have worked elsewhere. There is ample evidence in development literature about the dependency-producing outcomes of participation efforts sponsored by external agents, be they state or privately sponsored. How to take the most advantage from what the external agents have to offer and yet retain the autonomy and the momentum of self-development is a major issue that needs to be addressed.

Organization is a crucial element in all measures to strengthen the participation and empowerment of older people. The organization of older people for specific purposes such as consumer or housing cooperatives, voter registration, or income generation is a necessary instrument for empowerment, especially when older persons manage to determine the structure, decision making, goals, and the functioning of the organization rather than some outsiders. Initiation of new organizations and strengthening existing organizations of older persons deserves a high priority in international aid and cooperation.

PARTICIPATION AND EMPOWERMENT: PROSPECTS AND REALITIES FOR THE NEAR FUTURE

In the wake of the development initiatives that have swept the global scene since the founding of the United Nations, people's participation has increasingly acquired a dominant position. In addition, global policy instruments focused on specific population groups, as well as on primary health care, human settlements, population, rural development, and employment have expanded this theme to include emphasis on decision making, autonomy, and self-reliance of the people concerned. These global policy developments, which resulted from intergovernmental consensus, have been incorporated in many national policies. Rural community development in India, Harambee, and Ujamaa; movements in Kenya and Tanzania; Gotong Royong and Semaul Udong; efforts in Indonesia and Korea; and several other government-sponsored participatory programs have yielded valuable experiences concerning various aspects of participation. The remarkable successes achieved by women's and children's issues in attracting global attention, through declarations and conventions as well as funding and political support, also have lessons to offer to older persons and the issue of global aging. In addition, the expansion of democracy, relaxation of state controls, development of new "welfare mixes," privatization, and decentralization provide a more positive environment for progress on better integration of aging questions in development planning.

On the other hand, questions of participation and empowerment of older persons have to contend with many not-so-favorable factors. The perception of the aged as a passive, consuming, and economically unproductive population segment persists. The aging continue to be at the receiving end of remedial, institutionally based, and curative approaches. Unlike industrial workers or women, there is not a comparable uniting bond of solidarity among older persons, who are divided by social class, educational level, urban/rural residence, gender, and many other factors. There are also problems in seeking greater participation and empowerment in a world of continuing economic constraints, North-South divisions, and shrinking national resources. In addition, there are potential and real possibilities for competition and conflict from other population groups, also seeking to expand the base of their own participation and empowerment.

It is difficult and perhaps not even possible to balance these positive and negative factors. One might view these overlapping thrusts as evolving processes, nurtured and guided by outsiders until older persons themselves take greater hold, until they learn to set their goals, assess and harness the needed resources, and take commensurate risks in their social, economic, and political milieus. The precise ingredients and stages of participation and empowerment cannot be delineated, except in specific local contexts, as also the exact techniques, strategies, and skills involved in the participation and empowerment of older people. This paper has attempted to paint, through broad brush strokes, a canvas of the potential that this area offers for bold and innovative strides for the advancement of older people, within the larger framework of development.

REFERENCES

Bose, A. B. 1989. "Services for the Elderly in Development: The Role of Community Based Programs," in *Studies on the Integration of Aging in Development: Legislation, Social Security and Social Services*. Bangkok: United Nations, 140–152.

International Council on Social Welfare. 1976. *Self-reliance in Social Development*. Vienna: Author, 5.

International Federation on Ageing. "Final Declaration on the Rights and Responsibilities of Older Persons," in *Ageing International*, Vol. XXIII, no. 1. July 1991, 5–6.

Lloyd, Peter. 1991. "The Empowerment of Elderly People." *Journal of Aging Studies* 5(2), 125–135.

Margolies, Luise. 1990. *Issues of Cross-Cultural Transferability of Model Programs for the Aged*. Tampa, FL: University of South Florida.

Tout, Ken. 1989. *Ageing in Developing Countries*. New York: Oxford University Press, 151–200.

United Nations. 1969a. Declaration of Social Progress and Development, General Assembly Resolution 2542 (XXIV) of 11 December 1969. New York: Author.

United Nations. 1969b. Proceedings of the International Conference of Ministers Responsible for Social Welfare. New York: Author.

United Nations. 1975. Economic and Social Council Resolution 1929 (LVIII) 6 May 1975. New York, Author.

United Nations. 1981. International Strategy of the Third United Nations Development Decade. New York: Author.

United Nations. 1982. Popular Participation: Report of an International Seminar, Ljubljana, Yugoslavia. New York: Author.

United Nations. 1983a. Vienna International Plan of Action on Aging. New York: Author.

United Nations. 1983b. World Program of Action Concerning Disabled Persons. New York: Author.

United Nations. 1985a. Guidelines for Further Planning and Suitable Follow Up in the Field of Youth. New York: Author, 18.

United Nations. 1985b. Report of the World Conference to Review and Appraise the Achievements of the United Nations Decade for Women: Equality, Development and Peace, Nairobi, 15–26 July 1985. Sales No. 85. IV. 10. New York: Author.

United Nations. 1987a. Developmental Social Welfare Policies and Programs: Current Needs and Issues. E/Conf. 80/3 of 26 June 1987. New York: Author.

United Nations. 1987b. Guiding Principles for Developmental Social Welfare Policies and Programs. New York: Author.

United Nations. 1988. Handbook of Organizations Active in the Field of Ageing. New York: Author.

United Nations. 1989. Report of Secretary-General on Second Review and Appraisal of the Implementation of the International Plan of Action on Ageing E/1989/13. New York: Author.

United Nations. 1991a. General Assembly Resolution on "Implementation of the International Plan of Action on Aging and Related Activities," New York: Author.

United Nations. 1991b. *Integration of Ageing Women: Choice or Necessity*. Paper presented at the Expert Group Meeting on Integration Ageing and Elderly Women in Development, 7–11 October 1991. Vienna: Author.

United Nations. 1991c. Major Issues and Program Activities of the Secretariat and the Regional Commissions Relating to Social Development and Welfare and Specific Social Groups. Report of the Secretary-General. E/CN. 5/1991/3. New York: Author.

United Nations. 1991d. Report of Secretary-General on International Co-Operation on Ageing for 1992 and Beyond. New York: Author.

Chapter 12

The Aged and Development: Mutual Beneficiaries

Sandeep Chawla and Marvin A. Kaiser

AGING AND DEVELOPMENT

Through the 1980s, a growing literature has emphasized the idea that development is synonymous with expanding the capabilities of people (Sen, 1981, 1985; Dreze and Sen 1989; Ahmad, Dreze, et al., 1991). The notion of "human development"—as classic an example of a tautology as any—is now a paradigm in mainstream discourse. The tautology, however, is by no means fanciful: it has been necessary because goods and services were frequently treated as ends in themselves, rather than means to enhance human capability. Goods and services cannot, in themselves, constitute a better standard of living. They can do so only insofar as they provide a basis for the expansion of human capability. Thus, at the end of the 1980s, the United Nations Committee of Development Planning found it necessary to draw attention to this and to refer to human resource development as the "neglected dimension" (United Nations, 1988). Many of these arguments dovetail into the assertion that very similar levels of social development can be achieved at very different levels of economic development (Griffin, 1990). The empirical basis to substantiate this is growing. The United Nations Development Program now publishes an annual *Human Development Report* that compares countries on the basis of a composite human development index of three variables: life expectancy, education, and income (UNDP, 1992). Not surprisingly, country rankings differ considerably on the income scale, used, for instance, in the World Bank's development indicators (1992), and on the human development scale.

Within this same period it has become almost a truism to say that population aging is a global phenomenon. It is manifest in several parts of the world and incipient in all the rest. The elderly, those age 60-plus, are the fastest growing population group in the world. Their numbers are projected to increase sixfold, from 200 million in 1950, to 1.2 billion in 2025. The total world population is projected to increase at only half this rate over the same period, multiplying to about three-and-a-half times its size, from 2.5 billion to 8.5 billion (United Nations estimates, 1990, and medium variant projections). Even more significant than the rate of increase is the pattern of distribution around the world. In 1950, the world's elderly population was roughly equally divided between the developed and developing regions. Today, about three-fifths of the half a billion elderly live in the developing world. By 2025, nearly three-fourths of the world's 1.2 billion elderly are likely to be living in the developing countries.

When the two notions—development and aging—are conflated, the nature of the relationship between the two remains unclear in several respects (Chawla, 1993). What is clear is that the development process influences population aging, at least in terms of the well-documented, demographic phenomena of declining mortality and fertility. The reverse relationship is less clear: how does aging influence development? Do older people contribute to the process, or merely benefit from it? The kinds of answers offered frequently polarize the debate: somber prognostications about the "burden" and escalating costs of the elderly are contrasted with assertions about their productive contribution and developmental potential. While there is much empirical evidence to substantiate either position, or indeed to synthesize the two, the ambit of the evidence is generally confined to the developed or industrialized countries. For the developing countries, assessments of aging tend to be long on demographic and epidemiological data, but short on documentary evidence of what the elderly actually contribute, and what benefits they actually receive. Various bits and pieces of cross-sectional data and anecdotal evidence are then frequently summoned to supply the defect.

Any discussion about the empowerment of the elderly in an international context ought to be predicated upon a basis that is more rigorous than cross-sectional and anecdotal evidence. It was against such a background that a multicountry study was developed at the United Nations Office at Vienna/Centre for Social Development and Humanitarian Affairs (UNOV/CSDHA): it's aim was to identify some of the specific developmental implications of population aging, assess the contributions of the elderly to development, and suggest policy options to enhance these contributions. Four country studies—in Chile, the Dominican Republic, Sri Lanka, and Thailand—have been completed (Chawla and Kaiser, forthcoming), and some survey data germane to the question of empowerment is presented below.

EMPOWERMENT AND PARTICIPATION

The participation of the elderly is a necessary condition for their empowerment. Sometimes treated in the literature as synonymous with what is called productive aging, the concept of participation is, ipso facto, difficult to use because it is made up of so many subjective and objective elements that are hard to balance. Yet, if the concept is defined clearly, it can serve as a unifying framework which has considerable explanatory power in a cross-national, comparative context.

The concept of the *participation* of the elderly is thus considered here as a framework with at least three components: *contribution, reciprocity,* and *integration*. First, there is the notion of the elderly making contributions to others, which can, in turn, be seen at three levels, or in three forms: family (helping family and/or friends); community (helping others, usually at the level of the community, and sometimes called volunteering); and work. Second, the notion of reciprocity tries to measure the symmetry of exchanges in terms of what the elderly give to others, and what they get from them. Third, the notion of the integration of the elderly into society tries to examine the consequences of contribution and reciprocity in terms of the self-fulfillment and levels of satisfaction that the elderly derive from these activities.

In the survey results presented below, the concept of participation, with its triad of components—contribution, reciprocity, and integration—is thus used as the unifying framework. The specific activities described are organized within the three levels/forms of contribution: family, community, and work. Contributions at the level of family and community, because they are difficult to distinguish, are considered together, under the rubric of social participation. Contributions in the form of work are discussed under the rubric of economic participation. Each description of activity is accompanied, where appropriate, and where the data permits, by measures of the extent of reciprocity and integration.

THE FOUR-COUNTRY STUDY

Random samples of older persons age 60-plus were surveyed in each of the four countries. The number of subjects interviewed was 601 in Chile, 555 in the Dominican Republic, and 600 each in Sri Lanka and Thailand. The samples were stratified by gender, rural/urban location, and age group. Stratification by age group in the samples conformed generally to population structure of the four countries: three-fifths of the total elderly population in their sixties, a third in their seventies, and a tenth in their eighties.

A demographic profile of the four host countries, presented in Table 1, sets the basis for a discussion of the survey results. Population aging is a clearly identifiable, as well as rapid, phenomenon in each of the four countries. Two kinds of measures establish this quite clearly. The first is to consider proportions of each population age 60-plus in 1950, and contrast these with projections for the year 2025. Thus, the elderly population of Chile will grow from 7 percent of the total in 1950 to 16 percent of the total in 2025. Corresponding figures are 5 percent to 13 percent in the Dominican Republic, 6 percent to 17 percent in Sri Lanka, and 5 percent to 15.5 percent in Thailand.

The measure to assess the rapidity of population aging would be to look at

Table 1
Demographic Profile: Chile, Dominican Republic, Sri Lanka, and Thailand

	CHILE			DOM. REPUB.			SRI LANKA			THAILAND		
	1950	1990	2025	1950	1990	2025	1950	1990	2025	1950	1990	2025
Total Population (000)	6082	13173	19774	2353	7170	11447	7678	17217	24572	20010	55702	80911
Sex Ratio (Males per 100 Females)	98.1	97.6	96.8	104	103.3	103.1	115.4	100.7	97.9	101.3	100.7	100
Percent Urban	58.4	85.9	92.8	23.7	60.4	79.6	14.4	21.4	42.6	10.5	22.6	49.2
Elderly (60+) Population (000)	417	1169	3158	122	392	1506	457	1375	4184	954	3453	12559
Percent Elderly (60+)	6.9	8.9	16	5.2	5.5	13.2	6	8	17	4.8	6.2	15.5
Median Age	22.2	25.3	32.4	17.7	20.7	31.6	19.6	24.2	35.4	18.4	22.9	35.5
	1950-1955	1985-1990	2020-1925	1950-1955	1985-1990	2020-2025	1950-1955	1985-1990	2020-2025	1950-1955	1985-1990	2020-2025
Annual Population Growth Rate %	2.16	1.66	0.83	3.03	2.22	0.8	2.55	1.33	0.76	2.58	1.53	0.7
Life Expectancy at Birth	53.8	71.5	74.6	46	65.8	73.6	56.6	70.3	77.3	47	65	74.6

Source: United Nations, World Population Prospects, 1990.

growth factors of the total population, 1950 to 2025, and contrast them with growth factors of the elderly population. Thus, from 1950 to 2025, the total population of Chile would have grown by a factor of three, and it's elderly population by a factor of eight. Corresponding growth factors are five and twelve in the Dominican Republic, three and nine in Sri Lanka, and four and thirteen in Thailand. In other words, the elderly populations of the two Latin countries will grow at more than twice the rate of their total populations, and the elderly populations of the two Asian countries will grow three times as fast as their total populations.

Apart from population aging, other related demographic trends in the four countries are clear from Table 1. Rapid rates of urbanization characterize all the countries, though they are more pronounced in the Latin ones. By 1990, Chile appears as an overwhelmingly urban country. Sex ratios, the number of males per 100 females, are declining in all countries, in confirmation of a global trend, but we see a clear female majority only in Chile, and in the projections for Sri Lanka in 2025. This supports the decision to stratify the sample in each country to equal proportions of males and females. The median age is increasing in all the countries and will be over 30 years, in all cases, by 2025. Life expectancy also shows steady increases, though from different bases; it will, in every case, be over 70 years by 2025.

Household and Family Structure

Any discussion of participation must be predicated on establishing the context within which it takes place: this section accordingly details survey results to draw up profiles of the households and families within which the subjects live, participate, and contribute. The data are reported in terms of estimating household and family size and structure, patterns of co-residence, the nature of family links, and the specific position of the elderly subjects in the family and household.

The most likely living arrangements, in all four countries, are households of three to five persons, covering 41 percent of the sample population in Chile, and 44 percent each in the Dominican Republic and Sri Lanka, and 51 percent in Thailand (see Figure 1). Households of six to nine persons are more popular in the Asian countries, covering 40 percent of the sample in Sri Lanka and 35 percent in Thailand; this household size is also significant in Chile and the Dominican Republic, covering over a fifth of each population. Dual person households, by contrast, are more popular in the Latin countries, describing 22 percent of the study population in Chile and 17 percent in the Dominican Republic; in the Asian countries, they cover less than a tenth of the samples. Households of over ten persons are not very significant in any of the countries, accommodating 7 percent of the sample population in Sri Lanka, 6 percent in Dominican Republic, and 4 percent each in Chile and Thailand.

Proportions of people living alone are significant only in Chile, where a little more than a tenth of the study population lives in single person households. Neither gender nor location are important here, as there are roughly even proportions of

Figure 1

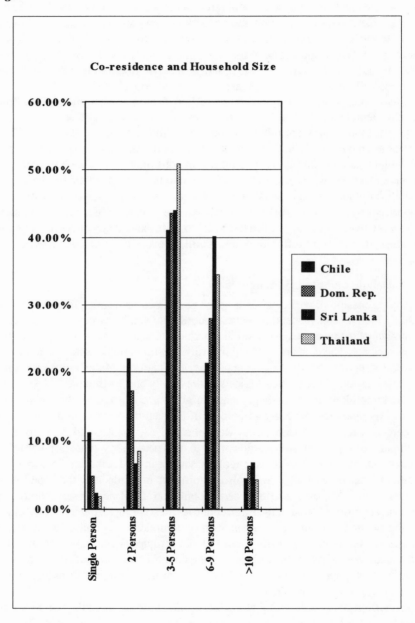

males and females in urban and rural locations. In the Dominican Republic, only 5 percent of people live alone, and in Sri Lanka and Thailand, the proportion is even lower, at only 2 percent. Isolated living arrangements among the elderly population, therefore, is not a categorization with much meaning in Sri Lanka and Thailand, though it does have some significance in the Dominican Republic, and a little more in Chile.

Given that the most likely living arrangement for the elderly in all countries is three- to five-person households, it is not surprising that many subjects report a wide range of family members co-residing with them. In Sri Lanka and Thailand over one-half of subjects have at least one daughter living with them; in the Dominican Republic and Chile the proportion is over two-fifths. Over one-half of the Sri Lankan sample have sons living with them; the proportion is over one-third in the other countries. The number of subjects living in multigenerational households, that is, with co-resident grandchildren, is notable in all countries, ranging from one-third in Chile, one-half in the Dominican Republic and Sri Lanka, and slightly over two-thirds in Thailand. Close to one-fifth of subjects reside with daughters- and/or sons-in-law in Sri Lanka and Thailand; the proportion is less in the other two countries.

Large proportions of the elderly in all four countries have living children and siblings: over four-fifths in the Dominican Republic, Sri Lanka, and Thailand; and over three-fourths in Chile. Of the subjects with living children, over two-fifths live with a son and/or a daughter in all four countries. Larger proportions live with a daughter, rather than a son, except in Sri Lanka, where the pattern is reversed. Of those with living siblings, few co-reside with them. Where children do not co-reside with the subject, the frequency of interaction remains very high in Sri Lanka, Thailand, and the Dominican Republic, with over three-quarters to nine-tenths of the subjects reporting daily contact with at least one child; in Chile, these proportions are considerably lower, covering a third of subjects. Another measure of interaction and reciprocity is the frequency with which children and siblings, living separately from the subjects, visited them. It appears to be extremely high: over 60 percent of all living sons and daughters visit their parents at least once a month in the four countries; siblings range from 29 percent in Sri Lanka, 30 percent in Chile, to 39 percent in Thailand, and 42 percent in the Dominican Republic.

Domestic Activities

In order to assess the contributions of the elderly to their families, the study attempted to document the multiple forms of involvement. Table 2 lists the domestic activities and numbers of subjects who reported performing them, by gender.

The most significant finding is the large proportions of elderly people who perform these tasks and therefore continue to contribute and, in this sense, be productive. There are surprisingly few activities in which less than a quarter of the study population does not participate. Expressed another way, there would be a low

Table 2
Selected Domestic Activities by Elderly by Gender

Domestic Activities: CHILE	Men 300 N	%	Women 301 N	%	Total 601 N	%
Child Care	66	22.00	96	31.89	162	26.96
Care for Sick/Disabled	25	8.33	40	13.29	65	10.82
Food Preparation	168	56.00	274	91.03	442	73.54
Household Cleaning	196	65.33	271	90.03	467	77.70
Sewing/Mending	30	10.00	110	36.54	140	23.29
Washing/Ironing	92	30.67	237	78.74	29	54.74
Household Repairs	215	71.67	119	39.53	334	55.57
Gardening	191	63.67	211	70.10	402	66.89
Tending Animals	104	34.67	128	42.52	232	38.60
Household Shopping	211	70.33	231	76.74	442	73.54
DOMINICAN REPUBLIC	**Men 260**		**Women 295**		**Total 555**	
Child Care	47	18.08	123	41.69	170	30.63
Care for Sick/Disabled	9	3.46	37	12.54	46	8.29
Food Preparation	60	23.08	226	76.61	286	51.53
Household Cleaning	55	21.15	214	72.54	269	48.47
Sewing/Mending	33	12.69	151	51.19	184	33.15
Washing/Ironing	40	15.38	184	62.37	224	40.36
Household Repairs	92	35.38	70	23.73	162	29.19
Gardening	44	16.92	83	28.14	127	22.88
Tending Animals	114	43.85	140	47.46	254	45.77
Household Shopping	94	36.15	144	48.81	238	42.88
SRI LANKA	**Men 308**		**Women 292**		**Total 600**	
Child Care	143	46.43	168	57.53	311	51.83
Care for Sick/Disabled	12	3.90	11	3.77	23	3.83
Food Preparation	26	8.44	171	58.56	197	32.83
Household Cleaning	140	5.45	190	65.07	330	55.00
Sewing/Mending	12	3.90	95	32.53	107	17.83
Washing/Ironing	82	26.62	162	55.48	244	40.67
Household Repairs	90	29.22	19	6.51	109	18.17
Gardening	131	42.53	41	14.04	172	28.67
Tending Animals	25	8.12	10	3.42	35	5.83
Household Shopping	149	48.38	115	39.38	264	44.00

Table 2 (continued)

THAILAND	Men	294	Women	306	Total	600
Child Care	129	43.88	149	48.69	278	46.33
Care for Sick/Disabled	9	3.06	7	2.29	16	2.67
Food Preparation	83	28.23	175	57.19	258	43.00
Household Cleaning	121	41.16	187	61.11	308	51.33
Sewing/Mending	22	7.48	92	30.07	114	19.00
Washing/Ironing	58	19.73	128	41.83	186	31.00
Household Repairs	135	45.92	45	14.71	180	30.00
Gardening	21	7.14	18	5.88	39	6.50
Tending Animals	139	47.28	126	41.18	265	44.17
Household Shopping	73	24.83	122	39.87	195	32.50

participation rate for a particular activity if less than a quarter of the sample populations reported that they do not perform it. The activities with such low participation rates are few. Care for the sick and the disabled is the only activity with low participation rates in all four countries. The only other activities with low participation rates are sewing/mending in Chile, Sri Lanka, and Thailand (in each country, however, over a third of females perform this activity); gardening in the Dominican Republic and Thailand; and household repairs in Sri Lanka.

On the other hand, the highest participation rates, that is, those performed by two-thirds or more of the sample population, were limited to relatively few of the domestic activities and in most cases to either males or females, not to both. In general, the highest rates of participation in domestic activities were reported in Chile. More specifically, women in Chile reported high participation rates in food preparation, household cleaning and shopping, and doing the laundry; food preparation and household cleaning in the Dominican Republic and household cleaning in Sri Lanka approached these highest levels of participation. Only in Chile did men report the highest levels of participation in household repairs, as well as in household shopping and cleaning.

Another way of assessing participation rates is to take an average of all the domestic activities being performed, thus collapsing them into one measure. If we average participation rates in eight of the ten domestic activities listed in Table 2, and exclude child care and care for the sick and disabled, we arrive at a measure which shows that nearly a third of the elderly in Sri Lanka (30 percent) and Thailand (32 percent), about two-fifths in the Dominican Republic (39 percent), and just under three-fifths in Chile (58 percent) are making domestic contributions. Care for the sick and disabled is excepted from this measure because, as noted below, this activity appears to be more extensive outside the ambit of the family. Child care is excluded because it seems to show a high participation rate on its own account (ranging from over a quarter to one-half in all four countries), and because it should properly be measured against the numbers of subjects that actually have co-resident grandchildren. If we take the numbers of subjects reporting the performance of child care from Table 2 and express them as proportions, not of the total samples, but of the subjects that report co-resident grandchildren (noted in the section on Household and Family Structure above), we find extremely high participation rates. Thus, of subjects with co-resident grandchildren, 93 percent in Sri Lanka, 73 percent in Chile, 69 percent in Thailand, and 60 percent in the Dominican Republic report caring for them.

Gender distributions in the performance of these activities reveal that women generally appear to be more active, as one might expect, in the performance of domestic tasks than men. For all countries, the number of females performing these domestic activities is proportionally larger than males in all except household repairs. In addition, there are some variations between countries. In Sri Lanka and Thailand, the two additional activities, gardening and caring for the sick and disabled, were performed by larger proportions of males. Only in Sri Lanka did more men than women engage in household shopping.

Age does not appear, by itself, to be a particularly significant determinant of domestic participation. While controlling these activities with the variable of age does show a general picture of declining activity rates with age, the declines are neither dramatic nor entirely consistent across all countries and activities. The picture is equally mixed in the contexts of marital status and education: neither of these variables appear to be significant determinants of domestic participation.

Very few of the elderly reported remuneration, either in money or in kind, for the domestic activities they performed for family or others. Responses to questions related to remuneration, however, are difficult to assess because they assume direct relationships between specific activities and some concrete return, such as remuneration, in cash or kind, accruing from them. In the context of the reciprocity and mutual aid that characterize so much of family and community life, such direct relationships are not always evident or clear. Getting to a realistic measure of reciprocity, therefore, makes it necessary to balance data on remuneration with responses to other questions about support that subjects received at the family and community levels. While some of this support is monetary (and discussed below), much of it may come in other ways. Table 3 shows the receipt of such support from children, other relatives, and others. Regular support from children is highest in the two Asian countries, and is reported by 56 percent of the sample in Thailand and 53 percent in Sri Lanka. Comparable figures for the Dominican Republic and Chile are 32 percent and 18 percent. These patterns apply equally to occasional nonmonetary support from children. Support from other relatives and from others is generally not very significant, except in Thailand and Sri Lanka, where about a fifth of the sample receive occasional support from other relatives.

Social and Cultural Activities

Further assessments of the contributions of the elderly to family and community life can be made on the basis of responses to questions that were designed to

Table 3
Number and Percentage of Elderly Persons who Receive Nonmonetary Support

Type of support:	CHILE TOTAL 601 N	%	DOMINICAN REPUBLIC TOTAL 555 N	%	SRI LANKA TOTAL 600 N	%	THAILAND TOTAL 600 N	%
Food								
Regularly	76	12.65	154	27.75	360	60.00	284	47.33
Occasionally	43	7.15	70	12.61	66	11.00	128	21.33
Shelter								
Regularly	61	10.15	69	12.43	216	36.00	120	20.00
Occasionally	8	1.33	21	3.78	14	2.33	24	4.00
Clothing								
Regularly	49	8.15	157	28.29	125	20.83	183	30.50
Occasionally	53	8.82	86	15.50	304	50.67	195	32.50
Medication								
Regularly	57	9.48	176	31.71	117	19.50	183	30.50
Occasionally	37	6.16	62	11.17	243	40.50	126	21.00
Transportation								
Regularly	20	3.33	120	21.62	63	10.50	98	16.33
Occasionally	13	2.16	37	6.67	181	30.17	77	12.83

document activities that had a wider ambit than the domestic ones. Although the distinction is somewhat arbitrary, these activities were listed as "social and cultural" (Table 4). The responses allow for some exploration of the wide range of roles that the elderly appear to adopt to maintain, or enhance, living standards of the family or community.

Using the rough measure of participation rates discussed above, it is significant that there are very few activities that a quarter, or less, of the study populations do not perform. In Chile, there is only one activity with a low participation rate: "Negotiating Matrimonial Arrangements." In the Dominican Republic and Sri Lanka, there are three such activities; in Thailand, there are four. "Teaching Vocational and Craft Skills" and "Traditional Health Roles" are both low participation activities in all three of these countries; "Special Roles in Community Functions" is low in Sri Lanka and Thailand; and "Leading Religious Rituals" is low in the Dominican Republic.

It follows from this that high participation rates, with over two-thirds performing them, are most evident in Chile, with five such activities: "Entertaining Children," "Discussing Family/Community Events," "Providing Emotional Support to Others," "Discussing Religious Matters," and "Special Roles in Family Functions." In the Dominican Republic, two activities, "Providing Emotional Support" and "Special Roles in Family Functions," show high participation rates; in Thailand, the latter is the only high participation activity; and in Sri Lanka, there is no activity reported with high participation.

Table 4
Income for Basic Needs (Percentages)

	Male	Female	Total
CHILE	(300)	(301)	(601)
Not enough	51	53	52
Just enough	39	38	39
More than enough	9	8	9
DOMINICAN REPUBLIC	(260)	(295)	(555)
Not enough	60	64	62
Just enough	37	33	35
More than enough	3	3	3
SRI LANKA	(308)	(292)	(600)
Just enough	38	40	39
More than enough	3	4	3
THAILAND	(294)	(306)	(600)
Not enough	14	11	13
Just enough	76	83	80
More than enough	9	11	6

Using the single measure for assessing participation rates established above, by collapsing all the social and cultural activities into one average, we find higher rates across all the countries. Thus, a third of the sample populations in Sri Lanka (33 percent) and Thailand (36 percent), little more than two-fifths in the Dominican Republic (43 percent), and over one-half in Chile (55 percent) report the performance of these social and cultural activities.

Gender distributions in the performance of these activities reveal considerable variation between the four countries. In Thailand, the proportion of males is greater than females in all activities. In Sri Lanka, the proportion of males is greater in all but two activities, "Discussing Religious Matters" and "Entertaining Children." In the other two countries, the pattern is reversed, with the proportions of females being greater in most activities. The only exceptions, where the proportions of males are significantly higher, are "Assisting in the Education of Children" and playing a "Special Role in Community Functions" in the Dominican Republic, and "Discussing Family/Community Events," "Teaching Vocational/Craft Skills," and playing a "Special Role in Community Functions" in Chile. The general pattern of higher male participation in the Asian countries, and higher female participation in the Latin ones appears more clearly in the average measure for all social and cultural activities. Thus, in Thailand, 41 percent of males and 31 percent of females report performance of these activities; in Sri Lanka, it is 36 percent of males and 30 percent of females. The trend changes in the Latin countries, with a clear female majority in the Dominican Republic (45 percent compared to 40 percent for males) and level participation for males and females, at 55 percent, in Chile.

When social and cultural activities are controlled by the variable of age, there is a general picture of declining activity. The declines are not dramatic, however, and there is an upswing in participation among the older age groups in all countries: the 80-plus group in the Dominican Republic and Sri Lanka, the age 75 to 79 group in Chile and the age 70 to 74 group in Thailand. Given that the average measure of life expectancy at birth, 1985–1990, ranges between 65 and 71 years in all four countries (Table 1), it is reasonable to consider people in the 70-plus age group as something of a survivor generation. In this light, the upswings in participation rates in the upper age groups are not surprising. However, the general conclusion about fairly high levels of reciprocity and mutual aid seems to be as sustainable here as it was in the context of the domestic activities.

Community and Family Participation

Several parts of the survey instrument addressed the complex question of community participation. Data on two of its dimensions—participation in religious groups and meetings and participation in associations of a nonreligious nature—are presented in Table 5. When both are considered together, the rates appear to be extremely high: 60 percent of the study population in the Dominican Republic, 67 percent in Chile, 70 percent in Sri Lanka, and 92 percent in Thailand report active involvement in these two kinds of association. When the two are considered

Table 5
Participation in Religious and Nonreligious Groups by Gender

Country	N	Male	N	Female	Total	%
CHILE		300		301		
Religious		123		177	300	49.92
Nonreligious		70		35	105	17.47
DOMINICAN REPUBLIC		260		295		
Religious		95		178	273	49.19
Nonreligious		27		32	59	10.63
SRI LANKA		308		292		
Religious		168		160	328	54.67
Nonreligious		68		25	93	15.50
THAILAND		294		306		
Religious		174		197	371	61.83
Nonreligious		111		69	180	30.00

separately, it appears that religious association involves a far larger segment—close to, or over half of the elderly population in all four countries. Nonreligious forms of association, on the other hand, cover from a tenth (Dominican Republic) to over one-fourth (Thailand) of the sample. Rural or urban location is not of much significance here, but gender distribution is: females are the larger proportion in religious association, though only marginally in Sri Lanka; males are the larger proportion in nonreligious association in Chile, Sri Lanka, and Thailand, and about even with females in the Dominican Republic.

Rates of participation in domestic, social, and cultural activities, in terms of contributions made by the elderly, were found to be reasonably high. Turning now to the question of reciprocity, and the symmetry of exchanges, an assessment can be derived from data on the extent to which the elderly participate in family decision making, presented in Table 6. The first category of data is a general one, covering participation, regular and occasional, in the making of major family decisions. It shows very high participation rates. Totals of regular and occasional participation reveal that 66 percent in Chile, 69 percent in Sri Lanka, 83 percent in Thailand, and 90 percent in the Dominican Republic are involved in making major family decisions. If only regular participation is considered, the rates are still high, with 46 percent for Chile, 35 percent for Sri Lanka, 43 percent for Thailand, and 57 percent for the Dominican Republic.

When specific kinds of family decisions are considered, with regular and occasional participation combined, the assessment of high participation remains valid. Decisions about food preparation are made by half to two-thirds of the study populations. In most of the other kinds of decisions, about a fifth, or more, of the elderly appear to be involved. The only major exception to this pattern are decisions

Table 6
Participation in Family Decision-making by Elderly

Decisions	CHILE	601	DOMINICAN REPUBLIC	555	SRI LANKA	600	THAILAND	600
	N	%	N	%	N	%	N	%
Major Family Decisions								
Regularly	279	46.42	314	56.58	212	35.33	258	43.00
Occasionally	121	20.13	182	32.79	204	34.00	242	40.33
Food to be Cooked								
Regularly	302	50.25	271	48.83	206	34.33	217	36.17
Occasionally	90	14.98	127	22.88	94	15.67	206	34.33
Clothing for (grand) Children								
Regularly	68	11.31	71	12.79	35	5.83	28	4.67
Occasionally	41	6.82	84	15.14	61	10.17	149	24.83
Agriculture Production Activities								
Regularly	69	11.48	120	21.62	53	8.83	105	17.50
Occasionally	40	6.66	55	9.91	70	11.67	119	19.83
Family Business Activities								
Regularly	121	20.13	104	18.74	52	8.67	139	23.17
Occasionally	43	7.15	130	23.42	56	9.33	122	20.33
Recreational Activities								
Regularly	96	15.97	48	8.65	50	8.33	41	6.83
Occasionally	68	11.31	104	18.74	88	14.67	119	19.83
Leading Religious Activities								
Regularly	76	12.65	110	19.82	163	27.17	101	16.83
Occasionally	32	5.32	123	22.16	170	28.33	145	24.17
Marriage of (grand) Children								
Regularly	28	4.66	71	12.79	93	15.50	114	19.00
Occasionally	40	6.66	117	21.08	134	22.33	196	32.67
Occupation of (grand) Children								
Regularly	47	7.82	41	7.39	42	7.00	81	13.50
Occasionally	47	7.82	91	16.40	75	12.50	109	18.17

about matrimonial and occupational choices of grandchildren and agricultural and religious activities in Chile, and family business decisions in Sri Lanka, though, even in these cases, over a tenth of the elderly reported an involvement.

In addition to actual participation in family and community decision making, the survey asked the elderly whether they were consulted regarding community problems (Table 7). The responses range from 17 percent in Sri Lanka, 26 percent in Thailand, to 29 percent in Chile and 40 percent in the Dominican Republic. When these totals are desegregated into regular and occasional consultation, the picture begins to look somewhat different. Regular consultation ranges from a low of 4 percent in Sri Lanka to a high of 12 percent in Chile; occasional consultation, by contrast, reveals larger percentages, from 13 percent in Sri Lanka to 29 percent in the Dominican Republic.

Different kinds of social association are also important measures of reciprocity at family and community levels. Subjects were asked whether they had attended weddings, funerals, family gatherings, birthday parties, religious festivals, or other

Table 7
Number and Percentage of People Consulted Regarding Community Problems

CHILE	N = 601	%
Regularly	73	12.15
Occasionally	102	16.97
Never	416	69.22
NA	10	1.66
DOMINICAN REPUBLIC	N = 555	%
Regularly	61	10.99
Occasionally	159	28.65
Never	326	58.74
NA	9	1.62
SRI LANKA	N = 600	%
Regularly	26	4.33
Occasionally	78	13.00
Never	467	77.83
NA	29	4.83
THAILAND	N = 600	%
Regularly	29	4.83
Occasionally	128	21.33
Never	424	70.67
NA	19	3.17

Table 8
Number of People Attending Selected Social Events in the Previous Six Months

SOCIAL EVENTS	CHILE	DOMINICAN REPUBLIC	SRI LANKA	THAILAND
Wedding party	123	123	339	384
Funeral mourning	320	328	447	440
Family gathering	178	115	97	80
Birthday party	175	85	75	56
Religious festival	175	238	323	324
Other social gatherings	74	42	18	133

social gatherings in the last six months (Table 8). The numbers of subjects reporting attendance were not insignificant in any of these events. Given the fact that the subjects, and therefore their peer groups, are all elderly, it is not surprising that funerals are the most frequently attended events in all four countries. More than half the study population in Chile, nearly three-fifths in the Dominican Republic, and nearly three-quarters in Sri Lanka and Thailand reported attending at least one funeral during the last six months. There is variance between the countries on the second most frequently attended event or events: in Chile, family gatherings, birthday parties, and religious festivals each cover about a third of the sample; in the Dominican Republic, religious festivals cover over two-fifths of subjects; and in both Sri Lanka and Thailand, more than half the subjects reported attendance at both weddings and religious gatherings in the last six months.

Visiting relatives and friends is another form of social association. In the survey, the elderly reported on the frequency of their visits from and to relatives and friends. Figure 2 illustrates a rough measure of the intensity and symmetry of interaction, showing numbers of subjects who visited friends and relatives, or were visited by them, within a given month. The highest frequency is in the Dominican Republic, where 74 percent of subjects visited relatives and friends at least monthly, and 85 percent were visited by friends and relatives. Comparable figures are 48 percent visiting and 58 percent being visited in Chile, 43 percent and 51 percent in Thailand, and 32 percent and 37 percent in Sri Lanka. These data suggest that, in the main, there is a great deal of social interaction and reciprocity between the elderly and their relatives and friends. The variance between the countries, that is, the high frequency of interaction in the Latin countries and lower frequencies in the Asian ones, can be explained, to some extent, by the fact that the incidence of co-residence is higher in the Asian countries.

Some measure of the extent of integration (the third component in the triad of participation) can be derived from questions that asked subjects how often they

Figure 2

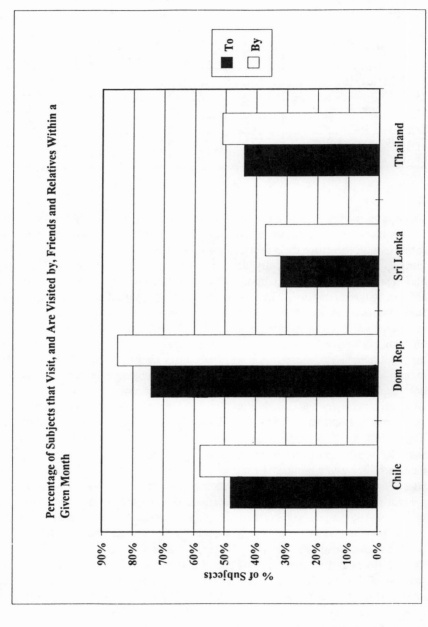

Percentage of Subjects that Visit, and Are Visited by, Friends and Relatives Within a Given Month

found themselves feeling lonely (Table 9). Those that reported feeling lonely quite often are the highest in Chile, at a quarter of the sample, 14 percent in the Dominican Republic, 13 percent in Sri Lanka, and only 6 percent in Thailand. Proportions of those that felt lonely sometimes, which is, of course, less significant, are highest in the Dominican Republic at 45 percent, followed by 39 percent in Thailand, 32 percent in Chile, and only 23 percent in Sri Lanka. Expressed another way, by excepting the numbers that felt lonely quite often and sometimes from the rest, we find that 64 percent of the sample in Sri Lanka, 55 percent in Thailand, 43 percent in Chile, and 41 percent in the Dominican Republic are not troubled by loneliness.

Continuing on the issue of the impact of social association on individual satisfaction and integration, subjects were asked whether their contact with relatives and friends occurred as often as they would like it, or whether it was too seldom (Table 10). Only in Chile did over two-fifths of the sample assess the contact to be too seldom; in the Dominican Republic, this proportion was less than a third; in Sri Lanka it was a fifth, and in Thailand it was less than a fifth. The proportions of subjects reporting contact as frequently as they wanted it are, expectedly, low in Chile (32 percent) and high in the other countries— 70 percent in the Dominican Republic, 61 percent in Sri Lanka, and 73 percent in Thailand.

Economic Status

Following a consideration of the first two forms and levels of contribution (family and community), this section focuses on the third one, work. Work contributions can then be set against assessments of reciprocity and integration. Data on sources of income are used to assess the symmetry between what the elderly give and what they get. Assessing levels of integration and satisfaction by means of correlating responses to questions about the desirability and necessity of working, and the adequacy of income to fulfill basic needs, concludes the discussion of economic participation.

The most significant finding from the several parts of the survey instrument dealing with work patterns is the large proportion of the elderly who, despite age, continue to work. Direct questions were asked about three categories of work: agricultural work, business enterprises, and cottage industry. These were followed by a fourth category covering other kinds of income producing work. Combining all four categories for the purposes of a general measure, we find that more than two-fifths of the study populations in Sri Lanka (41 percent) and Chile (43 percent) and about three-fifths in the Dominican Republic (57 percent) and Thailand (60 percent) are working (Figure 3).

Involvement in work, whether in agriculture, business, cottage industry, or other activities may or may not be income producing. While survey data on the relationship between the work patterns of the study population and remuneration, either in-cash or in-kind, is available, it is not presented here. In order to provide a context to locate the discussion on work, however, an average measure of remuneration will suffice. It can be derived by totaling the number of subjects reporting remuneration,

Table 9
Number and Percentage of Older People Who Feel Lonely

CHILE	N = 601	%
Quite often	151	25.12
Sometimes	193	32.11
Almost never	256	42.60
DOMINICAN REPUBLIC	N = 555	%
Quite often	80	14.41
Sometimes	248	44.68
Almost never	190	34.23
SRI LANKA	N = 600	%
Quite often	80	13.33
Sometimes	139	23.17
Almost never	331	55.17
THAILAND	N = 600	%
Quite often	38	6.33
Sometimes	233	38.83
Almost never	291	48.50

Country totals do not include respondents not answering.

Table 10
Contacts with Relatives and Friends

CHILE	Total M	6.01
As often as want to	195	0.3245
Too seldom	260	0.4326
DOMINICAN REPUBLIC	Total M	5.55
As often as want to	388	0.6991
Too seldom	161	0.2901
SRI LANKA	Total M	6
As often as want to	364	0.6067
Too seldom	126	0.21
THAILAND	Total M	6
As often as want to	435	0.725
Too seldom	90	0.15

Figure 3

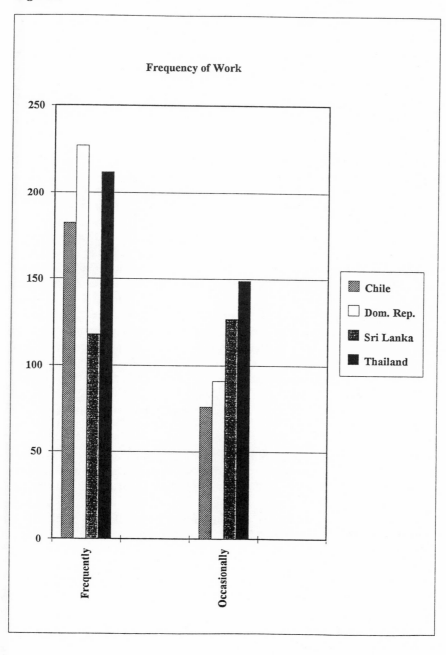

Table 11
Volunteer Work

Country	N	Sample Size	% of Sample
CHILE	80	601	13.31
DOMINICAN REPUBLIC	47	555	8.47
SRI LANKA	15	600	2.50
THAILAND	38	600	6.33

in cash and kind, and expressing them as proportions of the total number of subjects that are working. Thus, the highest average is found in the Dominican Republic, where 84 percent of those working report remuneration for the work. Corresponding averages for the other countries are 82 percent in Thailand, 69 percent in Chile, and 39 percent in Sri Lanka.

Beyond the more traditional forms of work, respondents were also asked to describe their involvement in volunteer activities. As seen in Table 11, volunteer work was not frequently cited by the study population. Only in Chile did over a tenth of the study population report such engagement. This discussion should, however, be qualified by the caveat that the concept of volunteer work does not have universal applicability. The previous sections on social participation showed that there are several activities performed, without remuneration, for the community. Such activities can be considered a part of the networks of mutual aid and reciprocity that characterize many communities, but, given the difficulties in identifying a definite remuneration for them, it seems equally reasonable to categorize them as volunteer activities. If this is done, it begins to look as though fairly high proportions of the study populations are engaged in volunteer work.

Income

Income, in its various forms, is a good measure of reciprocity if it can be used to assess what the elderly get in relation to what they give. Data on what subjects reported to be their main sources of income are presented in Table 12, with gender as the control variable.

Despite the large proportions working, formal and informal work, taken together, make up the main source of income for 13 percent of the study population in Chile, 17 percent in Sri Lanka, and much larger segments in Thailand (30 percent) and the Dominican Republic (39 percent). Informal work constitutes a slightly larger proportion than formal work in Chile and the Dominican Republic and is almost five times as large in Sri Lanka. In Thailand, the trend is reversed, as the proportion of formal work, as a main source of income, is nearly seven times larger than informal work. Males constitute the majority of those who derive their main income from work in all four countries: three times as many males as females

Figure 4

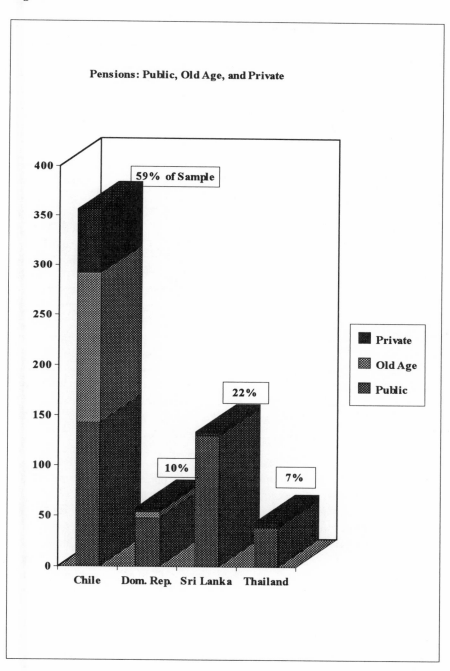

Table 12
Main Sources of Income by Gender

CHILE	Male 300		Female 301		Total 601	
	N	%	N	%	N	%
Formal Work	29	9.67	9	2.99	38	6.32
Informal Work	32	10.67	11	3.65	43	7.15
Savings/Investments	4	1.33	5	1.66	9	1.50
Public Service Pension	73	24.33	57	18.94	130	21.63
Military Pension	6	2.00	7	2.33	13	2.16
Old Age Pension	84	28.00	65	21.59	149	24.79
Private Pension	30	10.00	35	11.63	65	10.82
From Spouse	8	2.67	83	27.5	91	15.14
From Children	10	3.33	26	8.64	36	5.99
From Other Relations	5	1.67	1	0.33	6	1.00
Other Income	38	12.67	28	9.30	66	10.98
DOM. REPUB.	Male 260		Female 295		Total 555	
Formal Work	66	25.38	34	11.53	100	18.02
Informal Work	63	24.23	51	17.29	114	20.54
Savings/Investments	12	4.62	12	4.07	24	4.32
Public Service Pension	20	7.69	20	6.78	40	7.2
Military Pension	5	1.92	3	1.02	8	1.44
Old Age Pension	3	1.15	3	1.02	6	1.08
Private Pension	2	0.77	2	0.68	4	0.72
From Spouse	23	8.85	29	9.83	52	9.37
From Children	85	32.69	155	52.54	240	43.24
From Other Relations	14	5.38	16	5.42	30	5.41
Private Charity	1	0.38	0	0.00	1	0.18
Other Income	3	1.15	12	4.07	15	2.70

in Chile; twice as many in the Dominican Republic and Sri Lanka; but only slightly more in Thailand, where the proportions are about even.

Income accruing from work must be set against what is received for previous work contributions in the form of pensions. Segments of the study population that are covered by pensions—public service, military, old age and private pensions, taken together—are 59 percent for Chile, 22 percent for Sri Lanka, 10 percent for the Dominican Republic, and only 7 percent for Thailand (Figure 4). Breaking down these totals into the different kinds of pensions shows that a public service pension is the main kind of pension in Sri Lanka, the Dominican Republic, and Thailand, covering 21 percent, 7 percent, and 6 percent, respectively, and the secondary kind in Chile, covering 22 percent of the sample. An old age pension is reported to be available to 25 percent of those in Chile, to only 1 percent in the

Table 12 (continued)

SRI LANKA	Male	308	Female	292	Total	600
	N	%	N	%	N	%
Formal Work	14	4.55	3	1.03	17	2.83
Informal Work	56	18.18	26	8.90	82	13.67
Savings/Investments	11	3.57	3	1.03	14	2.33
Public Service Pension	89	28.90	39	13.36	128	21.33
Military Pension	2	0.65	0	0.00	2	0.33
Old Age Pension	0	0.00	0	0.00	0	0.00
Private Pension	3	0.97	1	0.34	4	0.67
From Spouse	10	3.25	32	10.96	42	7.00
From Children	55	17.86	75	25.68	130	21.67
From Other Relations	7	2.27	5	1.71	12	2.00
Private Charity	0	0.00	2	0.68	2	0.33
Other Income	28	9.09	50	17.12	78	13.00
THAILAND	Male	294	Female	306	Total	600
Formal Work	76	25.85	80	26.14	156	26.00
Informal Work	15	5.10	8	2.61	23	3.83
Savings/Investments	50	17.01	38	12.42	88	14.67
Public Service Pension	32	10.88	5	1.63	37	6.17
Military Pension	1	0.34	1	0.33	2	0.33
Old Age Pension	0	0.00	0	0.00	0	0.00
Private Pension	5	1.70	0	0.00	5	0.83
From Spouse	16	5.44	7	2.29	23	3.83
From Children	97	32.99	117	38.24	214	35.67
From Other Relations	1	0.34	7	2.29	8	1.33
Private Charity	0	0.00	0	0.00	0	0.00
Other Income	4	1.36	6	1.96	10	1.67

Dominican Republic, and to none in Sri Lanka, and Thailand. A military pension is not significant in any of the four countries. Private pensions are also insignificant in the Dominican Republic, Sri Lanka, and Thailand, but cover 11 percent of Chile's population. Gender distributions show that more males receive a pension in all these categories except private pensions in Chile, where the proportion of females is slightly larger (12 percent) than males (10 percent), and in Thailand, where one male and one female receive a military pension.

Children are generally a significant source of income for the study population. Forty-three percent of the Dominican sample, 36 percent of Thailand's, and 22 percent of Sri Lanka's received income from children. Only in Chile, with 6 percent of the sample, was income from children not significant. Females are the major recipients of this income in all four countries.

Income from a spouse is the main source of income for 15 percent of the subjects in Chile, 9 percent in the Dominican Republic, 7 percent in Sri Lanka, and 4 percent in Thailand. Gender distribution between husbands and wives receiving income from a spouse is nearly even in the Dominican Republic. In Sri Lanka, however, three times as many females as males receive such income; in Chile, the ratio is even greater, with ten times as many females. The trend is reversed in Thailand, where twice as many males as females receive income from a spouse. Income from other relatives is received by very small segments of the study population: 5 percent in the Dominican Republic, 2 percent in Sri Lanka, and 1 percent in Chile and Thailand.

The "Other Income" category is substantial in Sri Lanka, at 13 percent and Chile, at 11 percent, but only 3 percent in the Dominican Republic and 2 Lanka, the Dominican Republic, and Thailand, but a smaller proportion in Chile.

Personal savings and investments provide income for a substantial segment of the study population only in Thailand (15 percent). In the remaining countries, personal savings and investments cover insignificant proportions of the sample: 4 percent in the Dominican Republic, and 2 percent each in Chile and Sri Lanka.

To summarize the findings on income, notwithstanding some country variation, it appears that children, work, and pensions are the three most frequently reported sources of income for the study population. Two additional sources, spouses and savings, are identified in individual countries. Thus, the variations between countries, in different orders of magnitude, are: pensions, work, and spouses in Chile: children, work, and pensions in the Dominican Republic and Sri Lanka; and children, work, and savings in Thailand.

Several key questions in the survey instrument examined the subject's own assessment of his or her capacity to work, economic need, and income level. Limitations of space prevent these data from being reported here, and only one indicative example is presented. This concerns income to fulfill basic needs. Table 4 (on page 162) shows the number of subjects who reported more than enough income, just enough income, and not enough income to meet basic needs. In Chile, the Dominican Republic and Sri Lanka, an astonishingly high propor-tion—over half to three-fifths of the study populations—feel they do not have enough income for their basic needs. In these countries, over one-third to two-fifths put themselves in the border-line category of having just enough income. Thailand shows a completely different pattern: the largest segment of the study population (81 percent) put themselves in the borderline group of having just enough income. In the contrast to the other three countries, where those reporting not enough income ranged from three-fifths to a half of the sample, in Thailand this proportion was only 13 percent. Finally, the numbers of those with more than enough income are significant only in Chile and Thailand, covering 9 percent and 6 percent of the sample, respectively. In Sri Lanka and the Dominican Republic, these proportions are only about 3 percent each.

These results provide a basis for estimating levels of deprivation among the study populations. The estimations can be tested and validated by balancing the numbers of subjects actually working. While the argument cannot be detailed here, it has been done elsewhere, and shows that the estimations of deprivation based upon the income measure reported above appear to be reasonably accurate (Chawla and Kaiser, forthcomimg). Thus, in accordance with the numbers of subjects reporting insufficient income for their basic needs, we can estimate that two-fifths of the elderly in Chile, about half in Sri Lanka, and nearly three-fifths in the Dominican Republic live in conditions of deprivation. In the case of Thailand, because of the more objective measures noted above, and because of the largest proportion being in the borderline category of having just enough income, there is good reason to revise the estimate upward and conclude that about a third of the elderly appear to live in conditions of deprivation.

Given these estimations of deprivation, it is surprising how many of the elderly report making another form of contribution: giving financial support to their children, grandchildren, and other relations. The data are presented in Table 13, with gender as the control variable. Substantial proportions of the study populations provide financial support to their children, with the highest in Chile, at 44 percent, followed by 40 percent in Thailand, 30 percent in the Dominican Republic, and 27 percent in Sri Lanka. Proportions of males are greater than females in all four countries, with larger differences in the Asian countries.

Table 13

Number and Percentage of Older Persons Who Give Financial Support to Children, Grandchildren, and Other Relatives

CHILE	Male	300	Female	301	Total	601
Financial Support to	N	%	N	%	N	%
Children	147	49.00	117	38.87	264	43.93
Grandchildren	126	42.00	110	36.54	236	39.27
Other Relatives	57	19.00	51	16.94	108	17.97
DOM. REPUB.	Male	260	Female	295	Total	555
Children	96	36.92	71	24.07	167	30.09
Grandchildren	73	28.08	69	23.39	142	25.59
Other Relatives	47	18.08	42	14.24	89	16.04
SRI LANKA	Male	308	Female	292	Total	600
Children	107	34.74	55	18.84	162	27.00
Grandchildren	65	21.10	50	17.12	115	19.17
Other Relatives	37	12.01	15	5.14	52	8.67
THAILAND	Male	294	Female	306	Total	600
Children	146	49.66	91	29.74	237	9.50
Grandchildren	158	53.74	134	3.79	292	48.67
Other Relatives	70	23.81	54	17.65	124	20.67

Financial support is provided to grandchildren by about one-half of the sample in Thailand, two-fifths in Chile, a quarter in the Dominican Republic, and a fifth in Sri Lanka. These proportions are only slightly less than those who give support to their children. Males are in the majority, again, in all four countries. The proportions of those that report giving financial support to other relatives are also surprisingly high, ranging from 21 percent in Thailand, 18 percent in Chile, 16 percent in the Dominican Republic, to 9 percent in Sri Lanka. Again, males are more likely to make such contributions than females in all four countries, with the biggest difference in Sri Lanka.

Contrasting these data with those presented in Table 12, on main sources of income, allows for some interesting patterns. We find that the proportions that report receiving income support from their children are 6 percent in Chile, 43 percent in the Dominican Republic, 22 percent in Sri Lanka, and 36 percent in Thailand; those that give income support to their children (Table 13) constitute 44 percent in Chile, 30 percent in the Dominican Republic, 27 percent in Sri Lanka, and 40 percent in Thailand. Females are a majority of those that receive financial support, males a majority of those that give it. The patterns that emerge in the four countries are different. In Chile, significantly more elderly people (44 percent) give financial support than receive it (6 percent). In Thailand, 40 percent give financial support and 36 percent receive it. In Sri Lanka too, 27 percent of people provide support compared to the 22 percent that receive it. The pattern is reversed in the Dominican Republic: the numbers of those that receive support (43 percent) are larger than those that give it (30 percent). The most likely reason for these divergent patterns appears to be the availability of some public assistance and social security in Chile, and, to a lesser extent, in Sri Lanka. Public pensions cover over a fifth of the study populations in both countries. When old age and private pensions are added, two-fifths of the population in Chile is covered. This seems to limit the need of the elderly to get financial support from their children, and enables them to provide it. In Thailand, private assets in the form of personal savings and investments, combined with some public pensions, serve the same purpose. In the Dominican Republic, on the other hand, more elderly receive support than provide it because pension coverage and personal savings are limited to a very small proportion of the population.

CONCLUSION

Answers to questions about the main problems in subjects' lives provide a suitable summary to conclude this assessment of the survey results. The main problem in Chile, the Dominican Republic, and Sri Lanka is economic: three-quarters of the sample population in Chile, and over four-fifths in the Dominican Republic, and Sri Lanka report this. The second most important problem, again common to these three countries, is health, covering three- to four-fifths of the samples. In the case of Thailand, this pattern is reversed: health appears as the main problem, for over four-fifths of the sample, and the economic problem is in the second place, covering, nonetheless, two-thirds of the sample.

The fact that an overwhelming majority of subjects, in all four countries, consider their economic status to be their most serious problem (the second most serious problem in Thailand, but still covering two-thirds of the sample), is a confirmation of similar conclusions drawn from other sections of the survey. It was estimated above that about a third of the elderly in Thailand, two-fifths in Chile, one half in Sri Lanka, and three-fifths in the Dominican Republic live in conditions of deprivation. Given this, and the numbers of people that live on the edge of deprivation (those, for instance, who report having "just enough" income) it is reasonable to conclude that the primary target for any policy or program development for the aged should be the alleviation of this economic constraint.

The economic limitations of the elderly should, however, be contrasted with the other major conclusion emerging from the survey: that the elderly are both economically and socially productive. Data on domestic, social, and cultural activities, as well as those on family and community participation presented above, show that considerable numbers of the elderly continue to be productive and contribute significantly to the maintenance of their families and communities. This contribution is not merely social but also significant in economic terms, as data on work, occupation, and income reveal.

The contributions, moreover, do not appear to be asymmetrical. Levels of reciprocity and integration, in the various measures used above, seem to be high. Perhaps the best single measure of this can be found in the responses of subjects to a question about how satisfied they were with their own lives. Overwhelmingly high proportions of subjects pronounced themselves satisfied. Combining the categories of "satisfied" and "very satisfied" reveals 81 percent of the sample in Chile, 85 percent in the Dominican Republic, 68 percent in Sri Lanka, and 90 percent in Thailand. Despite the economic constraint, therefore, the contributions that the elderly make, and the reciprocity of the exchanges implied therein, appear to create a high degree of integration and satisfaction.

It is empirically demonstrable, therefore, that the elderly have both the desire and the capacity for productive occupation and self-help. Actual empowerment to be productive within the structure of a given society is quite another matter. Public policies and programs, if appropriately conceived and implemented, can enable precisely such an empowerment. If the quantum of enablement increases, then the elderly are likely to acquire more capabilities to do a variety of things, many of which would contribute greatly to the development of the society in question. By way of example, a determined public policy can ensure that the elderly continue in paid employment, find alternative forms of productive occupation, and have greater control over the community services from which they benefit, but to which they also contribute. Public policy, in other words, is a crucial determinant of empowerment.

While there can be no substitute for universal pension coverage—and the survey data demonstrates the capabilities generated by entitlement to a pension—there is no defensible reason for public policy to confine itself to the provision of formal income maintenance benefits. What is also needed is public policy that addresses the human resource potential of the elderly, in order to enhance their capabilities. If such policies are directed toward family and community support, to care for the elderly or to enable them to care for, and contribute to, the family and community, there is no clear evidence that the one public policy (family support) will short-circuit the other (government-provided welfare support). The popular belief that state welfare benefits "crowd out" family solidarity is being questioned in a growing literature (Tracy, 1993). The present survey results also show, quite clearly, that family solidarity is not "crowded out" by state-provided benefits.

Such a balance, then, between the provision of income security for the aged, and the expansion of their developmental potential, indeed informs the practical strategy on aging that the United Nations has adopted to ensure more extensive and intensive implementation of the International Plan of Action on Aging (United Nations, 1992). The setting of national targets on aging is one prong of this strategy. Among the various approaches, it is suggested that countries institute a national program on productive aging; establish schemes to provide income security to all older persons through a broad range of mechanisms appropriate to the economic and social infrastructure of the country; and provide a safety net for the most vulnerable of the elderly who are often overlooked because their position, ipso facto, leaves them in the interstices that are usually created between broad program areas and sectors.

REFERENCES

Ahmad, Ehtisham, Jean Dreze, John Hill, and Amartya Sen (eds.). 1991. *Social Security in Developing Countries.* Oxford: Clarendon Press.

Chawla, Sandeep. 1993. "Demographic Ageing and Development." *Generations: Journal of the American Society on Aging* XVII(4): 20–23.

Chawla, Sandeep, and Marvin A. Kaiser. Forthcoming. *Developmental Implications of Population Aging: A Four-Country Study.* New York and Vienna: United Nations.

Dreze, Jean, and Amartya Sen (eds.). 1989. *Hunger and Public Action.* Oxford: Clarendon Press.

Griffin, Keith. 1990. *Alternative Strategies for Economic Development.* London: Macmillan, 7–10.

Sen, Amartya. 1981. *Poverty and Famines: An Essay on Entitlement and Deprivation.* Oxford: Clarendon Press.

———. 1985. *Commodities and Capabilities.* Amsterdam: North Holland.

Tracy, Martin B. 1993. "Government versus the Family: The False Dichotomy." *Generations: Journal of the American Society on Aging* XVII(4): 47–50, and further references therein.

United Nations. 1988. *Committee of Development Planning, Report on the Twenty Fourth Session* (E/1988/16, Supplement No. 6).

United Nations. 1990. *World Population Prospects, 1990* (ST/ESA/SER.A/120); and *The Sex and Age Distributions of Population: The 1990 Revision* (ST/ESA/SER.A/122). New York: United Nations.

United Nations. 1992. *Global Targets on Aging for the Year 2000: A Practical Strategy.* Report of the Secretary-General to the General Assembly (A/47/339).

United Nations Development Programme (UNDP). 1992. *Human Development Report.* New York, Oxford: Oxford University Press.

World Bank. 1992. *World Development Report.* New York and Oxford: Oxford University Press.

Chapter 13

Older Persons in Pakistan: Their Major Problems and Empowerment Strategy

S. M. Zaki

Less than a hundred years ago, old age and retirement questions scarcely existed in the land now known as Pakistan. Only a few men and women lived long enough and were wealthy enough to avoid working until they died. With life expectancy less than 35 years, there was little need to plan for the future. Families were much closer than today and it was quite normal to have three generations in one home. Grandfather was the head of the family; grandmother helped bring up the grandchildren; adult children worked for a living. This "joint family" system provided shelter and care in health as well as sickness (Zaki, 1987).

The advantages of these close-knit families of the past may be exaggerated. Alongside the gains in real support for older family members by younger ones and vice-versa must be placed the terrible poverty endured by much of the population, the lack of privacy, the absence of proper medical treatment, and the need for children to forego an education and begin working at an early age.

Much has changed. People live longer, thanks to advances in medical science. Insurance is more widespread and pensions or retirement benefits are available to many retiring employees.

However, improvements in health and education combined with more business opportunities and growth in industry have resulted in a substantial increase in the numbers living in cities and towns, which in turn often results in scattered families. Traditional family units are breaking into nuclear families as young people find it difficult to keep their elders with them. The migration of the working-age generation to urban areas and foreign lands, where they can earn a livelihood, often keeps older people away from the families of their grown-up children. The aged often prefer to live in the quieter, more peaceful environments of smaller towns and rural districts. Finally, there is the generation gap often caused, or perceived to be caused, by the resistance of the elderly to the changing pattern of life in the present-day society.

Fragmentation of the family unit has exacerbated the problems of the elderly, particularly in big cities, and brings us face-to-face with a pressing problem for the growing number of older Pakistanis: having an equal right to live a decent life.

DEMOGRAPHY OF AGING IN PAKISTAN

In 1990, the population of Pakistanis age 55-plus stood at almost 10 million. The age group 55 to 64 accounted for slightly more than half of this number; those 65 to 74 made up almost three and a half million; those age 75 to 79 totaled more than 800,000. In the 35-year period from 1990 to 2025, the total number of those over 55 will more than double to almost 26 million people. Of that number, 14½ million will be the youngest of the old; almost eight million will be between ages 65 and 74; less than two million will be in the 75 to 79 age group, and more than a million and a half will be at least 80 years old or older (Kinsella and Taub, 1993).

When looking at these numbers, it is important to take into consideration the onset of early aging symptoms in the general population (particularly in the 50-plus group), largely attributed to low standards of living. This process is marked by a gradual withdrawal from active life and reduced earning capacity. Moreover, the low participation of females in the labor force and the general tendency not to use the skills and talents of physically fit senior citizens in different employment venues further aggravates the need to support a growing number of people.

MAJOR PROBLEMS

Following are the primary issues concerning Pakistan's elderly:

- Rapid growth in the population age 65-plus and comparatively scarce socio-economic resources.
- Absence of schemes to provide income security, health care, and social support and the urgency of putting these into place before the rapidly increasing numbers of older people makes the problem unmanageable.
- The burden on the working-age population of a high proportion of dependents under age 15 and over age 65, which is aggravated by low labor-force participation of women and the general exclusion of able-bodied seniors from salaried jobs (Zaki, 1991).
- Need to increase new technology, skill development, and training, with particular emphasis on including women and physically fit senior citizens in economic activity.
- Fragmentation of services offered by nongovernmental organizations (NGOs) and government agencies at all levels, which makes the service provision that does exist relatively costly and inefficient.
- Interest groups for seniors still in an early stage of development.

TRADITIONAL STATUS OF THE ELDERLY

Although the power of the elderly in Pakistan has declined, once it was not unusual for them to have the authority and influence of a "high priest" in the family and the community. By culture and tradition, older men and women were the final arbiters in family matters.

There can be no better example of the empowered elderly than the *Jirga* (feudal) system of the Northwestern Frontier province and the Northern Tracts. In this system, clan elders are vested with substantial powers including setting fines and compensation and sentencing. (Formerly, they pronounced the death penalty.) A similar type of authority is held by the *Panchayat* or village council, where great community power is exercised by chosen elders.

Other functions of the elderly are to arrange marriages, festivals, community feasts, burials, and family birth parties. They also consult on rural work programs such as building huts, planting crops, and harvesting.

The empowerment of the elderly in public life can be clearly seen by the fact that even the poorest Pakistanis often look with disfavor on the charitable aid—traditionally given on the occasion of a birth or a death—by the rich or by the state, but deem such assistance acceptable when it is arranged by elders.

CURRENT STATUS OF THE ELDERLY

At many levels of Pakistani society, old men and women are shown respect in theory but in fact are treated as "surplus and least serviceable" because of age and lack of income. The public support networks that exist in the West have yet to be developed, so the elderly have no solid pensions, no proper medical coverage, and no social security. Failure to have such support in their own right makes them dependent and practically subservient to the earning family member and the society as a whole. Thus, the show of respect and filial piety toward the elderly (and the so-called powers vested in them) becomes merely theoretical at times.

It is vital to ensure the elderly's participation in socioeconomic and other programs that offer help and guidance to them. This participation should not be based on humanitarian grounds but on developmental grounds, a principle already emphasized in the Vienna International Plan of Action for Ageing or VIPAA (United Nations, 1982). If freed from retirement age and other artificially created restrictions, the able-bodied elderly are capable of making sizable contributions to the society.

Tomorrow's elderly are in fact today's working-age adults. They are likely to live longer than their parents and their knowledge of modern science and technology stands to remain valuable to the society in general, making it likely that the concept of older people as a burden will be reversed, in distinct contrast to our present thinking (Zaki, 1993).

Another handicap is that many older people in countries like Pakistan live in isolation, without anyone fully understanding their social needs. They are considered "marginal" to society and hence often ignored in the socioeconomic context. Serious empowerment efforts are needed to bring them into the mainstream of society.

Campaigns to change attitudes toward the elderly are being waged by various organizations through print and electronic media, radio and television programs, observance of International Day of the Elderly and International Volunteer Days, as well as reorientation of public opinion in the light of international efforts to address the concerns of an aging population.

A few words of caution about the relationship of older people to the family, the economy, and the state may be emphasized here. These are not merely problems of adjustment on the part of the elderly. In fact, these are "socially structured" and the economy and the state play a crucial role in this process of restructuring. This vital issue has been summarized by Townsend (1981) as follows:

> There is the imposition and acceptance of earlier retirement; the legislation of low income; the denial of rights to self-determination in institutions; and the construction of community services for recipients assumed to be predominantly passive.

AGING POPULATION

According to the latest statistical data, the population of women is nearly the same as for men. Most Pakistani women do not choose to work outside the home. In general, they have low levels of education and lack access to family planning; the resulting successive childbearing makes them prematurely old. The general poverty, which, when combined with the high likelihood of being widowed, creates a life-long struggle that is especially onerous in advanced age, when many women have no male family members to support them. A number of social welfare NGOs, run by women and operating mostly in cities, work on their behalf. However, women's participation in seniors' organizations has not been very forthcoming because there is still a stigma in being classified as a senior citizen.

There is another class of elderly deserving of special consideration—those with disabilities or other limitations, who require special facilities. Pakistan is fortunate to have the state-funded Ministry of Special Education and Social Welfare in addition to several NGOs working for the welfare of these people. Factually speaking, age itself can be classified as a disability, especially for the very old (70-plus), and coverage could be provided to them for the time being from the funds already available at the federal level.

Another social problem is becoming more visible, the abuse of the elderly within the home and in public. Abuse takes different forms—neglect, forced labor, malnutrition, abandonment, segregation, and so on. This problem should be addressed by careful study and prompt action by state agencies and NGOs.

RIGHTS FOR OLDER PEOPLE

The emerging problems of the elderly and the need for greater coordination between the private and public sectors in addressing these problems led the Pakistan government to prepare an Action Plan for Ageing in 1980. Pakistan participated in the World Assembly on Ageing held in Vienna (Austria) in 1982. In addition, concerns for the well-being of the elderly also led to the founding of the Pakistan Senior Citizens Association in 1985, which is affiliated with international professional organizations. Added two years later, the Senior Citizens Foundation works to create a public awareness of the needs of older people.

The achievements of the young but growing seniors' movement in Pakistan show the potential of senior power and provide a glimpse of what can be achieved by empowering the elderly through popular participation. Some of these achievements are:

- An entrenched pattern of paying low pensions, which made it impossible for retirees from state employment to live with any dignity, compelled the Pakistan Senior Citizens Association to sponsor filing a civil suit in the Supreme Court. The suit was joined by the All-Pakistan Pensioners' Association and certain victimized individuals, all of whom were senior citizens. The final verdict, though not completely favorable, forced the government to increase retirement pensions by 30 percent for the most very old, low-paid pensioners and 10 percent for the recently retired. Pressure for additional benefits is continuing and a further sizable increase in pensions is anticipated for the fiscal year 1994-95, with some marginal benefits and possible tax relief.

- Public support of senior citizens convinced the government to nominate a Working Groups on Senior Citizens in 1986 with active participation of the Pakistan Senior Citizens Association, which presented its report on recommendations on short- and long-term planning. Little tangible action could be taken to implement the proposals due to continual financial constraints caused by restricted flow of funds from the U.S. government, currently suspended for want of specific results. The future plan is for such funds to be made available directly to the bona fide NGOs for specific high priority welfare projects, with those benefiting disabled persons and the poorest senior citizens topping the list.

- Active follow-up has resulted in 15 percent of the beds in government hospitals in three out of four provinces in Pakistan being reserved for the ailing, impoverished elderly.

- The government has agreed to grant a 50-percent concession to the elderly traveling on public transport in the two provinces where such systems function.

- Five percent of the houses and apartments to be constructed by the government for housing its employees will be reserved for older retirees unable to build on their own.

- A scheme introduced several years ago with International Labor Organization expertise makes fairly substantial pensions as well as other types of social security coverage available to workers in state-controlled industries and their family members, especially widows. Contributions are made by the employers as well as employees with a government contribution and overall management under the Old Age Benefit Scheme and Social Security Institutions.
- Introduction of Bait-ul-Mal, Ushr and Zakat (state-controlled charities funded by compulsory deduction of 2.5 percent on all savings of all Muslims) amounting to nearly seven billion Pakistani Rupees (U.S.$230 million) to be used for assistance to the poor and needy, including to non-Muslims.

These steps show that progress can be made through a subtle empowerment process closely akin to inducement that leads to public and private efforts to provide care for the aged and other vulnerable groups. The fact that legislators in Pakistan are now demanding draft legislation to assist them in getting appropriate laws passed to address these concerns is an important sign that senior power has made its presence felt (from a voting viewpoint).

OBSTACLES AND BARRIERS

In the face of far too many socioeconomic problems and heavy defense expenditures, allocation of funds for welfare projects—especially those for the elderly—are severely limited. This lack of funds is partly offset by the voluntary work of charitable organizations, NGOs and religious bodies, financial assistance from Bait-Ul-Mal, Ushr, and Zakat funds, and foreign aid for socioeconomic development.

There is a conspicuous shortage of health care facilities as well as trained staff to provide such services. There is also an absence of any infrastructure or trained personnel to deal with geriatric and gerontological problems. A detailed proposal presented by the author to establish the National Institute of Geriatrics and Gerontology with financial assistance from the UN Trust Fund for Aging was unanimously approved at the National Workshop for Welfare of Aging convened by the federal government in Islamabad in July 1987, in collaboration with the World Health Organization. Paucity of funds has held up implementation.

Another issue deserving of attention is the generation gap. Measures need to be implemented to strengthen family ties and support family caregivers rather than rely on the concept of residential care for the elderly, a concept far more common to industrialized nations than to Pakistan. Several seminars and study groups on the subject of elder care within the family have been convened by the Pakistan Senior Citizens Association in Karachi and other places during the last several years.

LEGISLATIVE AND TRAINING NEEDS

The fact that legislators and the public alike are now demanding draft legislation to assist them in getting appropriate laws passed to address these concerns is an important sign that senior power has made its presence felt, at least from a voting point of view. This is evident from the latest private circulation of a draft bill to enact the Pakistan Senior Citizens Act for providing long overdue relief to the needy elderly population.

Credit goes to the Pakistan Senior Citizens Association for having organized, in affiliation with several international organizations, a number of seminars and workshops on different aspects of elder care during the last eight years. A national workshop on elder care was convened by the Federal Ministry of Social Welfare in Islamabad during June 1991. It attracted participants from different NGOs from all parts of the country, who attended at government expense. For this type of training to continue, there is a need for financial and professional assistance from national as well as international sources.

CONCLUDING RECOMMENDATIONS

1. Design and implement effective measures to check the high growth rate in the general population.

2. Enact elder-care legislation and undertake programs that will ensure economic support, health care, housing, and social services for the poor aged, starting with those 65-plus and gradually extending to other groups.

3. Make specific arrangements for the welfare of women (especially widows and those without support) and other vulnerable groups such as the disabled or terminally sick.

4. Introduce effective voluntary and part-time paid work for able-bodied elderly to reduce costs and obtain better results.

5. Take effective measures in support of family caregivers, such as flexible employment practices and opening of skills retraining and recreational centers for the elderly, limited initially to provincial capitals.

6. Increase cooperation and coordination between the state, the NGOs, and the international aging community, specifically to obtain funds and expertise for programs for the elderly.

7. Activate the Federal National Committee on Ageing to secure greater implementation of the Vienna International Plan of Action on Ageing (VIPAA), to which the government of Pakistan is a signatory.

8. Convince the Federal Ministry of Social Welfare to coordinate with the specialized NGOs and obtain advice from international sources to prepare feasibility plan for establishing the proposed National Institute of Gerontology and Geriatrics for research, training, and specialized treatment, as already done in Bangladesh with a substantial financial grant from the UN Trust Fund for Aging.

9. Encourage federal and provincial governments, large corporations, and public limited companies to grant concessions, tax relief, facilities, and ancillary benefits to employees age 60-plus.

10. Establish state grants for research work on aging and for publishing age-care literature in local languages, particularly that which encourages self-help.

11. Survey the elderly in all provinces to assess bona fide needs and the extent of pressing problems faced by different groups of older persons.

The latest encouraging development has been the presence of Dr. Julian Mamo from the International Institute on Ageing, Malta, who conducted a WHO workshop on the elderly. The workshop was held in Khyber Medical College, Peshawar. Participants assessed the current aging situation and proposed a Plan of Action for the Elderly in Pakistan. His final report is yet to be completed.

According to the latest official information, a budget allocation of approximately Rupees 1.23 billion (U.S.$41 million) is anticipated during fiscal year 1994-95 to cover various social welfare measures. These are expected to include measures for the welfare of the handicapped and disabled poor but no provisions for impoverished senior citizens. Such assistance will not be forthcoming unless financial aid from the United States directly to deserving NGOs is restarted.

Finally, a word of caution may be added with regard to the concept of empowerment. Leaving aside the actual dictionary meaning, it is worthwhile to realize that this word implies force or arbitrary power to many and it may not appeal to everyone working on behalf of the elderly. An appropriate substitute worth careful consideration could be "entitlement" or "inducement." The author leaves this matter to the wisdom and foresight of others concerned with age care.

REFERENCES

Kinsella, K., and Cynthia Taub. 1993. *An Aging World II*. International Population Reports P95/92-3. Washington, DC: U.S. Department of Commerce.

Townsend, P. 1981. "The Structured Dependency of the Elderly: A Creation of Social Policy in the Twentieth Century." *Ageing and Society* 1(1), March.

United Nations Center for Social Development and Humanitarian Affairs.1982. *Vienna International Plan of Action, Humanitarian and Development Aspects*. New York.

Zaki, S. M. 1987. *The Ageing Population in Pakistan*. 4th ed. Karachi, Pakistan.

———. 1991. "Old Age in Pakistan: A Serious National Problem." *BOLD Quarterly*. August.

———. 1993. *Life-Style Guide for Senior Citizens in Third World Countries*. Karachi, Pakistan: One World Publications.

Part 5

ROADS TO EMPOWERMENT

Chapter 14

Research as a Tool
for Empowerment

Valerie Møller

There are many ways in which research can empower older people. Nevertheless, its emancipatory effects have often been overlooked, especially in developing countries. Research findings typically shape public opinion, influence policy, and contribute toward a better understanding of groups excluded from the mainstream. The research process lends itself to building individual and group capacity. It lies close at hand that wherever individuals or groups of seniors renounce disengagement from society, they may wish to avail themselves of research as a tool for empowerment.

This article addresses three aspects of research for empowerment: uses and abuses of research on aging and the elderly, research roles that build capacity, and research for policy formation to promote the cause of the older generation. The discussion and illustrations draw exclusively on South African material, which provides an instructive case for the discussion of research for empowerment. Similar to many developing countries around the world at the beginning of the 1990s, South Africa is in transition to a new social order. The ideology of apartheid belongs to the past. Empowerment and democracy are concepts that spell hope for the future for the formerly oppressed majority. At the same time, values of filial piety and veneration are fast becoming abstract concepts rather than practical moral guidelines; this is a source of uncertainty and anxiety for the middle and older generations.

South Africa has a heterogeneous population and is socially divided along racial, ethnic, and language lines. Apartheid exaggerated and entrenched these social divisions, which correspond to economic ones. The most urgent task of the new government is to seek more equitable solutions to accommodating the needs and expectations of all South Africans.

South Africa's black elderly represent only one of many oppressed groups whose causes were taken up during the apartheid era by activist research groups such as the South African Institute of Race Relations, the Back Sash, and the Human Awareness Program, to name a few, along with university and commercial research organizations. Investigative journalism and descriptive reports compiled by these bodies played an important role in identifying the inequities of the apartheid system, the failure of its policies, and their negative influence on the quality of daily life for discriminated groups of society.

During the apartheid era, attitude surveys and opinion polls were among the few channels available for reaching out to the oppressed black population and amplifying their needs and aspirations. Social research created a legitimate forum for the grievances of black South Africans who were voiceless even though they made up the numerical majority.

The research agenda is now less restrictive. However, given the limitations on finance for research and development, most social research efforts tend to be problem specific and policy oriented. Research that addresses equity and under-development issues is a priority for community groups and nongovernmental organizations.

For historical reasons the black elderly, who make up almost three-fifths of the 1.3 million South Africans over age 65, may benefit most from research for empowerment.

In former times, black elders were venerated and enjoyed the considerable power and prestige paid the elders in most traditional societies. In more recent times, labor migration and urbanization have disrupted the traditional way of life and disempowered the older generation. Loss of self-confidence and dignity among the black elderly is cause for concern. A recent survey of older South Africans conducted by the Human Sciences Research Council/University of Cape Town (HSRC/UCT) Center for Gerontology found that the vast majority of the black elderly perceived that they lacked respect from younger persons (Ferreira, Møller, Prinsloo, and Gillis, 1992).

In old age, the accumulation of the hardships experienced under 340 years of apartheid rule has taken its toll. "To be black, poor and aged in South Africa" captures the essence of this multiple discrimination (Lawton, 1981).

GATEKEEPER ROLES IN RESEARCH

Although most South Africans have great respect for good social research that subscribes to the basic principles of scientific inquiry, there is considerable public debate about the benefits to be derived from basic and applied research. During the apartheid era, tribal elders occupied key functions in the screening of research projects to be conducted in their jurisdiction. During the 1980s, community elderly in urban areas lost this gatekeeper role to activist youth, a situation that still prevails today in many township neighborhoods.

From the vantage point of disadvantaged groups, many research endeavors do not address issues of immediate concern. Although there may be a high regard for scientific integrity, there is also a partisan interest in research outcomes. Target research groups are particularly concerned about the selection of foci of research and personnel, and about the manner in which the research is conducted.

To date, the greypower movement has provided direction for gerontological research. However, the movement is not fully representative of disadvantaged groups of seniors; its following is mainly among white pensioners (Ferreira, 1991). The greypower lobby is currently seeking to expand its constituency at the grassroots level. Elder Voice is an advocacy council representing views and interests of elders countrywide. Its mission is to identify, coordinate, and integrate grassroots issues of concern (Elder Voice Forums Under Way, Thambodala 1993:2). Elder Voice may be the appropriate body to take up the gatekeeper function in research on behalf of regional groups of seniors, or to initiate research. The countrywide network of Elder Voice forums would ensure two-way communication between local communities and their national council on research efforts and outcomes.

NEW RESEARCH PARADIGMS

Partnership is the dominant research paradigm of the new South Africa. Target groups, who were patronized in many projects in the past, are emancipating themselves. Contemporary social researchers are assuming more humble roles. They are acting as technical consultants rather than initiators and directors of social inquiry (Zulu, 1990). The principles of good research are not in question. The researcher is entrusted with upholding the values of the professional community to ensure the legitimacy of the product and its worth for all parties involved. But the target group may insist on participating actively in all stages of research, including the definition of goals and the tools of inquiry. In particular, disadvantaged target groups wish to make the research product their own.

The partnership model was first pioneered in South Africa among township youth in the 1980s (Lund, 1982). The community self-survey method is a form of social investigation carried out by members of a community to gain better knowledge and understanding of their situation. Although professional expertise may be available to guide the process, the community members control it and "own" the product. They serve both as the object of the inquiry and as co-investigators. Their participation provides an opportunity for community members to learn. It also reduces costs and eliminates external influence, which might be contested. The method has become so popular that it has become a standard tool for community research.

To sum up, senior-driven research is not yet an established practice in South Africa. However, variations of the partnership model of research have already been tested in different regions of the country with encouraging results.

Partnership Roles in Research

Empowerment through research suggests the notion of older persons adopting roles as equal status subjects and research partners. Individual and group participation can be built into most research designs by enlisting the assistance of elderly people in the formulation of questions, the development of appropriate instruments, and the interpretation of results. Elders are ideally placed to evaluate reports. Advice of seniors may be useful on the formats and style of language that preserve the dignity and integrity of the subjects in media reports and policy recommendations. Scientific research reports need to be translated into local languages and styles that are accessible to target groups. The extensive life experience of the elderly can be put into good use in a variety of roles.

Partnership Roles in Conventional Research Designs

The majority of black South Africans were formerly excluded from active participation in conventional sample survey projects, which tended to patronize rather than engage subjects. Until recently, few opportunities existed for training lay persons in research techniques and methods. The Human Sciences Research Council currently offers courses on research methods countrywide. Third Age education in research, which is available in Western Countries (e.g., Garms-Homolova, 1988), is considered too ambitious an undertaking at present. A Durban study of housing conditions among elderly whites may have set a precedent when members of the target group were trained to conduct interviews for a sample survey. Education levels of older black South Africans lag behind those of their white counterparts. Only about one in two older black South Africans age 60-plus will have received formal education. Interviewing tasks are usually assigned to the younger, better educated generations.

Currently, retired black teachers and nurses are taking up volunteer work in their communities. There may be scope for Third Age education in research methods in this category of retirees. The case of a former schoolteacher from Soweto near Johannesburg is a case in point. The retired school teacher was recruited by a regional association for the aged to conduct in-depth interviews with older subjects for a study of lifestyles in retirement (Møller, 1984). The teacher had no formal training in social research and was initially fearful of her new role. She quickly mastered interviewing techniques by practicing in the office. In the field, the ex-teacher developed interviewing styles that were peculiarly adapted to the local situation and cannot be learned from books. For example, she contacted subjects for a convenience sample by boarding a bus destined for the target residential areas, seated herself next to a likely research subject, and casually engaged that person in conversation, as is the local custom. By the time the bus arrived at the subject's destination, he or she was usually prepared to give a full interview on experiences in retirement. The material produced by the older teacher-turned-fieldworker was far richer and more empathetic than that of younger interviewers working in other survey sites. The older interviewer took great care to cover the prescribed issues and to follow leads. By the time the fieldwork was completed, this lay researcher felt fully confident and satisfied with her work, which she felt had brought happiness not only into her life but also into the lives of her research subjects. She reported that she and her interviewees had benefited from the experience.

Partnership Roles in Community Research Designs

Obviously, there are limited roles for older South Africans as specialists in conventional research. There may be more scope for new roles in community research, which more readily fits popular notions of grassroots democracy. As reported earlier, community action research captured the imagination of South African township youth in the early 1980s. More recent examples of community-based research suggest that the partnership mode is also gaining momentum with the older generation.

Research into health care for older people recently undertaken in Duduza, a black township in Transvaal province, is an example of partnership between professionals and lay persons in which both parties are dependent on one another for a successful outcome. Local residents were trained to carry out the fieldwork for a conventional sample survey to elicit baseline data on the social circumstances of older Duduza residents. The survey also identified the needs of the elderly. The second round of research designed a structure by which individuals and groups in the community could meet some of these needs. The project addressed solutions that could be integrated into existing programs and could be generated from within the community with popular involvement and modest financial outlays. The model guided individuals and groups through the process of starting a new program to support the elderly and their families in caring for themselves. "It empowered those involved to move beyond just hoping for change or being puzzled by its elusiveness" (Hildebrandt, 1993:i).

A second example of partnership research concerns a community action project still under way in Khayelitsha, a black residential area near Cape Town. Living conditions are stark with many newcomers finding accommodation in primitive shacks without water, sewerage, and electricity. An earlier sample survey of older residents of Khayelitsha revealed that older women, in particular, were at risk of neglect and nonclinical depression. Subsequently, a subsample of the survey participants in the baseline study who could be traced, were invited to participate in focus-group discussions to discuss their needs and problems. Service delivery agents operating in the area were called upon in a separate session to give their perceptions of the situation. Several rounds of discussions with members of the target group and service providers were summarized in practical recommendations for action to alleviate some of the most pressing problems of the elderly in the area (O'Brien and Gillis, forthcoming).

These examples show some of the common characteristics of the partnership model of community research involving seniors.

1. To date concerned outsiders, usually research professionals, rather than insiders, are the imitators of the projects. Nevertheless, these professionals play less authoritative and more humble roles in community research than is the case in conventional research designs. Researchers act as consultants, facilitators, and mediators of viewpoints and actions.

2. In the transition to democracy, many South African communities are split into rival or warring factions. It is not possible to engage all sectors of seniors in equal manner. Suspicions and fears are allayed and participation levels increased if the researcher role is made transparent.

3. The focus of community research is on the process rather that the outcome. Progress in completing research tasks may be slow and involve numerous steps, such as meetings to establish the legitimacy of the project, several rounds of inquiry to identify community needs, and regular feedback to interested groups to refine research tools and translate research findings into action. Community research is participant driven in the sense that the target group sets the pace of research.

4. Lastly, community research typically involves members of the younger generations as well as the senior target group. The research process is conceived as a learning experience to promote mutual trust and respect between research partners and the generations.

Further, it is worth noting that community research programs, which provide practical lessons in research democracy, may supplement the voter education made available to senior citizens in South Africa's first nonracial elections. Crash courses in voter's rights have been conducted countrywide to assist black citizens who will go to polls for the first time in their lives under the new political system.

RESEARCH TOPICS FOR EMPOWERMENT

Research content is critical for the empowerment process. The choice of research questions will obviously determine the usefulness of the research product and its impact. The transition phase may call for topics of gerontological inquiry that go beyond identifying and redressing the inequalities of the past. There is a need to shift away from purely problem-oriented topics to ones which demonstrate that older persons are capable of adapting to rapid change in society.

In South Africa, the trend has been to exclude older cohorts in general population surveys. While numerous case studies have been conducted to redress this oversight, special inquiries have tended to focus on problems, issues, and groups. As a result, the elderly have been identified mainly as a homogeneous group at risk. Problem reports are often considered newsworthy and contribute to wider social awareness. At the same time, they reinforce negative popular stereotypes associated with aging and the elderly. Once older people are type-cast as a problem group in society, it may be difficult for them to shed this label. An antidote of positive social reports on the elderly may serve as a measure to boost morale and self-confidence, and create positive reference concepts for older people.

Although talk of democracy and equal opportunities is everywhere in the air in South Africa, there has been a marked increase in levels of violence and social intolerance. Older South Africans are not immune; they have become targets of violence and age discrimination. Better knowledge of their vulnerability and the image they project to society may assist the elderly in their fight against prejudice. It is foreseeable that the competition between the generations for goods and services will increase during the economic adjustment phase ahead. Studies that identify divisive issues as well as common interests will supply useful tools for revising the social contract between the generations in the new era.

An example of a project that straddles the generation divide is the development of a practical manual for lay caregivers by University of Natal researchers (Lund and Madlala, 1991). The manual, which addresses the needs of adult caregivers and elderly care recipients, is the result of two years of community research in which community members were actively involved. In the first stage of the inquiry, the researchers enlisted the assistance of health workers and lay persons in a postal survey and focus-group discussions in identifying high priority topics for training sessions. The topics identified were the aging process, treating bedsores, mobility, and nutrition. Worksheets in Zulu and English were prepared for each module, then tested and revised in several rounds of workshops attended by trainers and lay caregivers in the urban and rural areas. The contents of the manual were also broadcast over the radio to reach caregivers in the remote rural areas. The worksheets were bound in a looseleaf notebook so that they could easily be removed for photocopying and distribution to the wider community. The resource file proved so popular with caregivers and recipients that it has since been published in other African languages.

THE EMANCIPATED PENSIONER

The older section of a population is rarely a homogeneous group, which poses problems for participatory research and collective action (Pratt, 1993). Among developing countries, South Africa may be unique in that older South Africans, and the majority of the older black population, are entitled to a noncontributory, state old-age pension that is means-tested. The concept of a pension as a reward for life-long service to the family and community is consistent with the ideals of a society in which the aged are venerated.

It follows that, ideally, pensions should enhance the power of the elderly and their own prestige as well as that of their family. In practice, the application procedures and the pension delivery system violate the dignity of black elders.

The state pension system has attracted extraordinary attention from social researchers over the last decades. Much development research has concentrated on problems experienced by pensioners. Knowledge of the plight of pensioners has no doubt contributed to reforms of the social security system. The achievement of parity between pensions paid out to both black and white pensioners is a milestone in the history of South Africa's greypower movement.

Pensions may not be sufficient to empower state pensioners. The pensioner role still projects an image of weakness and vulnerability rather than strength. Although, on aggregate, pensions have enhanced the quality of family and community life, their real value has not been fully recognized.

At present, social pensions operate as an effective mechanism to redistribute wealth and inject cash into development areas (Ardington, 1989). During the recession, rural pensioners may represent the only income earners in the household. As such they are considered creditworthy in impoverished remote areas. Pensions are considered a right and not a privilege in the popular viewpoint (Møller, 1986). The government may be reluctant to dismantle the noncontributory pensions system for fear of losing popular support, in spite of competing demands on public funds to redress the social injustices of the past. However, future pensioners cannot be certain that this situation will hold indefinitely.

The case of the South African state pensioner typifies the situation of elderly in developing countries where traditional respect for the elderly has been reduced to an abstract principle (Zaki, 1993:15). Like their Western counterparts, the South African elderly may need to demonstrate their entitlement to social benefits and social recognition. In some regions of South Africa, the pension bill currently represents up to 80 percent of social welfare expenditure.

A future challenge for research in gerontology will be to justify and empower the pensioner. A review of past and present research on pension issues shows progress made toward empowering pensioners by involving their concern in highly visible, mainstream research endeavors.

Trends in research on social pensions issues over the last decade demonstrate the remarkable shift from patronizing to participatory research for empowerment. In the early 1980s, the Second Inquiry into Poverty (Wilson and Ramphele, 1989) engaged university and community-based researchers in collecting information on the state of poverty, including the social pensions issues. Problem accounts submitted on behalf of pensioners concentrated on negative experiences with applying for a pension, irregularities of payments, and incidences of corruption at pay-out points. Reports were typically compiled from observations at pensions pay-out points and records held at pensioner advice centers. The material collected in this manner paved the way for the compilation of practical manuals for prospective pensioners (an example is Association for Rural Advancement 1990) and lobbying for parity of pension payments. The current inquiry into South African statistics on economics and poverty has engaged not only researchers but representatives of all interested parties at the regional and national levels as reference groups. Built into the research design are opportunities for building research skills in the community. A nationwide household sample survey inquires into economic and social activities of household members of all ages. A wide range of data on households and lifestyles will be recovered. An anticipated research outcome is comprehensive information on the contributions older members make to the welfare of their respective households. This detailed information may prove critical for improving the weak image of social pensioners and safeguarding their interests in the future.

CONCLUSIONS

The South African experience shows that both the research process and its products can empower older people. The transition to majority rule has opened up a new research agenda for the emancipation of formerly disadvantaged groups, including the elderly. The new research paradigm moves beyond conventional research designs to include more active participation from subjects and target groups. Research topics address problems of aging and the elderly as intergenerational and community issues of concern. The outcome provides a sound basis for policy and action to improve the well-being of the elderly target groups and society in general. The South African examples cited may suggest applications for research for empowerment in other settings in the developing world. The scope for social research that will emancipate older people is wide open and needs to be explored in many different times and places.

ACKNOWLEDGMENTS

The author thanks Director Dr. Monica Ferreira and her staff at the Human Sciences Research Council/University of Cape Town Center for Gerontology for assistance in processing this chapter.

REFERENCES

Ardington, E. 1989. "Developing Appropriate and Effective Welfare Policies for the Aged." in M. Ferreira, L. S. Gillis, and V. Møller (eds.), *Ageing in South Africa: Social Research Papers*. Pretoria: Human Sciences Research Council.

Association for Rural Advancement. 1990. *A Guide to Pensions/Izimpesheni*. Pietermaritzburg, South Africa.

Ferreira, M. 1991. "Consumer Rights, Service Provider Responsibilities and Consumer Forums." *Senior News* 24(2): 1–2.

Ferreira, M., V. Møller, F. R. Prinsloo, and L. S. Gillis. 1992. *Multidimensional Survey of Elderly South Africans, 1990–91: Key Findings*. Cape Town: HSRC/UCT Center for Gerontology.

Garms-Homolova, Y. 1988. "Retirement Roles: Volunteers in Gerontological Research," in S. Bergman, G. Naegele, and W. Tokarski (eds.), *Early Retirement: Approaches and Variations: An International Perspective*. Jerusalem: JDC-Brookdale Institute of Gerontology and Adult Human Development, 137-149.

Hildebrandt, E. 1993. *Self-Care Strategies for the Aged in a Black Township*. Cape Town: HSRC/UCT Center for Gerontology.

Lawton, M. P. 1981. "To Be Black, Poor and Aged in South Africa." *The Gerontologist* 21(3): 235–239.

Lund, F. 1982. *Community Self-survey in Lamontville*. Durban, South Africa: Center for Applied Social Sciences, University of Natal.

Lund, F., and N. Madlala (eds.). 1991. *Caring for Elderly People: A Resource File*. Durban, South Africa: Center for Social and Development Studies, University of Natal.

Møller, V. 1984. *Images of Retirement: An Exploratory Study among Black Domestic and Service Workers*. Durban, South Africa: Centre for Applied Social Sciences, University of Natal.

————. 1986. "State Old-Age Pensions: A Blessing or a Burden?" *Indicator South Africa* (Rural and Regional Monitor) 45(1): 56–59.

O'Brien, A., and L. S. Gillis. Forthcoming. *The Perceived Needs of Elderly Residents of Khayelitsha*. Cape Town: HSRC/UCT Center for Gerontology.

Pratt, H. J. 1993. "The Emergence of Seniors' Organizations: An International Perspective." *Ageing International* 20(1):9–11.

Thambodala, Newsletter of the HSRC/UCT Center for Gerontology and the Co-operative Research Programme on Ageing, 1993.

Wilson, F., and M. Ramphele. 1989. *Uprooting Poverty: The South African Challenge*. Cape Town: David Philip.

Zaki, S. M. 1993 "Older Pakistanis Lobby for Better Lives." *Ageing International* 20(1): 15–16.

Zulu, P. 1990. "Social Contracts: From Trustee to Partners, a Corporate/Community Accord." *Indicator South Africa* 9(1): 15–18.

Conclusion of the Working Group on the Empowerment of Older Persons

Sally Greengross

"Older adults, as full citizens and participating members of their society, should have the same rights and their voice the same power and influence as other groups living in their community."

The Working Group on the Empowerment of Older Persons took this statement as fundamental to its argument. According to this principle, which underlies concepts of empowerment and self-determination, older people must make choices about their lifestyle and their priorities. In order for them to do this, they must have by right a standard of living similar to that enjoyed by other groups in their community. If not, they will not have *real* choice, and the options available will either bear no resemblance to their own preferences or will be a choice between predetermined decisions taken by other people, which may not reflect their own views.

The above argument is correct in principle, and many would agree that it is one of basic justice. The acute need for this workshop on empowerment arose because, in fact, older people across the world tend to be severely marginalized, a trend that accelerates as the older population itself grows older.

In times of limited resources, older people tend to be given lower priority, and the resourcing of services for them and work with them lags behind that devoted to others in need. Recognizing this reality, the working group made a number of different recommendations. Specifically, it highlighted the fact that many of the recommendations in the UN Program on Aging and Development Research Project could only transform the lives of older people, particularly in developing countries, if a commitment is made to concrete policies and programs. The members of the working group were adamant that agreements in principle will achieve nothing if not translated into action, and that all the appropriate United Nations agencies, such as the UN Fund for Population Activities (UNFPA), the UN Development Program (UNDP), and the UN Women's Fund (UNIFEM), should include issues concerning older persons in their development projects and programs.

They urged everyone responsible for relevant international conferences and events, such as those celebrating the International Year of the Family and future conferences on human rights, on population issues, on the situation of women, among others, to put as a main item on their agenda the full integration of older persons in development.

The group also recommended that the UN member countries and funding agencies, national and international nongovernmental organizations, and others include in their programs the development and strengthening of organizations governed and run by older people. These organizations often need technical assistance, training, or initial start-up support, or help later on in order to maintain their growing strength. Such support was felt to be the key to empowerment. The reality today is that, in countries moving toward industrialization, older people are often the last group to seek or to obtain empowerment, so a basic set of rights should be adopted by member governments that would help to ensure the development of interest groups and associations run by seniors.

The group agreed that a prerequisite to empowerment is that basic needs in terms of income maintenance must be met through adequate social security measures, guaranteeing a minimum income for individual older people. If not, acute poverty will continue to overwhelm other possibilities for progressive change.

In areas where a high level of poverty persists, older people are likely to suffer more than other age groups. Therefore, short-term programs as well as systems to address the needs of older people in the longer term need to be established as a matter of urgency. In all such cases, older people must be participants in integrated policies and practices and not an isolated group. If this does not happen, they will continue to be discriminated against and fare badly in relation to other groups in need.

Women, in most parts of the world, lag behind men in education and are relatively disempowered. Their potential in the process of empowerment and their importance as catalysts needs to be harnessed. Networking at an informal, local level can lead to the formation of effective movements and, through networking, feed into more formal organizations and facilitate radical change.

Only through action by individual older people and by collective empowerment will the integration of an aging dimension into all policy and practice in the economic, environmental, educational, as well as health and social fields be achieved. The working group made a point of emphasizing that both developing and more industrialized regions can learn from each other, and organizations of seniors in all parts of the world would benefit from the sharing of knowledge, research, and training.

In industrialized countries, where basic needs are more likely to be met and where the population balance is rapidly changing, concepts such as self-determination and fulfillment, choice, full participation, and equal rights of citizenship are now beginning to emerge as major issues on the social agenda. In those countries, the resource offered by the increasingly fit, healthy, and active majority of older people is not fully utilized. Stereotyping and prejudice keep many skilled people in the margins and prevent the continued use of their knowledge and experience. This is a particular problem in countries where rising unemployment has ousted many older workers from the economy without taking into account the resulting need to replace their skills and the effects of enforced exit from the workplace on individuals unprepared for 20 or 30 years of "leisure." Older workers often face the consequences of inadequate savings, a culture that may well stigmatize them for not being in the paid labor force, and the subsequent toll on their physical and mental well-being.

One way of utilizing the resources of older people is to make adequate opportunities available for volunteering. The group emphasized the importance of prioritizing this and of giving tangible recognition of such work to older volunteers. The working group proposed the idea of some type of service credit to provide such an acknowledgment. Comprehensive training programs for older volunteers were considered equally important. Older people as mentors, trainers, and consultants could be themselves very significant actors in ensuring that this happens.

Participants also drew attention to the point that increasing the rights of older people must be balanced by increasing their responsibilities. If increased opportunities become available in education, training, and employment, older people must themselves be responsible for taking up these opportunities. Older people cannot, however, participate fully or take an active role in their communities unless their environment is conducive to such a way of life. Ideally, people's own homes should be designed in a way that enables them to stay there throughout their lives, calling upon flexible systems of domiciliary support as and when needed. Adequate and appropriate housing, suitable transport and access to local facilities, leisure, and cultural programs play an important role in enhancing older people's lives. Research has not yet established how to provide the best environment and, of course, this depends on the level of development of each country. More work needs to be done to address this complicated and important range of issues.

Nevertheless, participants agreed that one of the most important ways of ensuring that older people can stay in their own homes whenever possible is to provide support for families and carers. If older people are to be truly integrated into mainstream society, they need to be involved with younger generations, not isolated from them. Religious institutions, which are natural focus points in local communities and are multigenerational in character, are important in promoting intergenerational activities and need to incorporate such work as a priority.

The group also considered that the media should pay more attention to the portrayal of older people and to activities in which they are involved. The voice of empowered groups of older people will eventually grow stronger, but meanwhile, patronizing, stereotyped, or negative images of older people should be actively discouraged. The media, on the other hand, by taking up the cause of older people and their empowerment, could effect massive change.

Demographic and family changes, especially in developing countries, mean that the social expectations of older people, particularly women, are undergoing rapid change. Through the employment of increasing numbers of working women, older people are likely to become even more isolated. Older people in need of social, emotional, or practical support must be able to plug into local community network: here, in particular, the resources of active and fit seniors will be even more essential than now. In this respect, some of the less industrialized nations can share a wealth of experience and take the lead in showing other parts of the world how to better integrate and maintain the roles, value, and dignity of older people.

At every level of operation, mechanisms are needed to prevent elders from being disempowered by their own organizations as they become more established.

The group recommended, therefore, that all participants in the UN Program on Aging augment the resources of the UN Center for Social Development and Humanitarian Affairs (CSDHA) and other key focal points. They have always suffered from being underresourced and need significantly more funds in order to implement fully the key policy, instruments on aging. As the world population ages, plans, policies, and practice must be established in advance of a crisis to which the very success of family planning and health policies will otherwise inevitably lead. The group stressed that the ll member states participating in the UN program should ensure that the relevant UN bodies no longer suffer from such restricting of funds. It also recommended that older people have full access to the benefits enjoyed by other groups, whether these are in terms of training, program development, or financial aid.

Members also felt strongly that, where possible, coalitions should be formed as a means of collective empowerment and of promoting intergenerational solidarity, with special attention given to older women and to the use of older volunteers. The concept of empowerment must be core to the planning of all human services, that is, older people must be part of the initial and ongoing process of planning. Their priorities and their preferences must be taken into consideration; this is necessary if the democratic principle is to include a large group of people, itself progressively growing in numbers, who become increasingly excluded as they get older.

The conclusion of the working group was clear. Empowerment is not merely a concept: it is increasingly recognized as fundamental to social justice. Without it, older adults will continue to be negatively stereotyped, through, at best, patronizing goodwill and, at worst, denial of opportunities, of adequate income support measures, of acceptable standards of health and welfare services, of housing, transportation and other essential factors making for a lifestyle comparable to others in their society.

Empowerment alone will go a long way to avoid these inequities. It is, therefore, an imperative. It is about today's older people and younger citizens who themselves will be older people tomorrow and better educated, better informed, and more demanding than all previous generations. They will ensure, that it happens tomorrow. We must facilitate its more rapid introduction today.

Index

Witmer, Melvin, 117
Women: in aging organization, Mexico, 123–25, as caregivers, 43; needs, 204, organization of single caregivers, Great Britain, 83–90; participation in development, 134; power in family, 39–40; social expectations of, 206; studies of aging, in Pakistan, 186
Women's Group for Improvement of an Aging Society (WGIAS) (Japan), 92, 94–95

World Bank, development indicators, 151
World Council of Churches, 107, 108
World Employment Conference, 135
World Health Organization, 188

Youth, participation in development, 135–36

Zeigler, L. Harmon, 78 n.1

Editors and Contributors

DANIEL THURSZ recently retired as president of the National Council on Aging, Inc. and is international vice president of the International Federation on Ageing. He has served as executive vice president of B'nai B'rith International and was Dean and Professor at the School of Social Work and Community Planning at the University of Maryland at Baltimore. Dr. Thursz co-edited *Reaching the Aged, Social Services in 44 Countries.*

CHARLOTTE NUSBERG is coordinator for international information for the American Association of Retired Persons, editor of *Ageing International*, former secretary-general of the International Federation on Ageing.

JOHNNIE PRATHER is senior editor of *Ageing International*. She has an extensive background in publishing.

JULIA TAVARES DE ALVAREZ is Ambassador and Alternate Permanent Representative of the Dominican Republic to the United Nations. Internationally recognized as an advocate for the elderly, Amb. Alvarez served as her country's chief delegate to the Third Committee of the UN General Assembly, which is charged with humanitarian, social, and cultural issues.

SANDEEP CHAWLA is an expert on development policy. He conducts development policy research for the UN and has written extensively on social policy and development issues. He serves as Visiting Professor at the Diplomatic Academy and adjunct professor at Webster University, both in Vienna. He was, until recently, senior technical adviser to the United Nations Centre for Social Development and Humanitarian Affairs, Vienna.

BRIGID DONELAN is Social Affairs Officer at the United Nations Centre for Social Development and Humanitarian Affairs, Ageing Unit in New York City.

SALLY GREENGROSS is director of Age Concern England and secretary-general of Eurolink Age, a European, community-wide organization. Author of numerous books and articles on policy and practice regarding the elderly, Ms. Greengross was voted U.K. Woman of Europe in 1990.

BJARNE HASTRUP is managing director for DaneAge Foundation and DaneAge Association. He has written several books on economic history, a subject he teaches at the University of Copenhagen.

MARVIN A. KAISER serves as Dean, College of Liberal Arts and Sciences, Portland State University, Portland, Oregon. Dr. Kaiser has served as staff consultant to the House Select Committee on Aging of the U.S. House of Representatives, the U.S. Agency for International Development, and the United Nations Centre for Social Development and Humanitarian Affairs at Vienna. He is the author of numerous articles, book chapters and monographs on rural and international aging issues.

HEATHER McKENZIE qualified as a Barrister at Law, Grays' Inn, London. From 1975 to 1985, she was Chief Administrative Officer of the National Council for the Single Woman and Her Elderly Dependents, later the National Council for Carers and Their Elderly Dependents. Ms. McKenzie, author of several books on caregiving and other issues, currently consults internationally and is co-director of Family Care Resources.

VALERIE MØLLER is a professor in the Centre for Social Development Studies at the University of Natal, Durban in South Africa. She holds a Ph.D. in Sociology from the University of Zurich, Switzerland. She has been engaged in social research in Southern Africa for 20 years. Her research interests cover a wide range of quality-of-life topics, including ones related to the well-being of the elderly, youth, and the unemployed.

JANE MYERS is a professor in the Department of Counseling and Educational Development at the University of North Carolina at Greensboro. She has directed projects for the U.S. Administration on Aging and has written numerous books, book chapters, articles, and monographs about aging.

HENRY J. PRATT is a professor of political science at Wayne State University in Detroit and Associate Provost. He has written numerous scholarly books and journal articles on politics, aging, and organizational structure.

MUKUNDA RAO was chief of the Social Welfare and Social Integration Section, United Nations Centre for Social Development and Humanitarian Affairs from 1983 until his recent retirement. He now works as a consultant. Dr. Rao has been a featured speaker and panelist at a number of international conferences on social development and has written extensively on the social aspects of development.

CELIA RUIZ is a psychologist and psychoanalyst in private practice in Mexico City. She works closely with VEMEA (Vejez en Mexico, Estudiar y Accion).

TAKAKO SODEI teaches sociology at Ochanomizu University in Tokyo and is a founder of Women's Group to Improve an Aging Society. She has served as visiting scholar at the National Council on Aging in Washington, D.C. and is the author of many books and articles on the elderly.

JAMES T. SYKES is a gerontologist currently teaching in the medical school at the University of Wisconsin-Madison. A nationally recognized advocate on behalf of the elderly, Dr. Sykes is chairman of the National Council on the Aging's Public Policy Committee.

KEN TOUT has been involved with aging programs since the late 1940s when he set up some of the first British day activities for the elderly. He has worked extensively with aging programs in the developing world and currently serves as consultant to several programs. He is author of *Ageing in Developing Countries*, published by Oxford University and *Elderly Care: A World Perspective*, published by Chapman and Hall. In recognition for his "services to the elderly," Dr. Tout was made an Officer of the Order of the British Empire in 1994.

S. M. ZAKI is the founder and vice president of the Pakistan Senior Citizens Association. He has written extensively on the subject of aging in Pakistan and is the author of *The Life-Style for Senior Citizens*.